HARD TIMES
IN PARADISE

Also by the authors

HOMESCHOOLING FOR EXCELLENCE

HARD TIMES IN PARADISE

AN AMERICAN FAMILY'S STRUGGLE TO CARVE OUT A HOMESTEAD IN CALIFORNIA'S REDWOOD MOUNTAINS

DAVID and MICKI COLFAX

WARNER BOOKS

A Time Warner Company

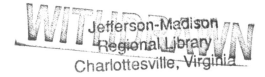

1304 9901

Warner Books, Inc., 1271 Avenue of the Americas, New York, N.Y. 10020

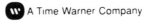 A Time Warner Company

Printed in the United States of America
First printing: July 1992
10 9 8 7 6 5 4 3 2

Library of Congress Cataloging-in-Publication Data

Colfax, David.
  Hard times in paradise : an American family's struggle to carve
out a homestead in California's redwood mountains / David and Micki
Colfax.
      p.   cm.
  ISBN 0-446-51489-6
  1. Mountain life—California—Anderson Valley.   2. Anderson Valley
(Calif.)—Social life and customs.   3. Colfax, David.   4. Colfax,
Micki.   5. Colfax family.   6. Anderson Valley (Calif.)—Biography.
I. Colfax, Micki.   II. Title.
F868.M5C65   1992
979.4'24—dc20   91-50414
                                                                     CIP

Book design by Giorgetta Bell McRee

For Grant, Drew, Reed, and Garth

ACKNOWLEDGMENTS

We'd like to thank Virginia Nash, Margaret K. Simmons, Pam Abramson of *Newsweek*, and Nanscy Neiman of Warner Books, for their encouragement; Susan Suffes, our editor, for her invaluable insights and suggestions; and Irene K. Davis and Gerd Schroeter, who so helpfully commented on the manuscript.

CONTENTS

PROLOGUE

Why would a couple of happy, presumably intelligent adults give up their comfortable home in a midwestern suburb, abandon their careers as teachers, and move with their three young children to a wild and remote mountaintop in northern California and spend the better part of the next twenty years there trying to make a living off the land?

It's a question we've been asked—and asked ourselves—hundreds of times over the years. Even now, when it seems that things have turned out better than we could have ever hoped, now that three of our four boys who were so much a part of it all are grown up and off on their own, in medical school, in Africa, and in Cambridge, we still sometimes ask ourselves what it would have been like if we had not taken to the hills back in 1973. Now that our homestead—Shining Moon Ranch—has come together, now that the towering redwoods and firs on our mountaintop are interspersed with well-established gardens, pastures, aging sheds, and a house that was much too long in the making, we can look back at the years of only partially self-imposed exile, of excruciatingly hard work, and of mind-numbing isolation with something that resembles philosophical detachment. It is a little easier now to recall in relative tranquillity those difficult years in which we were struggling to survive as a family in the face of what we viewed as an increasingly hostile, inhumane world.

Even now we often wonder why, of all the things we *might* have done back in the early seventies, we chose to go into the mountains and, more preposterously, remained there, trying to make a living at something for which we were, on the face of it, painfully unprepared.

Over the years there were times—such as those dark winter evenings when we found ourselves sloshing in water up to our ankles, tripping over scattered piles of two-by-fours, and climbing over water-soaked and crumbling cartons of hardware and boxes of tools in the half-built, kerosene-lighted house, cringing in fear as the howling storms roared up out of the canyon, pounding against the felt-paper walls and threatening to topple the giant firs and redwoods that encircled us—when we cursed ourselves for being so stupid, so insufferably self-righteous and arrogant, as to have gotten ourselves into such a mess. If only we had compromised a bit, we told ourselves, if we had not been so outspoken, had not taken it all so seriously, gotten so involved . . . And years later, when our commitment to surviving on the land had taken such hold of us, when the house still was far from finished, when we were flat broke and were working ourselves, all of us, to near exhaustion every day just to keep things together, we would have had to admit, if anybody had bothered to ask, that we'd made a colossal mistake in thinking that we would be able to eke out a living on our beautiful, unyielding mountaintop.

But there were moments, during even the hardest of times, on those brilliant spring mornings, when the fog formed a many-fingered cotton-candy lake that reached back into the hills and glimmered below us, when the sounds of lambs and goat kids gamboling in the pastures we'd so painstakingly cleared drifted down from above the orchard, where the trees, shimmering and heavy with lush new growth, waved in the wildflower-scented breeze that floated up the ridge and we could hear the voices of the boys somewhere off on an adventure in the woods, when we knew that we hadn't made a mistake in coming into these hills. However inchoate our reasons for being here, no matter how much work it had entailed, and even if it seemed that we seldom had the time or inclination to step back and take in all its glory, we knew, as we did from the beginning, that we were living in what could only be characterized as a sylvan paradise. And then, almost as if to jolt us into a realization that, after all, it was not the idyllic beauty or the charm of country living that had brought us to and kept us on the mountain, the harsh realities of ranch life would rudely surface—an all-night session with a sick sheep, a few days working on the Chevy pickup, an afternoon spent chasing down a waterline break.

When our oldest son, Grant, who "had never gone to school" was admitted to Harvard at the end of our first decade on the land back in 1983, we were bemused and, indeed, fascinated by the way in which the media characterized our adventure. We were portrayed as one of those families that had been part of the back-to-the-land movement of the early seventies, that had blithely taken to the hills to build a house with our own hands, plant a garden, grow our own food, teach our kids at home—and send them to Harvard. It was a success story with a great "sound bite"—"Goat Boy Who Never Went to School Goes to Harvard." It was a bright and shiny version that conveniently left out the hard parts, one that overlooked our long struggle to prove to ourselves, if not to those in the outside world, that despite everything we could make a go of it, on our own terms, in the rugged hills of northern California.

AUTHORS' NOTE

Hard Times in Paradise is both the story of a family and a partial biography of six individuals. Since many of the conversations contained in this book occurred years ago we have done our best to reconstruct them from memory. Generally, in the pages that follow, the two of us, David and Micki, speak as one—about what we have jointly experienced and recall. Occasionally, however, there are points in the narrative where it becomes necessary to abandon the collective "we" and to present the events at hand from the point of view of one or the other of us. The reasons for this should be clear from the context.

Everybody knows you can't make a living on forty acres of hill land.
—CALIFORNIA AGRICULTURAL EXTENSION AGENT

I guess you'd have to call this, what? Paradise?
—TELEVISION NETWORK CORRESPONDENT

PART ONE

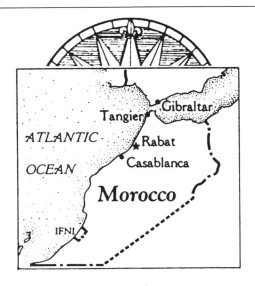

Breaking Away

CHAPTER ONE

St. Louis Blues, 1971

David hung up the telephone, sighed, and returned to the dining room. Micki and the boys were almost done with the dinner the call had interrupted. Micki was poised, spoon in hand, her elbow resting on the high-chair tray, waiting for an opening in which she could parry another spoonful of yellow puree into six-month-old Reed, who sat there giggling as if to indicate that he knew he was winning the battle. Micki put down the spoon and looked up expectantly as he slid his chair back and sat down between Drew and Grant.

"What *is* that stuff?" David asked.

Drew and Grant had stopped eating, had put down their forks, and were watching him intently. Micki must have told them it was an important call.

"Squash," said Grant. "It's good."

"*He* doesn't seem to think so," said David, looking across the table at the baby, who let out a gleeful shout. "I don't blame him." He took his napkin, spread it on his lap, and reached for one of the serving dishes.

"It's cold now," said Micki. "You were on the phone for at least a half hour. I didn't know whether to put it in the oven or what."

"It's okay," said David, taking a bite of chicken.

"Well?" Micki asked after a long moment. "It's all over, isn't it?"

David shook his head. "Worse than we'd expected. They handed the administration what it needed. Three for, three against, and three abstentions. The liberals copped out at the end."

"That's it, then, isn't it? No tenure," said Micki, her voice rising. "Again." She wiped Reed's face carefully and pulled her chair around to the table. "At least it took them three meetings to get what they wanted."

"I can't believe the administration was so heavy-handed," David said as he pushed away his plate. "But they want to get all the activists out of the place. The powers that be are going after Barry Commoner next. At least at Connecticut the faculty stood firm."

"And a lot of good it did you," Micki said bitterly. She stood up and began clearing the table. "There's ice cream for dessert."

"Dad?" Grant said softly. "Does this mean we'll have to move again?"

"Not for a while," said Micki. "Maybe not at all. Don't worry about it, honey. Everything'll be all right, won't it, David?"

"It'll be okay," David said distractedly. It didn't mean anything to Reed and Drew who were too young, but Grant knew what was happening. It had been bad enough the first time around, two years before, thought Micki, after we'd been chased out of our home by right-wing vigilantes and then denied tenure because of our involvement in the civil rights and antiwar movements—and while colleagues who hadn't published, hadn't gotten the research grants, and hadn't come anywhere near winning the teaching awards David had, were routinely granted tenure, that lifetime guarantee of a job in the university, almost as a reward for doing nothing at all.

"It's really gotten to me," David confessed that night as we were getting ready for bed. "I didn't expect anything better, but did you see the look on Grant's face? Even though he knew what was coming? No matter how many times we try to explain it to him, it's hard for him to understand why we're involved in all of this and his dad's lost his job again."

"He's only seven, David. And you know as well as I do that he'll never forget that night we had to leave our house, even though he thinks he understands it."

"We need to get away from this," said David. "Away from academia, Vietnam, the whole thing. It's going to eat us up if we continue this way."

It was an old topic, one we'd discussed a hundred times. After a half dozen years of teaching, antiwar activism, and community organizing in Hartford that culminated in our being quite literally run out of town, we had hoped that St. Louis would be a new beginning, a place where we could raise the boys, teach, and continue the community and antiwar activities that the times demanded. After all, we reasoned, St. Louis was a big place, Washington University had a reputation as being liberal and, in the McCarthy era, even something of a bastion of academic freedom, and we'd do our best to make sure that we never became as prominent as we had in Connecticut. But, inexorably, as the decade marked by urban riots and student revolts came to an end, as the inner cities festered and the war in Vietnam intensified, we found ourselves becoming involved more than ever before. In the year and a half since we had moved into the massive old house on the tree-lined chained-off street on the edge of the ghetto, we'd become more involved than ever. We soon realized that in this dying city, where the worst of midwestern and deep south values commingled, academics such as ourselves were expected to possess the proper attitudes about social and political matters but were quickly and fatally categorized as lacking the soundness and judgment required of professorial colleagues when they involved themselves too deeply in matters relating to poverty and peace. And now the vote was in, and David had a year to find another job.

"We can stay here and I can keep on teaching while you do the organizing," said Micki, even though she knew that was an option we'd rejected in previous discussions. She was teaching at a nearly all-black junior high school, and we'd managed to continue our community and antiwar activities almost unabated by taking the boys with us to the seemingly endless night-after-night meetings and, after we found a preschool program for Drew and a Montessori-inspired school for Grant, having Reed accompany David to his classes, where he almost invariably dozed his way through his father's lectures on race relations and political sociology, to the amusement of his students.

Only six months earlier the idea of remaining in St. Louis might have made some sense. After all, we had a great house and were doing important work in the community and on campus. But the work we'd been doing with a group of social workers, lawyers, and health activists whom we'd met shortly after arriving in the city was having a far greater impact on the community than we'd ever anticipated, and before long all of our careers, in one way or another, had been put in jeopardy. We had been publishing a monthly newspaper that documented the failure of local government agencies and so-called political leaders to deal with what was then euphemistically termed "urban blight," and we'd produced a series of reports that showed how the local political and economic elite benefited from these arrangements. The reaction of those in power was swift and unsubtle. Our social worker friends suddenly found themselves out of jobs, health activists discovered that their programs were not being re-funded, our public interest lawyer friends were being urged to relocate their practices, and David was denied the tenure that ordinarily would have been routinely granted. There was nothing conspiratorial about it: The word had gone out that powerful people didn't want or need the kind of trouble that these social activist professionals were creating, and their subordinates—deans, agency heads, program managers—got the message and responded as they were expected to and, in so doing, confirmed our widely broadcast and not very original thesis that old St. Louis was, indeed, a tightly controlled, corrupt little city.

"You know we're not going to be able to accomplish much more here without the university connection," said David. "Especially with everybody else having to leave."

"You're right," Micki said. "We really don't have any reason for being here except the job. And now that's gone."

"We've still got a year and a half to work things out. We can do a lot before we go."

A year and a half later, in June of 1972, David went down the block to the preschool to pick up Drew for the last time.

"So," the teacher said brightly. "Drew says you're off to . . . is it Kenya?"

"Uganda," said David.

"Really?" said the teacher. "Last week he mentioned Singapore and . . . what was it, Hong Kong. I have to admit that for a while we thought that we were dealing with a rather confused little boy."

"No," said David, doing his best to be affable. She knew all about him from the newspapers, of course: PROFESSOR CHARGES "ACADEMIC FREEDOM VIOLATIONS," CONTROVERSIAL PROFESSOR TO LEAVE WASHINGTON UNIVERSITY.

We jammed more than we'd ever thought possible into that lame-duck year and a half in St. Louis, becoming even more involved in campus and inner-city politics almost as if to compensate for our imminent departure. But even so, while organizing rent strikes, leading the campaign to force the city to close down lead-paint-infested tenements, demonstrating against the war, and fighting welfare program cutbacks, our minds were elsewhere. David dutifully served out the remaining three semesters of his contract and, then, in the last days on the job, in what would ultimately prove to be a short-term victory and a long-term blunder of immense proportions, contested his denial of tenure. And while the seventeen-man committee that heard his case over a period of six weeks deliberated, we packed books into cardboard boxes to be mailed to Uganda, where David had secured a two-year position as a professor of sociology.

We'd had time to consider the options, the most obvious one of which was a teaching job for David at yet another college or university. They were out there, untenured positions at respectable enough places. But no matter where he went, according to the rules of the academic game designed to protect—but now being used against—mavericks like him, as an associate professor with a half dozen years at that rank, he'd have to be considered for tenure within two years of being employed.

Micki was adamant about not going through it again. She'd been through it once at UConn, where some of her best friends, already made uncomfortable by the risks the two of us had taken by being so intensely involved and frightened when we were run off, backed away when they learned that David, unlike their mindlessly right-thinking, reflectively professorial spouses, was going to be denied tenure. She'd learned to avoid the type by the time we moved to St. Louis and hadn't made any friends among the faculty wives.

But it was harder now, keeping up a good front around the boys, not letting it get to her, reassuring Grant and, more and more, Drew, that this turmoil wouldn't go on forever, that things would turn out just fine, that she and Dad hadn't really done anything *wrong*. This was what happens, she'd told them over and over from the time they were old enough to begin to suspect that their parents were different from others, when you "try to help the poor people and stop the war." As he had grown older we'd spent hours with Grant, discussing the war and social injustice and why we were involved. He loved being taken seriously, his big brown eyes wide as we explained what had gone on at a meeting or why a particular development was or was not newsworthy, and he'd gotten good at asking questions that sometimes forced us to confront our own assumptions or double-check a fact or two. And sometimes he surprised us with his grasp of it all, such as on that spring afternoon when a neighbor appeared on our doorstep with a shopping bag full of canned goods.

"I'm sorry," she told Micki, "but I didn't have anything when Grant came by, so I ran down to the market." She pulled a can of bing cherries from the bag. "I hope these are all right."

"Grant?" said Micki.

"He came by a little while ago," said the neighbor as she handed the bag to Micki. "He said he was collecting food for the poor people." She looked puzzled for a moment. "I *assumed* that it was something you were doing."

"Oh, sure," said Micki, doing her best to disguise her confusion. "Thank you very much, we really appreciate it."

An hour later Grant pulled his big red Radio Flyer wagon with the tattered blue "Eugene McCarthy for President" bumper sticker on it into the driveway. It was heaped high with canned goods, and a half dozen of his friends followed him in, their arms filled with cans and boxes of food.

"It's for the poor people," explained Grant, his eyes shining, as Micki came out into the yard. "Look at all this. And we only went around the block."

"That's wonderful," said Micki. "Whose idea was it?"

"Mine," said Grant. "Tori and Jeff and everybody helped."

"That was really nice of all of you," Micki said to the children who had gathered around her, beaming. "Let's stack all of it on the back porch and we'll take it to the poor people tomorrow, okay?"

"I don't know where he ever got the idea," she told David that evening when he got back from one of his meetings. "We've never collected food for anybody, have we?" She grimaced. "My God," she exclaimed. "I just thought of it. You don't think that the neighbors thought that Grant was collecting food for *us*, do you? That *we* need it?"

"Probably," said David. "Isn't that what happens when you lose your job? Think of how happy it made them all feel, helping us out."

"Oh, no." Micki laughed. "And Grant was so serious about it."

David looked at a couple of job offers that came loaded with conditions: Teach a few more courses than you've been doing for a little lower salary, take over our statistics classes, keep a low profile, and we'll vote on tenure in the middle of the second year of your two-year contract. The message was clear: He might be a good teacher and researcher, perhaps, but he was damaged goods, a two-time loser who, if necessary, could be dumped after a couple of years.

We weren't about to make any promises. We knew that wherever we went, no matter how obscure the school or however isolated the community, we'd find ourselves becoming involved in the same kinds of issues that had preoccupied us since our graduate school days at Chicago.

There was no way we could stand in front of a classroom and pretend that what was going on all around us didn't have anything to do with us or our students. We were tired of being humiliated by college administrators and let down by our colleagues. We had to get far away from all this, settle down. The civil rights and antiwar movements—and certainly academia—could manage without us for a while.

We'd been made at least dimly aware of something called the "back-to-the-land movement" through one of Micki's earliest and most successful projects, the setting up of a bulk-buying, natural-foods cooperative designed to serve both the university and inner-city communities, and, in ordering, we'd come into direct contact with providers of environmentally sound, organic produce all across the country—Deaf Smith grains, Erehwon ("Nowhere") vegetables, cheeses, and even organic beef and veal. We'd begun to spend our Saturday mornings at the crowded St. Louis Farmers' Market, getting to know the farmers who came up from the Ozarks, backed their trucks up to the stalls in the old glass-roofed pavilion, and displayed their produce—butter and eggs, cheeses, vegetables, live chickens and rabbits, skinned-out possums and raccoons. A couple of families, one of which made the best cottage cheeses, and another that had the best potatoes, caught our attention from the outset if only because of the way in which their preteenaged children were so obviously a part of their operations—moving produce out of the truck, making change, stacking boxes, weighing, and sorting. Perhaps it was their example that somehow inspired us to buy a dozen Leghorn pullets that the father told us were "just about ready to start laying" and house them in a room in the old unused carriage house at the end of our driveway. Heartened by our success—ten eggs a day!—we went out a few weeks later, bought a couple of rabbits and a duck for our backyard menagerie, and began thinking that perhaps it might be good to take off to the country for a few years, raise some animals and the boys far from the din and stress of city life and American politics in the seventies.

Perhaps because we had seen it up close as children, neither of us entertained much of a romantic view of country living or farm life. David had spent his childhood summers on the abandoned hundred-acre farm in northwestern Pennsylvania that his grandparents had bought during the Depression, where they'd eked out a living growing corn and hay, milking a dozen cows, plowing and seeding and mowing with rusted, worn-out horse-drawn equipment. It had been a great place for a kid, but he never developed any interest in becoming a farmer. Both Micki's parents had grown up on farms, and she had spent many happy summers on her grandparents' farm in Illinois. But farming was hard, and neither of her parents returned to the land after college. Still, the idea of finding a piece of land, growing our own food, and raising the boys in the country had a certain intrinsic appeal. Anybody could see how much the boys enjoyed feeding our small menagerie and collecting the warm eggs every morning.

One afternoon Micki brought home a ragged copy of something called the *Mother Earth News*, which she had come across at the co-op, and we leafed through articles entitled "Living on $6,500 a Year," "The Plains Indian Tipi" ("the best movable shelter ever developed"), and others on how to make yogurt and "digger bread." It was pretty corny, we agreed, and certainly nothing to be taken very seriously. Nevertheless, Micki went out the next day and found another copy of the magazine, a special issue entitled "How to Get Out of the City and Back to the Land." We ordered the "highly recommended" United Farm Agency catalog, which listed "hundreds of reasonably priced properties across the nation," as well as a book by a former professor named Scott Nearing who had moved to the country decades before, where he was, according to the title of his book, *Living the Good Life.*

We spent a couple of weeks that next summer traveling up and down the East Coast, checking out United Farm Agency listings and following up leads that took us to a dairy farm in Nova Scotia ("Do *you* want to milk sixty-five cows twice a day for the rest of your life?" asked Micki as we stood there in the barn surrounded by throbbing milking machines. "*I* don't.") and to a commune run by affable simpletons that we could buy into for a few thousand dollars ("These people aren't like us, are they, Mom?" said Grant as we drove away from the waving, smiling crowd that had gathered to see us off). And later, after a couple of telephone calls in response to an ad placed by a group calling itself the California Agrarian League that offered "land in Mendocino County from $300 per acre," David flew out to San Francisco and hitchhiked his way up the coast, only to discover that the Agrarian League consisted of several hippie realtors who had only a few parcels that they were trying to sell at considerably more than $300 per acre.

"It was a waste of money," David said when he returned and Micki met him at the airport with the boys. "But it's probably the most beautiful place I've ever seen. There are redwood trees coming right down to the ocean, the waves crashing on the rocks."

"Did you see anything we could consider buying?" asked Micki as she reached across the backseat of the Volvo to strap Reed in.

"It's really expensive out there, even for what I thought was some pretty useless land. Nothing like the prices in New Hampshire or the Ozarks. And the economic situation is really bad. They've got one of the highest unemployment rates in the country. Just about the only work is logging and sheep ranching, and there's not even much of that. I don't know how we could ever make a living there, even if we could afford the land."

"So it's out of the question?"

"Pretty much so," said David. "But if we ever *did* move to the land, that's the place to go. God, it's beautiful. We ought to take a trip out there together someday."

Micki's diary, May 1972: David spent the last two weeks in northern California. Didn't find anything. Seeing the way things are going in academia and the world (just heard Nixon's madman speech tonight), a mountaintop in California might be one of the more sensible places to be about now.

Hearings on his tenure begin next week now that the students are safely out of the way, the semester having ended. The committee is a real hanging jury, but we don't have anything left to lose and might even get in a few good punches.

It didn't take us long to realize that we really were neither financially nor psychologically prepared to give country living a try. The few places we saw that we liked were far too expensive, and we didn't have any idea of how we'd manage to make a living off in the boondocks somewhere. It was one thing to be young and unencumbered and head off into the hills to live in a tepee or a yurt, as the *Mother Earth News* and the *Last Whole Earth Catalog* suggested. Or to be independently wealthy, or to adopt the kind of austere life-style old Scott Nearing had. It was quite a different matter to be the thirty-five-year-old parents of three young boys with all the needs that children have. Going off somewhere and living off the land was something we might be able to consider doing someday, but it was out of the question now. Besides, there were other, interesting things that we could do, such as going off to another country to live.

David sent his résumé off to a half dozen British Commonwealth universities that advertised in the *New Statesman*, which we had been reading ever since we'd spent a year together at the London School of Economics in the early sixties. The University of Nairobi in Kenya, Amando Bellow in northern Nigeria, the University of Hong Kong, Makerere University in Uganda, the University of Singapore: We knew next to nothing about any of them, really, except that they were all very British and very far from St. Louis. And far enough away, apparently, to consider David's credentials apart from his political life, for we soon found ourselves sorting through a half dozen telegrammed offers. A two-year professorial appointment at Uganda's Makerere University—generally regarded as "the Harvard of Africa"—was the most attractive. Makerere offered plenty of good research opportunities, and Uganda, in addition to having a good climate, was home to some of the best game reserves in Africa. A new government, led by a former army officer by the name of Idi Amin, was in power, but our colleagues who specialized in African affairs assured us that his regime was essentially reformist and populist and nothing we needed to be concerned about.

We sold the house—"the best part of living in St. Louis," Micki said many times before and afterward—for barely more than what we'd paid for it just three years earlier, a price that didn't begin to compensate for the work we did that first politics-free summer when, soaked with sweat, we scraped and painted most of the fifteen dingy rooms of the seedy old mansion. It took several days for us to pack dozens of cardboard boxes with scholarly and children's books to be mailed—the cheapest way of getting them there—to Uganda. And as a part of the deal with the buyer of the house, we filled one room with furniture and personal belongings that we planned to pick up when we returned from Uganda in two years. After saying farewell to our friends and neighbors, we deposited our $12,000 equity from the house—just a bit less than David's yearly salary as an associate professor—in the bank and headed east in our seven-year-old Volvo, our Coleman pop-top camper in tow.

A week later we were on the SS *France*, steaming for Southampton, where we planned to catch a plane to Uganda. As things were to turn out, we were en route to California—the long way.

CHAPTER TWO

African Sojourn

The five of us leaned up against the rail of the upper deck of the *France* and waved good-bye to America as the tugs nudged us out into the Hudson River. The boys, holding hands and having been warned not to get separated, were a study in contrasts: Grant at seven, solemn, big-boned, with Dutch-boy straight blond hair; Drew a curly-headed imp of four; and at two and a half, his black puffed-up Afro framing his delicate features, tiny Reed, who was visibly intent upon giving the impression that he understood what was going on. They were appropriately enough attired in matching khaki safari shorts, oversize-looking hiking boots, and the forest green shoulder packs they'd crammed full with the books, drawing paper, and Magic Markers we'd told them they'd be in charge of for the duration of what they, at least, regarded as a great adventure. They'd spent hours looking through the *World Book* and leafing through tourist agency brochures that depicted the jungle, people, and animals of East Africa, and had done nothing else but talk about where we'd go and what we'd see once we arrived in Uganda. For us, though, no matter how bright a face we tried to put on things, no matter how self-imposed our exile might be, our leaving meant that we had at least temporarily conceded defeat in a battle that directly and indirectly had cost us friends, our home, and a couple of jobs and had left us worn out, angry, and unsure that our efforts had made any difference at all. It was with mixed feelings that we watched the New York skyline recede.

"You're a little choked up, aren't you?" asked Micki, glancing over the heads of the boys at David as the ship came around into the wind and the tugs backed off.

"A little," he said. "You are, too."

Drew pulled at David's arm. "I gotta go to the bathroom," he said with a pained, urgent look. "Bad."

"Now?"

"Right away," said Drew.

David glanced over at Micki, who shook her head. "I'll stay up here with Reed and Grant," she said. "We don't want to miss this."

David and Drew made their way through the crowd and down the empty corridors and stairwells of the ship to their stateroom.

Twenty minutes later, when they came back up on deck, the crowd had thinned, the sun had gone under, and it had turned cold.

"Maybe I should feel guilty about this, but I don't at all," Micki stated after the waiter had taken our order. We'd arranged for the boys to eat at the first sitting and had had dinner by ourselves for the four nights we'd been at sea. "I think I earned this." She smiled, raising her wineglass.

"You did," said David. Micki was looking better than she had for a long time. It had been hard these last few years, he thought. Ever since everything fell apart in Connecticut. Harder for her than for him.

"You don't think there's anything to worry about, do you?" she said, suddenly serious. "About what that Englishman said?"

We'd met him that afternoon as the boys bobbed in the tiny indoor pool. A big, friendly walrus of a character, he'd been to Uganda. "A wonderful place, a beautiful country." Then he frowned. "You do know there's been something on the ship's wire about it, don't you? Something about the Asians, the shopkeepers, there. Frightfully hardworking people, the Asians. Seems this new bloke, this Amin fellow, wants to boot them out."

"It'll be all right," David said as the waiter appeared with the appetizer. "It has to be a ruse of some kind. There's no way he can expel them."

We got the rest of the news when we docked in Southampton. As the other passengers bustled around us, rounding up their luggage, porters, and cabs, we stood huddled together next to the terminal newsstand, skimming through the *Times*, the *Mirror*, the *Guardian*, and the *Daily*

Telegraph, the full political spectrum. It was true: Idi Amin had decreed that all Asians had to leave Uganda within thirty days. The editorial consensus was that Amin would be forced to rescind the order shortly since it blatantly violated commonwealth agreements, and Amin, after all, was a creature of Her Majesty's government, since it had quite openly helped him to overthrow the previous government of Milton Obote, who happened to be a troublesome socialist.

"It doesn't look very serious," David assured the boys, who had been standing by patiently while we perused the newspapers.

"I'm not so sure about that," Micki said quietly, with her back to the boys so they couldn't hear her. Grant had already sensed our concern aboard ship and wondered if we "might not be going to Africa after all." She turned back to the boys. "It's all going to turn out fine," she told them. She took Reed's and Drew's hands, and we strode across the terminal together to the Cook & Sons agency. We arranged for the shipment of our three big steamer trunks to Mombasa and rented a car to drive to London, where, after a week or two, we planned to catch our plane to Kampala.

Agadir was a coastal town on the edge of the Sahara, two thousand miles south of London. It certainly was not where we had expected to find ourselves that fall. The situation in Uganda had proven to be more serious than we'd feared, and we'd decided to wait it out by taking a two-week trip to France in a Volkswagen camper that English friends had loaned us. The two weeks had lengthened into a three-month stay in Morocco.

At first we had meandered down the west coast of France and into Spain, picking up the *Herald Tribune* every time we came to a town of any size and anxiously seeking out fresh news about Uganda. But eventually, on a drizzly evening in a gloomy roadside campground in the Pyrenees, after we'd read about the murder of a Peace Corps volunteer and the disappearance of yet another Makerere teacher, we agreed that no matter how much the situation there seemed to improve, as we had been expecting it would ever since our arrival in England, it still would be dangerous to go there as an employee of a government that was run by an obvious madman.

We had the choice of simply biding our time someplace where the cost of living was low until Amin was overthrown—as we were sure he soon would be—or heading back to the United States. The latter wasn't very appealing, partly because we had spent so much getting to Europe and wouldn't be reimbursed if David didn't take the job, and partly because we had neither a job nor a home to return to back in the States. We decided to wait it out.

The consensus of those we'd talked with about our predicament was that we should continue south to Morocco. It was cheaper than Spain, and we could live there for a long time on very little money. Morocco was only a place on a map that we knew nothing about. But it *was* in Africa, and we convinced the boys, who were becoming increasingly unhappy about this latest turn in our plans, that even though there were no big animals or game preserves there, it would be "really interesting." Besides, we'd be there only until it was safe to go on to Uganda.

Morocco proved sufficiently interesting at the outset to make the boys almost forget about Uganda. A land of contrasts in which biblical scenes were superimposed against backdrops of gleaming corporate hotels and seaside discos, of camels tethered next to fourteen-wheel semitrailer trucks, of bikinied tourists and veiled natives. Our plan was to explore the country before settling down, and we spent several days driving along the Mediterranean, past young boys waving bags of *kief*—marijuana leaves—for sale, camping outside Berber villages, and then cutting south to Fez, Casablanca, and Marrakech.

Micki's diary, October 1972: *Reed, who looks "Maroc," is a curiosity here. The veiled women in the medinas come up and ask if he is "Maroc," the implication being that if he is, what's he doing with us? We are, of course, a high-status family since we have three boys: here they have only one child and a girl if one happens to be a boy and the other a girl.*

When Saud, a young Moroccan who was anxious to practice his English and befriended us at a Fez campsite, learned that we were looking for a place to stay, he told us he had exactly the place and, one hot afternoon, took us to a dusty, rock-strewn, and barren-looking farm that a friend of his had for rent. It was only after being served mint tea, bread, and pomegranates by the old woman caretaker that we asked to see, among other things, the water supply. She proudly led us through a maze of stone-and-mud walls to a courtyard where a couple of scrawny chickens sat on the edge of a waist-high, circular enclosure. She said something to our friend.

"There is much water here," he told us.

We looked into the dark pool. It was alive with tiny red worms swimming near the surface.

"Oh, my God," gulped Micki. "The tea water."

Two nights later Reed, the only one of the boys who had drunk much of the tea—Grant and Drew found it too syrupy sweet—awoke screaming with stomach pains and diarrhea. At daybreak we rushed him to Agadir, a coastal resort town to the south, where the only doctor we could find told us that he had a "serious stomach disorder" that would "probably pass," and there was really nothing he could do for him. For two days we sat around the camper, watching the waves wash over the campground beach, as Reed lay sprawled in a near stupor on one of the camper mats, shaded by the van from the glare of the sun, his eyes glazed and unseeing. Back in Agadir we found a different doctor, who prescribed some medicine, and by the end of the week Reed was on his feet again, but only barely, and he was thin and emaciated. We had gotten to know the city well in our search for a competent doctor. With its relentlessly modern white poured-concrete apartment buildings, hotels, plazas, and shops, what it lacked in character it made up for in sanitation and convenience, for it had been rebuilt a dozen years before after a devastating earthquake. It was not the kind of town in which we would have ordinarily chosen to settle, but Reed's illness had drawn us up short and made us realize just how lacking in resources and local connections we actually were. After a couple of months of camping we were more than ready to trade local color for some stability. With the help of an Anglophile real estate agent we found an apartment in a low-income Berber neighborhood. "We could get the same thing in St. Louis for half as much," Micki whispered, when the agent told us the rent. Still, from one of the rooms, if you looked carefully between the line of luxury hotels down on the coast, you could see the ocean, and it did have a flush toilet of sorts and running water that, presumably, wasn't worm infested. We paid two months' rent in advance and settled in to wait for the fall of a dictator three thousand miles across the continent.

From Micki's diary: October 1972: *We have a five-room flat with a big courtyard, sparkling white with marble floors, a tub, and a toilet, though no furniture. We've been sleeping on mats from the van and cooking in a tagine over charcoal like our neighbors. Today we have three Berbers tearing out the toilet, which hasn't worked since we moved in, and as I write, they have disconnected it and are tipping it, full of shit, into the drainage sewer in the middle of the courtyard. Lots of local color here! And now a boy from downstairs has appeared to say that the shop below is being deluged with shit. What a romantic place.*

As the days passed it became painfully obvious that sitting and waiting for something to happen was harder than we'd anticipated. When we left England we hadn't planned to settle in Morocco or anywhere else, and we'd brought with us only the sorts of things you take on a family camping trip—a few books and toys, some clothing, and cooking utensils. We had a couple of African histories and some novels, but none of the boys' read-aloud favorites, since those had long since been mailed ahead to Uganda. The picture books the boys had stuffed into their backpacks were tattered and boring by now, and the Magic Markers no longer worked. Contrary to what we had promised, Morocco wasn't interesting at all. The way the Berbers dressed and talked, the trips to the *souk* for groceries, the outdoor marketplaces, buying sardines off the boat, and picking up fresh-baked bread at the bakery around the corner, all had become commonplace. There was nothing to do except wait until afternoons when the neighborhood children came home from school and go down into the little cul-de-sac and kick a soccer ball around with them for a while. But even that was no fun, they complained, because there was not enough space to get a real game going, and nobody ever kicked the ball to Reed. Back in St. Louis, Grant reminded us, there was a big field, and even the little kids got a chance to play.

"If they could read, or if we had something we could read to them, it would be different," Micki said one evening, after we'd spent most of dinner out in the courtyard talking about when and if we'd be able to get down to Uganda. "They're bored silly, and I don't blame them."

"We should have brought more reading material," said David, looking up from one of the novels.

"Sure, and we both knew that we'd end up here in Morocco."

"Maybe we ought to see about getting them into some kind of school. At least it would give them something to do."

"Maybe Grant could learn to read," said David. "Then at least one of us will have accomplished something while we're here."

Grant had spent two happy years in a new Montessori school in St. Louis where bug collecting, story-telling, and building fanciful structures out of scrap materials were encouraged more than learning the three R's. Now, as he approached his eighth birthday, Grant—who his teacher had repeatedly assured us was very bright and "exceptionally verbal"— couldn't read. Now, it would seem, might be as good a time to learn as any.

As foreigners the boys couldn't enroll in the government schools, we quickly discovered, and it was too late to enroll them in the French school, which served the children of the local middle class. "You *could* send them to the Hebrew school," the principal there told us with a look that said it was something *she* wouldn't do. "I *think* it's somewhere over in your neighborhood," she sniffed.

It was in an old, nearly windowless mud-plastered building that must somehow have managed to survive the earthquake and sat forlornly in the middle of a hard-packed dirt courtyard. The principal—who, we quickly discovered, was the sole teacher and the proprietor as well— seemed happy to see us. She escorted us into the back of a dark classroom, where twenty children of all ages huddled intently over their books, only a few of them daring to sneak a glance at the visitors. An old man sat hunched in the corner and barked something at one of the neighborhood boys who had greeted us with a small wave. "*Pour la discipline*," said the principal, gesturing toward the old man.

"Do you think you can handle it?" Micki asked Grant once we were back outside. This gloomy, almost medieval classroom was a far cry from what he'd known back in St. Louis. For one thing, there would be language problems: the principal spoke French, but course work was in Arabic and Hebrew, and the children spoke Berber. Grant nodded apprehensively.

"What about you, Drew?" He had spent two years in preschool, where, engrossed in projects that only preschoolers might appreciate, he didn't speak a word for the first year and a half. He shrugged. "What else is there?"

The teacher assured us that they'd have no trouble fitting in. "No problem, no problem," she said as she stuffed the first month's tuition— six dollars—into her pocket and shooed the boys back into the building. "No problem."

Drew lasted until noon. They had come home for the usual Laughing Cow cheese and French bread lunch. "I just sat there all morning with my hands folded while that old man walked back and forth and smacked kids who looked around or talked." He hadn't been hit, had he? No, but he hadn't looked around or talked, either. "I'm not *stupid*," he pointed out indignantly.

Maybe it would be better in the afternoon, we suggested. It might be better after he got used to it.

"*I'm* not going back," Drew said adamantly. "The stupid place."

"It's really not a good place for him," Grant said. We'd noticed how the boys had just begun to back up each other in situations like this.

"Well, what about you?"

"I'll try it for a while."

Grant came home a week later and announced that his teacher had gotten very angry with him that afternoon. It seemed that after looking through his notebook she had waved it in his face and shouted something at him and the whole classroom that he couldn't understand. "She acted kind of crazy," he said. Drew nodded his head. *He'd* known she was crazy right from the beginning.

The three of us were met at the schoolroom door the next morning by the teacher and the old man, who, in the morning sunlight, looked to be at least eighty years old. Was there something wrong with Grant's work? Both began nodding vigorously. Yes, there was, said the teacher. She snatched Grant's notebook from his hands and held it up.

"*Vois!*" she exclaimed, waving it and pointing to a page. "*Vois!*"

We said we didn't understand, couldn't see anything wrong.

"*Vois!*" she shrieked. "*Vois!*" She turned to the old man, who was jerking his head up and down at what appeared to be a life-threatening pace.

"*Vois!*" he agreed. "*Vois!*"

"Wait a minute," said Micki, taking the notebook back from the teacher. "Something strange is going on here. My French can't be *that* bad."

She flipped through it. There was nothing there that we hadn't seen the night before: French words carefully rendered in childish block letters and some indecipherable marks that we presumed were Arabic.

Micki tried again. "*Je ne comprends pas,*" she said, handing back the notebook.

"*Vois! Vois!*" the two of them began again.

"Let's get out of here," urged Micki, taking Grant by the hand and carefully backing away. It was like a scene out of a comic opera. We stumbled backward a few more steps as the two of them advanced on us, and then, as one, turned abruptly and scurried across the yard as their angry cries rang out after us.

"What," exclaimed David, "was *that* all about?"

"Maybe he wrote something obscene in Arabic," said Micki.

"Or French," Grant added. "All I did was copy what was on the blackboard. I couldn't even read it."

We never did figure out what Grant had done to precipitate their reaction, but the episode prompted us to take yet another hard look at what was beginning to look like a disaster. Morocco had turned out to be no bargain: The fees and bribes we had to pay to transfer money from the United States to the local bank ate up whatever we might have been able to save in living costs. And according to our only link to the outside world, the *Herald Tribune*, things were not getting any better in Uganda; what we thought would be settled in a month or two now looked as if it could stretch out for years. If we called it quits and returned now, we'd have to pay for the trip over and back for the five of us. We began to think about what for months had been the unthinkable: cutting our losses and going back to gather the roomful of belongings we'd stored in what used to be our house, the old Volvo, and the camper. We'd tried to get away, and now, for all of our planning, we were worse off than when we'd left St. Louis.

Micki's diary, November 1972: *After a month the plumbing is finally fixed. Every night the plumber would say, "Ça va," "It works," and every morning I'd search him out to say, "Toilet kaput." Now we marvel with each clean flush. Speaking of shit, the university is getting some flack about David's case—"the victim of a railroading that has not been seen since the days when the Wabash Cannonball careened through the Midwest," according to a piece in the student newspaper, which last year characterized his case as "boring."*

"Why not California?" Micki said to David. "You said Mendocino was beautiful. At least we could be doing *something* there, instead of sitting here watching our money dwindle away." We were seated around a cast-concrete table—one of our few pieces of furniture—in the corner of the courtyard and had just finished recounting for Drew and Reed's benefit our encounter with the crazy teachers. It had begun to sound like a reprise of the St. Louis story: We didn't have any reason for staying on in Morocco now that Uganda seemed out of the picture and the boys couldn't even go to school. Where did we go from here?

"What would we do, live in the camper?"

"Why not?" she answered. "We could do it. Look at all the camping we've done. And how we're living here, for heaven's sake. You know we can't keep bouncing around like this."

"You know how much this fiasco has cost us, don't you? We can't even think about getting some land."

"What about Wash U?" she asked. A colleague of David's had written to say that the administration was anxious to work out a settlement in the face of an American Association of University Professors move to censure them for violating his academic freedom.

"It's probably a ruse," said David. "I wouldn't believe anything those sons of bitches say."

Micki's diary, November 1972: *Things aren't working out here, partly because of the kids' isolation and partly because of the cost of living. We've heard from friends who have been scouring the field for jobs for David; they say there's little chance of his getting anything decent, and besides, we think it's time to kick that whole damn racket.*

"I *knew* we wouldn't go to Uganda," Grant moaned. "I knew it."

"There's nothing we can do about that, Grant," said Micki. "You're old enough to understand that."

"In California you could have your own animals," said David. "A dog and cat. Chickens and rabbits, and maybe even a goat or two. We could have a garden and everything. How about it, Drew? Reed?"

"It sounds okay to me," Drew said unenthusiastically. In St. Louis we'd already had all of those, except for the goats.

David turned to Reed. "It'll be fun, going to California and living in the woods, won't it?" Reed shrugged noncommittally.

"Poor Reed," said Grant. "By now he doesn't know what to think."

"That's just it," said David, turning to Micki, annoyed by the boys' passivity. It was as if they were saying they weren't buying into this one, this latest adventure. "We really need a place we could always come back to, instead of having to bounce around like this," he told Micki, ignoring the boys. "Look at how it's getting to the kids. They don't know what's happening. We need to get a place somewhere and dig in. So that no matter what happens, it's *home*, a refuge from all this crap."

"A refuge." Micki thought for a minute. "Do you really think we could do it?"

"The only alternative is to stay here. Or start looking for another teaching job in some godforsaken town."

"Let's talk about it some more later," said Micki, getting up. "How soon do you think we could leave?"

"Tomorrow," said Grant, perking up again.

"Yeah, yeah, tomorrow," Drew piped up.

"Tomorrow or the next day," said David.

Later that night, when the boys were asleep, we sat in the courtyard sharing what was left of a bottle of harsh Moroccan red wine. "If we go back, we'll really have to go on to California, you know," said Micki. "No matter what. We just can't keep doing this to the kids. Grant especially. I think he's beginning to wonder if he can believe *anything* we tell him."

"I know. Let's just hope California makes up for all of this and doesn't turn into another disaster."

"We can't let it," said Micki, her voice rising. "No matter what happens."

"Right," agreed David. "Can you have everything ready by tomorrow?"

"There isn't much to pack up."

"Then let's get out of here."

Micki's diary, November 1972: *Packed camper, late start, last stop at "Banana Village" for two kilos of bananas and one kilo of green oranges. Ate hard-boiled eggs and cheese for supper and decided to continue driving on to border, anticipating hassle but went through with ease. Caught ferry within twenty minutes and had the first cold beers in three months. A civil engineer on board just back from Uganda told us things there were terrible, a good thing we didn't go on down.*

PART TWO

Coming
into the
Country

CHAPTER THREE

Not a Place for Children

We arrived in the Bay Area on one of the coldest days in its history, in the midst of snow flurries and an unprecedented, tree-killing frost. The weather was the least of our concerns, however, and we immediately began searching for a place we could use as a base while we looked for land farther north. A week later, after locating a tiny furnished house in the Berkeley hills that commanded a spectacular view of San Francisco and the Golden Gate Bridge, we set off for Mendocino. It was not a particularly auspicious beginning, for on that cold and rainy December day northern California didn't look like something worth traveling six or seven thousand miles to find. The churned-up sea was a forbidding slate gray, the wind blustery and raw, the hills olive drab, and the sky became forebodingly darker as we traveled north. Even the usually majestic redwoods looked dull and ominous in the dim winter light.

"So this is Mendocino," Micki said as we rounded a bend on the coast highway and the town came into sight.

"It's beautiful when the sun's out," said David. Nobody responded. "It really is."

We drove into town and pulled up in front of a real estate office that David had visited briefly the year before. Inside, portly and garrulous, a walking caricature of a country realtor, "Fast Phil" ("See Phil and Getta Deal," proclaimed his business card) greeted us as if we were old friends. *Of course* he remembered David, *of course* he had something to show us, *of course* he could take us out to look at some properties. Braving the wind and cold rain, we climbed into Fast Phil's Bronco and visited a small redwood house close by, with a view of some offshore rocks and swirling white water.

"White water's worth more," said Fast Phil. " 'Course if you're interested in an ocean view *without* white water, I got those, too." He told us the price of the house with the white-water view. We didn't know anything about California real estate, but we did know that a tiny wooden house with a white-water view couldn't be worth three times what we'd sold our big red-brick St. Louis house for just six months earlier. Not to us, at least. Did he have something a bit less expensive?

"Well, if you're not interested in an ocean view, why pay for it, I always say," Phil said expansively as he helped Micki into the Bronco. "We can go back inland a ways and I'll show you some real buys."

A few minutes later we were standing next to the Bronco and staring down into a canyon that looked as if it had been bombed, a landscape of limbless and broken trees scattered among blackened redwood stumps, of muddy orange clay trails that were washing away before our very eyes, of huge tangled piles of roots, brush, and shattered logs. Fast Phil must have sensed our horror at the scene. "I suppose maybe they did a bit of a job on this one," he said apologetically. "Some of these fellas just aren't too careful about the work they do." Mendocino County realtors, we soon learned, were remarkably adept at sizing up their clients and adjusting their sales pitches accordingly. There was a pitch for the trust fund hippies, another for Sierra Club members seeking sites for their second homes, and yet another for near retirement Orange County couples who aspired to a double-wide mobile home on a half acre. Phil had quickly figured us for a bunch of environmentalists, somewhere between the first and second groups.

"Dad, we don't want a place like *that*, do we?" Grant whispered as we headed back to the road.

"Don't worry," said David. "It might take a while, but we'll find what we want."

"We better," Drew said emphatically. He'd stayed behind to take another look at the scene and had just caught up with them.

"Sometimes they just get carried away," Phil was telling Micki as we piled back into the vehicle. "It was just logged last fall, so it doesn't look like much," he continued, "but, listen, you know, with a little work it could be turned into a real pretty place."

He showed us two more "sleepers"—a field of wrecked cars that had "a good little spot over there where you could put a house" and a lot next to a junk-strewn, recently abandoned commune. After driving past a few more listings without stopping, we told Phil we really weren't interested in rehabilitating a rural slum or spending our lives cleaning up after a devastating logging operation. All we wanted were a couple of acres where we could put up a house and have a garden, then perhaps sell it and move on to something a little bigger.

"That's what everybody wants," said Phil, shaking his head. "Maybe you ought to look inland, where property is cheaper. 'Course you won't get the views or the resale value . . ."

Back in Berkeley, Micki scanned the "Country Property" ads in the *San Francisco Examiner* while David spent most of the next few days on the telephone. Upon returning from Morocco, we'd discovered that both Washington University and the American Association of University Professors desperately wanted to be done with David's academic freedom case. President Danforth was anxious that his handling of the case not result in the University being censured, and the AAUP was uncomfortable in the role of taking on one of the more powerful families in American education. Bill Brown, an attorney for the AAUP, had been trying to bring about a settlement for months. The offer was now up to $15,000—a little over a year's salary—and once again Brown urged David to take it. "It's not going to get any better," he warned. "They might back out altogether if you keep pushing." David reminded him that tenure would have guaranteed him upward of thirty years' employment, something worth well over a million dollars according to even the most conservative of estimates. And they were offering $15,000? "Nobody's ever done any better," said Brown. David told him to go back for more.

"What about Lake Berryessa?" Micki said that night at dinner. "There seems to be a lot of land up there." We checked it out on the map. Too far inland. No redwoods and probably too hot. And the Sierras were out: too hot in the summer and too cold in winter, worse than Missouri or Connecticut.

"We could get a hundred acres in Idaho for twenty-five thousand. Or forty acres of vineyards in Napa for five hundred thousand with a small down payment."

"Not small enough, though," said David. For six months we'd been living off what we'd gotten from the sale of the St. Louis house and hadn't dared calculate what the Uganda-Morocco adventure had cost. We figured that a down payment of about $5,000 on a piece of land would leave us enough to frame up a small house and forgo any outside income for perhaps a year, which was what back-to-the-land guru Scott Nearing recommended. We hadn't given much thought to what we would do after a year or so, since now, after the turmoil of the last few years, all we wanted was a place of our own, a place to which, no matter wherever else we might travel in the years to come, we could always return and call our own.

For the next two months we looked at dozens of parcels up and down the coast, but everything we saw was either too expensive or had something seriously wrong with it—next to a junkyard, recently logged, lacking any sign of water in what was an exceptionally wet spring, or, most often, so steep that it was hard to imagine setting a house on it, much less putting the land to any kind of use.

Micki's diary, January 1973: *Saturday we drove into San Francisco to celebrate the Vietnam ceasefire. We all felt good about it, but especially Grant, who has known and understood all about the war and its profound effect on his (our?) life.*

We'd long since given up on Fast Phil, but his successors weren't much better, ranging from the hippie realtors in their new, mud-splattered pickups and vans who always seemed to have a "right-on" piece of property that was "perfect" for us, to the good ol' boys in their air-conditioned Cadillacs who started off by showing us their expensive pieces "ideal for a nice family like yours" and then, visibly, ran out of patience as we worked our way down the list to what we could afford—but didn't want. One of the most memorable was the long-haired, fast-talking young realtor who told us that he had "been into confrontational politics in Berkeley" but was now "into saving Mother Earth" and was going to give us an opportunity to be "part of that trip, too." When we told him that the rocky ledge, deep in a gorge and utterly inaccessible except by foot, that we'd spent an hour climbing down to was not *our* idea of "a great house site" and definitely not, as he had promised, our "life's dream," he took it as an insult and didn't speak again until we'd climbed back out, at which point he informed us curtly that he had nothing else in which we'd be interested. Some people, it seemed, just weren't into saving Mother Earth. Then there was the especially glorious sunny day when we conferred under the trees high above the Pacific in Sonoma County, trying to figure how we could afford the monthly payments on what was the cheapest parcel on a newly divided ranch; when we asked the realtor about a couple of acres on a nearby ridge that seemed to be in the process of sliding down into the ocean, he became highly agitated and told us that he "resented the implication" that the land was in any way *unstable*.

By March we had a pretty good idea of what was available in our price range and had narrowed our search to an area in the southern part of Mendocino County called Anderson Valley. A couple of miles across at its widest point, flanked by redwood-covered ridges, and bisected by the Navarro River, which flowed northwest some thirty-five miles to the coast, Anderson Valley was generally regarded by those who knew anything at all about it as a real backwater in a backwater county. It lay halfway between Highway 101, one of California's major north-south routes, and the village of Mendocino, on a narrow road that twisted tortuously through rolling hills at one end and, on the other, into dense redwood forest that ran right up to the ocean.

After a few days of searching, we found a subdivision in the lower end of the valley called Rancho Navarro and selected a ten-acre parcel that was in our price range. The land was uncluttered, with open, rolling hills dotted with redwood groves. It was a bit too suburban, perhaps—we could see the beginnings of a half dozen minihomesteads from the middle of our plot—and a bit overorganized, with its community center and tiny swimming pool. But it would be a good place to start out, we agreed. In our ruminations about how we were going to finance our stay in the country, we'd decided that we might have to put up a "spec" house— we'd discovered that self-taught carpenters were doing just that all over the county—sell it, move on, and live off the profits while building another house on a parcel more to our liking. Rancho Navarro certainly wasn't our "life's dream," but it would do, at least for the time being. We signed the papers and returned to Berkeley, only to get a call from the realtor. He'd neglected to tell us that there might be some problem with electricity. The owner of an adjacent parcel had been refusing to give anybody the right-of-way to run power lines across his place, saying that he didn't want them spoiling his view.

"He'll probably change his mind once he gets to know you," the realtor tried to assure us.

"And if he doesn't?" asked Micki.

We tried to arrange a meeting with our would-be neighbor but couldn't find him. The deal was off. We couldn't risk it, especially if we were thinking of doing a "spec" house and moving on. Nobody wanted a place that didn't have electric power.

According to the Anderson Valley Chamber of Commerce brochure, Boonville, twenty miles up the Navarro at the south end of the valley, was its "Commercial Center and Home of the Mendocino County Apple Show and Fair." It had a population of 714 and was noteworthy for its apple orchards, timber, sheep ranches, and a language called "Boontling," which had been invented by local hopfield workers a century earlier, was still spoken by some old-timers, and had been the subject of a recent University of Texas Press scholarly monograph. In the language of Boontling, the brochure explained, the county seat and lumber mill town of Ukiah, twenty miles over the mountains to the east, was known as "Uke," valley residents who lived downriver from "Boont" were "deep-enders," and city slickers who ventured into the valley from San Francisco were "bright lighters." The town's three public telephone booths were "Buckey Walters," a derivation based on the original after the price of a call (an Indian-head nickel) and the name of the first person in the valley to have had a telephone.

We'd passed through the town a dozen times to and from the coast and had stopped there several times for groceries and gasoline. Now, as our search carried us farther inland, we had gotten to know the valley's "commercial center" better. Coming south on Route 128 from the coast, we'd pass by Schoenahl's apple orchards and big tin-roofed packing sheds, the highway maintenance yard, the green Caltrans sign ("Population 714, Elevation 400"), the turnoff to the high school ("Home of the Panthers"), Hiatt's logging truck yard, the Redwood Drive-In, a broken-down hotel, and an abandoned shack in a weed-infested lot with a sign hanging over the door that identified it as the "Boonville Recreation Center." In the center of town stood a big empty warehouse that a realtor told us had "been in escrow for years, a family split of some sort"; the Boonville Lodge, which was the last of the fifty or so bars that dotted the valley during the fifties timber boom; and, opposite the post office and the white stucco building that housed Rossi's Hardware ("Estab. 1931"), the Anderson Valley Market. The grandstand, parking lot, and county fairgrounds took up most of the western side of the road and faced a strip of ramshackle vacant buildings, the ruins of a badly maintained Laundromat, Jeff's Union Station, and a one-story frame building that was the unlikely home of the First National Bank. A few hundred yards south of the bank stood a sign next to a driveway guarded by a locked gate, which marked the entrance to the "International Ideal City," referred to by the locals as "the Moonie camp."

Lyle was a bit different from the realtors we'd come to divide into two categories—hippies and good ol' boys. He had grown up in the county and obviously liked Anderson Valley, and he patiently showed us one place after another, each of which we rejected as too expensive, too close to the road, too ugly, too steep, too logged over. After four days of combing the hills and the valley, we were in Lyle's office behind the Redwood Drive-In, where he was leafing through his listings and we were about to move on. That was it, he told us; he'd call if anything else came along.

"Were we up here?" David asked as the boys started toward the door. He was pointing to a spot on the topographical map taped on the wall, outlined in green ink, and marked by a stick-pin flag. It was on Mountain View Road, past the high school. "I don't remember being out that far."

Lyle dismissed it with a wave. "No," he said. "You wouldn't be interested in that. It's way out there, up on a ridge where you can't get power."

"How many acres?" asked Micki.

"Forty-seven." He pulled out the listing. "There are a couple of building sites, but it's pretty steep and wild. There's nobody around for miles. The county road out that way wasn't even paved until five or six years ago. It's not a place for children."

Micki glanced at David. We didn't have anything scheduled for the rest of the day. "Let's take a look at it," she said to Lyle. "If it isn't too much trouble."

Twenty minutes later we were bouncing up the deeply rutted dirt road in Lyle's open jeep, the kids clinging to the roll bar and screaming with delight. The ridge dropped off sharply to our left, and we could see a creek far below.

"There was a big slide here a year or two ago," Lyle shouted as we came around a blind curve and the road twisted steeply above us. He shifted down, and we passed under a canopy of overhanging oaks, firs, and redwoods. "No way in or out until they cut this new section." At the top, a mile up, he stopped and gestured to the overgrown embankment. "This is it," he said. "Now you all get out while I try to get this thing up there."

The embankment was about six feet high and practically vertical. Lyle swung the jeep around, backed up into the brush on the opposite side of the road, floored it, and charged into the earthen wall. For an instant it looked as if the vehicle were about to tumble backward, but the momentum carried it up and over the ledge. He stopped in a tangle of brush and waved for us to come up and get back in. "Just keep your head down and watch for branches," he instructed. "It's pretty thick in here. They can really hurt."

Micki got back into the passenger seat and pulled Reed onto her lap, ignoring his demand that he be allowed to ride in the back with his father and brothers, who were crouched down behind them. "This is fun, isn't it, Dad?" Grant exclaimed as the Jeep crunched forward.

We were on a narrow ridge so densely overgrown that it was impossible to imagine where Lyle intended to take us. He started down what seemed to be an old logging trail and then, finding it blocked by a cluster of fir saplings, backed up and started down another, while shouting for us to look out for the branches that slammed against the Jeep, snapping and cracking, as it pushed through the brush. The ridge seemed to slope to the south and east, gently at first, and then it fell off sharply. Redwoods, firs, tan oaks, black oaks, and madrones—we had learned to recognize all kinds of local flora in the course of our search for land—loomed up out of the manzanita and musk-bush brush that seemed to surround us. Eventually, after maneuvering the jeep around and through obstacles of every shape and form, Lyle pulled up to a spot just below a rise dominated by a huge old fir tree. "Come on up here," he said, hurrying ahead as the five of us examined each other, marveling that none of us had any serious cuts or bruises. We stood on the edge of a precipice, and there, across the canyon, in a sweeping panorama, were the ragged lines of a dozen ridges, stretching out before us one after the other. The nearest was perhaps a mile away and sloped downward into an open pasture. Behind it, two other ridges formed a deep V that twisted back into the hills.

"Somewhere down there is the Rancheria River," said Lyle, pointing. "It runs into the Navarro near Philo. And over there you can see the top of Goat Peak. Way out there is Fish Rock Road, and over there"— he pointed to the west—"is Breadloaf Mountain. On the other side of that a way is the coast." He stood there for a minute while we took in the view. "I'd put my house right here."

An hour later, as we slowly climbed up out of the deep canyon where Lyle wanted us to see the year-round creek, Drew took David by the hand and led him off to the side of the deer trail, out of hearing from the others. He looked up at him very intently. "We *are* going to buy it, aren't we, Dad?" It was as if they were sharing a secret.

David stopped to catch his breath. This part of the land was as steep as anything we'd seen. "Do you think we should?"

"It has a creek, and lots of firewood," he said. "And a good place where we could build the house. You said the price is pretty good." He gave what he'd just said serious consideration for another moment, then nodded. "Yeah," he said very seriously. "I think it's a good deal." After two months of tagging along with us, he figured that he knew as much about real estate as the rest of us.

"Drew says we should buy it," David called up the hill to Grant and Micki. "What do you think?"

Micki waited for them to catch up. "There's no pasture," she said. "And it'll take a lot of work to clear it."

Grant was farther up the hill with Reed and was showing him a piece of obsidian he'd found in the creek. "I think this might be Indian," he said, scraping the dirt off it and holding it up to the light.

"What do you think of the land?" said David.

"Sure we should buy it," Grant said distractedly, as if there were no question about it. "There might be an old Indian campsite around here somewhere," he told Reed as he scanned the ridge above us.

"It's by far the best we've seen yet," Micki said between breaths as we climbed up the trail. "But won't it be a lot of work?"

Lyle and the boys had gone on ahead and turned off into brush so thick that even though they were only a few yards away, there was no sign of them. "A *lot* of work," David agreed.

We peppered Lyle with the usual questions as we headed back to town to write up an offer. What about rattlesnakes? David was terrified of snakes, having almost been bitten by one he had surprised while throwing stones off a bridge near his grandparents' farm thirty years earlier. "Never saw one up there," said Lyle. We knew, of course, that his chances of seeing one were pretty slight since he'd told us earlier that he'd been on the property only once before, but it was close enough to the answer we wanted. Was he sure the creek ran year-round? We shouldn't count on it, he cautioned us: we'd have a hard time getting water from way down there up to the top of the ridge where we'd probably put the house. If it was up to him, he'd develop one of those little springs we'd seen on our way back up out of the canyon. And how much would it cost to have a power line run in if we decided that we really needed electricity?

"Don't even *think* of buying that place if you think you're gonna get power up there somehow," he said. "Why do you think it's so underpriced? You're over a mile from the main line, and it doesn't make any difference if you could afford to pay for it or not, the people who own the land in between won't give you a right-of-way." It was Rancho Navarro all over again, except that this was no suburb and certainly not the kind of place we'd be able or inclined to live on for a couple of years or so and then move on. If we bought it, it'd be for keeps.

"Do you think we can live without electricity?" asked David. "That means we won't have any appliances, you know. Kerosene lights, no washer or dryer."

"Or hair dryer or toaster or vacuum cleaner," added Micki. "I know. I can handle it if *you're* up to it."

"And we won't have a telephone, will we?" inquired Grant.

"No telephone," said Lyle. "Same problem."

"Good," said David.

Heading back to Berkeley that evening, exhilarated, Micki observed that we'd made up our minds before we saw the property, as we drove up the ridge toward it. "I could tell right away that Dad liked it," she said to the boys. "Up there far away from anything, no electricity, no neighbors, no telephone. I like the way Lyle took us up under the fir tree and said he'd put the house there. It was like Brigham Young in Utah proclaiming, 'This is the place.' "

"Who was Brigham Young?" asked Grant.

"A pioneer."

"Like us, huh, Mom," said Drew.

"A little bit," she agreed.

"It's going to be fun," said Drew.

"And a lot of hard work," she answered. "You realize that we can't even drive the car onto it now, don't you? And then we're going to have to cut a road down to where we'll build the house, right, David?"

"Right," said David. He glanced into the rearview mirror and could see the boys, their faces flushed with excitement.

"And we're going to live there forever," said Grant.

"Well, for a while, at least," Micki said, glancing over at David. He seemed almost as excited as the boys. Now was not the time to raise the question of how we were going to make a living up on that wild and lovely mountaintop. But Lyle's words, when David asked him about the piece back in the office, kept running through her head: "It's no place for children," he'd said. "Not a place for children." And we'd have the three of them up there with us. What were we *really* getting into? she wondered. But David didn't seem to be having any second thoughts. Or if he did, he was keeping them to himself.

Bill Brown telephoned from Washington a week later. "You got it," he said. "Twenty-five thousand. You agree not to take any legal action, and they'll put the check in the mail. That's the deal."

"Good," said David. He'd talked to Brown a dozen times over the last two months and had insisted that Washington University come up with at least two years' salary before he'd settle. "It still isn't enough."

"It's the largest amount we've ever gotten," Brown said. "And I have to tell you, they're not very happy about it. I just hope you haven't burned your bridges in all this."

"Meaning what?"

"They're just not very happy at being pushed like this. College presidents don't like having to admit that they might not take academic freedom as seriously as they should. Especially a liberal place like Wash U. And there are some pretty influential folks there, you know that."

"Hey, they're the ones who are in the wrong here," said David, his voice rising. "Not me."

"Yeah, I know, you're right. Well, you've got your money, and I'm only sorry there wasn't a damn thing we could do to make them give you your job back."

"We both knew that from the beginning. And I appreciate your help, I really do." He'd been pretty hard on Brown over the last few weeks. There was silence on the other end of the line for a moment.

"Are you by any chance looking for another job?" Brown asked hesitantly.

"No," said David. "We just bought forty-seven acres in the mountains north of here, up in Mendocino County, and plan to get just as far away as possible from academia for a while."

"Your family's going with you, too, of course?"

"Everybody. My wife and three boys. It's pretty wild. No telephone, no electricity."

"I envy you. It's everybody's dream, isn't it? Giving up the nine-to-five job and getting back to nature?"

"Yeah," said David. "But I didn't exactly *give up* my job."

"Of course. Well, anyhow, best of luck. You're entitled to some."

David hung up the phone and turned to Micki, who had come into the room with the boys when she realized that Brown was on the line. "Twenty-five thousand," said David, shaking his head. "I guess now it's pretty obvious that we should have sued them."

"It would have taken years," said Micki. "At least now we don't have to worry about anything except the land and getting a house up."

"We won, then, didn't we, Dad?" Grant said with a puzzled look on his face. He thought that they should be celebrating. "You made them pay us."

"Of course we won!" said Micki, forcing a smile. Twenty-five thousand dollars. It would make things easier for a while, she thought, but it wouldn't go very far. Not after they made a down payment on the land and put up a house. Living on the land with a family of five. For how long? she wondered.

Micki's diary, March 1973: *I'm still recovering from the shock of receiving that check. I've had to swallow my pride and admit that David was right about fighting back; I didn't think we had a chance of winning. Didn't even celebrate it except to drink a bottle of Paisano; deprivation destroys hedonistic impulses, it appears. We've heard that Danforth's mad as hell, which gives us some satisfaction.*

CHAPTER FOUR

A Wild and Lonely Place

"I'd go for the heavy-duty one," said Grant. "We're going to be digging a lot of fence post holes." At $29.95 it was more than we'd ever paid for a tool, and David was skeptical.

"We're not going to wear out a *fence post hole digger*," he said. "I think the lightweight one'll be okay." He turned to the rest of us for support.

"No," stated Drew, "I think we should get the heavy-duty one while we're at it. It's only thirteen dollars more." David gave Micki a look: they always backed each other up; them versus Mom-and-Dad. It was okay; what did we know about this stuff, anyway?

"Okay, let's get the big one, then," said David, capitulating.

We'd had to learn one new vocabulary when we were looking for land and had learned how to ask reasonably intelligent questions about such things as rights-of-way, water rights, liens, escrow, and second mortgages. Now, as we made preparations to move onto our forty-seven acres, we'd had to learn others. Like most back-to-the-landers of the time—and we had quickly learned there were enough of them to sustain a couple of Bay Area establishments that catered exclusively to what was apparently, if their prices for everything ranging from shovels to wind systems were any indication, a remarkably affluent clientele—we'd come to rely upon

Stuart Brand's *Whole Earth Catalog* and the now slick *Mother Earth News* in much the same way that we'd depended upon *Consumer Reports*, to point us in the right direction. Not that we entirely *trusted* these back-to-the-land bibles, of course: from the moment we'd begun to think about getting away from what we'd become embroiled in for too many years with such disastrous consequences, we'd been a bit put off by the smarmy, apolitical tone of these publications, which glorified the back-to-the-land movement. From our perspective, what America needed, in those Nixonian seventies, were not "tuned in and dropped out" disciples of muddle-headed millionaires such as Timothy Leary, not self-indulgent escapists, but younger versions of ourselves, people who got involved in the issues of the day. We were different, we told ourselves: Our moving to the land was as necessary—and as out of character—for us as it had been for old Scott Nearing so many years before, and for remarkably similar reasons. We might be moving to the country but were not inclined to romanticize what was, at bottom, something we felt we had to do. But even though we were offended by their seeming obliviousness of social and political issues, *Mother Earth News* and the *Whole Earth Catalog* contained the information we needed, and they, along with the newly discovered Sears Farm Catalog, seed catalogs, and house plan books, became our reading materials of necessity, if not choice, in the weeks before we moved up to the land.

We knew we needed such things as shovels and picks, saws and brush loppers and axes, to cut our way onto the land and through the brush, and we spent days searching out bargains—a shovel for $3.98, a Swedish bow saw for $6.98—at the local Sears and K mart. Right from the start we'd resolved to do all the clearing and road building ourselves and by hand, and that didn't require much in the way of equipment. We'd seen the devastation wreaked by heavy equipment—cats and backhoes and graders. Any damn fool could hire a bulldozer to come in and tear a road through the brush. We'd seen too many once beautiful spots that had been destroyed by people who, in an effort to get on with things, had hacked out roads and cut in building sites without regard for the lay of the land and had left it irreparably scarred. And we'd seen enough to know that our forty-seven acres, wild and isolated as they were, was no wilderness. It had been heavily logged two decades before, and the vegetation that made it so nearly impenetrable was the opportunistic result of that intrusion. Now, coming onto it as its most recent intruders, we resolved that the trade-off would be our efforts to restore it, even as we lived upon it, and that this could be best accomplished—if at all—only by hand. We knew it would be a slow process—we never imagined just *how* slow—but we sensed that if we did the clearing and construction ourselves, if we proceeded slowly and deliberately, as we had to under such circumstances, we'd be better able to relate to the land, to respect its integrity, and to help restore it to the condition it had enjoyed before it had been logged. In the spring of 1973, before we'd cut out a musk bush, limbed a fir, or thinned out a deformed redwood grove, this was little more than an intuitive, half-formed, and unarticulated notion; but once on the land, and as we became more and more a part of it, it emerged as a guiding principle that shaped and informed our efforts and to which, with only a couple of well-considered exceptions, we remained faithful.

Only the chain saw, the one powered piece of equipment we'd own until we started work on the house, was a problem. We'd never run one and, in fact, could recall seeing one being operated only once, when a St. Louis neighbor came over and greatly impressed us as he quickly dispatched a mulberry tree branch that had fallen on our fence. Sam down at the Navarro Saw Shop seemed to sense our trepidation as we stood in his cluttered workshop behind the Floodgate Store, surrounded by intimidatingly large saws of all kinds, their qualities touted on the posters that lined the walls—Homelites and McCulloughs, "American Made, American Tough," Husquavarnas and Stihls, "A New Era of Power." David gingerly examined a big Homelite.

"You don't need one of them big 'uns," said Sam, a jolly-looking ex-logger who'd "quit workin' in the woods twenty years ago and never regretted it." "That one there's got a forty-eight-inch bar. That's for fallin' the big ones."

"We only need something for clearing brush," said David. "And not too expensive." He'd just checked the price on the Homelite.

"I'd go with a used one, then," said Sam. He reached under a workbench and pulled out a battered blue Homelite. "This has a twenty-inch bar and enough power for what you'll need it for. And it's only seventy-five dollars. A new one this size'd cost you four hundred bucks."

"If you think it'll be okay," said David. "Now you've got to show me how to work it."

The five of us followed him outside, where, when he pulled on the starter cord, the saw roared to life in a cloud of blue smoke. "Here," he said, handing it to David and pointing him in the direction of a big log chipped and crosshatched with grooves from previous tests. David set the saw on the log and opened the throttle. The whirring teeth spewed sawdust back at him as it bit into the log for a few seconds, until Sam signaled him to turn it off.

"You got the idea," praised Sam. "C'mon in here now and I'll show you how to sharpen it."

As we left the shop that morning with our first piece of what we thought was, as Drew called it, "our first heavy-duty equipment," we didn't know that old Homelite we'd be using over the next couple of years was underpowered, worn out, and too heavy for the job we'd bought it for. Only later, when somebody stopped by with a better one, did we realize that we could have saved ourselves hours of backbreaking work if we'd only bought a new, lightweight model at the outset. But how was Sam to know that we were going to cut in a road through some of the heaviest brush in the area and clear a building site? We'd thought it had been a bargain.

We'd never had a real garden before; we'd grown a few radishes and some lettuce in Connecticut and a half dozen tomato plants in one of the old flower beds next to the St. Louis house, but we agreed that one of the first things we'd do when we moved onto the land would be to put in a garden. Lyle had warned us about the deer—"They can clear a six-foot fence without a running start"—so we picked up a couple of rolls of seven-foot-tall Red Top fencing over at the Ukiah Farm Supply, along with rakes, hoes, and some old-fashionedly familiar red and blue kerosene lanterns. For all of its advocacy of "country living," *Mother Earth News* had featured surprisingly few pieces on gardening, and we'd turned to something called *Organic Gardening*, a publication that seemed to have been around almost forever and whose message seemed to be pretty much the same from issue to issue and could be summed up in three words: compost and mulch. Somehow that was not enough, so we loaded up with the first batch of what soon became an extensive library of how-to-do-it books—the *Western Garden Book*, the *Basic Book of Organic Gardening*, the *Reader's Digest Complete Book of the Garden*, and what quickly became our gardening bible, a five-dollar paperback entitled *Grow It! The Beginner's Complete in Harmony with Nature Small Farm Guide from Vegetable and Grain Growing to Livestock Care*. It didn't quite cover everything but was more than adequate for those of us who didn't know acid from base, nitrogen from phosphorus, or, we soon discovered, poor soil from the extraordinarily bad soil in which we intended to grow our food.

And so on that late spring day in 1973, armed with shovels and rakes, a worn-out chain saw, and books on how to grow our own food and one on how to build a house, we came onto the land when it was lush, after a series of rains had cut even deeper gouges into what we'd come to call the access road. It was pouring rain the afternoon that we'd towed the Coleman camper up from Berkeley, and we had managed to get a half mile, halfway, up the ridge before the road became all but impassable.

"You're not going to try to make it up there, are you?" Micki asked as we peered through the steamed-up windshield of the Volvo.

"Let's check it out," said David. The boys pulled on their new ponchos, climbed out of the backseat, and followed us up the steepest stretch of the road.

"It's going to be hard to keep out of the gulleys," Micki said through the roar of the steady downpour. "There are some really big tree roots exposed in those gulleys that you're going to hit no matter what you do. It's going to be hard on the car."

"Just make sure the kids are way out of the way," said David, getting back into the car. "I might have to back down, and I won't be able to see anything."

Micki gestured to Reed, who was standing next to the car, shivering. "Get over here. Your dad's going to make a run for it."

David revved the engine a couple of times, then floored it, and the car jumped forward, fishtailing crazily as it charged up the hill, the camper lurching and bouncing wildly behind it, its small wheels slamming in and out of the deep yellow-clay ruts. Then, abruptly, it was over: he'd made it to the protected, almost level stretch at the top. He got out and walked around to the back of the car to check the camper, then waved his arms in triumph as Micki and the boys, soaked to the skin, hurried to catch up with him.

"Pretty good job, Dad," Reed said as they piled into the warm and steamy comfort of the Volvo.

"Pretty good?" exclaimed Micki. "Your father's a *great* driver."

"I didn't think it was *that* great," Drew said.

"Neither did I," said Grant. They were becoming a pretty formidable pair, David thought. Nothing got by them.

At the top of the ridge, just beyond our farthest property line marker, we backed into a small flat place—the only such spot the entire length of the access road—and cranked open the camper under some scrawny oaks. Crowded together in the tiny space—as we would be for months to come—we pulled on our work clothes and headed out into the unrelenting rain, with shovels, mattock, and rakes in hand. We had intended to spend the day trying to cut an incline into the embankment where Lyle had nearly toppled the jeep so that we could pull the camper up onto our land, but we succeeded only in churning up the sticky orange clay and getting soaked to the skin. We called it quits after an hour. Back in the camper, we stripped off our sopping wet, mud-streaked clothes, the boys huddling in blankets on their side of the camper until the propane stove turned the place into a sauna.

"This is a historic moment," David called over to the boys as we climbed into our sleeping bags, the boys on one side of the camper and we on the other. "Our first night on the land."

"We're not on our land," said Grant.

"Well, we're on our ridge," David growled. "It's still a historic moment."

But we were all too worn out by our efforts to dig out the hillside to debate the point and were quickly lulled to sleep by the steady drumming of the rain on the fiberglass roof of what was to be our home in the woods for the next nine months.

Micki's diary, April 1973: *Today each of the boys went through four different sets of clothing working in the rain. Can't imagine how I'll ever get them clean; already missing a washer and dryer. Had lentil soup and Cuban bread for dinner.*

We abandoned the digging project the next morning—it would be days before the earth would be dry enough to work—and began what would claim our time and energies for the next fifteen years: restoring the land by clearing and burning the brush that had grown up in the twenty years since it had been logged. Ironically, the job would have been infinitely easier if the woods had been in worse shape—that is, if it had been logged more recently. Then we could have spent our days burning redwood and fir bark, branches, and unusable logs—loggers called it "slash"—that had been bulldozed into huge piles, and there would have been plenty of open spaces where the giant trees had recently stood, as well as drag roads and loading docks, those large flat spaces cut into the hillsides where freshly cut logs were stacked until they were loaded on the trucks. The land would have been scarred, raw, and ugly, of course, like those first parcels we'd viewed with such horror, but then the brush that we now had to deal with wouldn't have had a chance to gain a foothold. Of course if the land had *never* been logged, or logged in the very distant past, our work would have been even easier, for then the tall trees of the mature, or "climax," forest would have created a canopy that kept the underbrush to a minimum and left the forest floor relatively open.

But our land was neither freshly logged nor a mature forest. When it had been logged some twenty-five years before during the post–World War II logging boom, new equipment—including the then revolutionary lightweight chain saw—and a flourishing timber market made it worthwhile for independent loggers—called "gypos"—to go into the hills and "harvest" redwoods that had been bypassed in earlier eras because of their inaccessibility. It was a time of relatively unregulated, wasteful, and destructive logging, in which it was common practice to drag logs down the ridges and into the canyons, where rough roads had been cut, often alongside and across creekbeds. Even then only the biggest and more accessible trees had been taken out, but in their taking others were damaged, and large logs, some four and five feet across and sixteen feet long, knotty or in some other way defective, were left strewn across the land or left in creekbeds, where they lay half-buried in the silt or thrown together into massive log jams by the rushing waters of a quarter century of winter storms.

The loggers had left only one small stand of virgin—"first growth"— redwoods untouched, a half dozen trees that were bypassed only because they were situated on the edge of a cliff, where they could not be felled without being shattered worthlessly as they crashed into the canyon far below. The other groves—and there were several dozen of them scattered around the forty-seven acres—consisted of anywhere from two or three large stumps to six or eight smaller ones, ringed by telephone-pole-size "suckers" and a few big trees that had been too small to harvest twenty-five years earlier and were now larger than most of the trees that had been logged.

By the time we came upon it, the ridge was a logging-induced mixed forest, tangled with a dozen varieties of "opportunistic" shrubs and trees that were engaged in what was a foregone losing battle for survival. Eventually the redwoods would come again to dominate the area, and even now some of those that had evaded the chain saws towered above the hardwoods. They had been here from the beginning of time, these redwoods, and if you looked carefully, you could see how some of the groves were really circles of big trees arraigned around a space in which an unimaginably huge prehistoric forebear once stood. Others stood in solitary splendor like the even bigger firs, which, if the natural order of things was not disrupted, they would someday displace.

But where the redwoods and firs had not succeeded in reestablishing themselves, we had to contend with mighty, rotten-topped tan oaks, big, orange-barked madrones that lurched up out of the brush at gravity-defying angles, manzanita—"little apple"—bushes, and the ubiquitous musk bush, a tumbleweedlike combination of shrub and vine, which was the first, on these dry ridges, to claim any space exposed to sunlight by logging. Now, as it yielded to the taller-growing, crimson-barked manzanita, it left behind a brittle, impenetrable mass of silver-gray, pencil-thick branches that exuded a sticky, milklike sap when cut. The manzanita, with its gracefully twisting branches, delicate white flowers, berries that the Indians once ground into a bitter flour, and half-exposed, basketball-size root that stored water for the dry season, was long-lived in the chaparral-covered hills farther inland. Here its fate was prefigured by the scrawny firs whose spindly tops were just beginning to penetrate the leafy canopy that had protected them from the sun until they were sturdy enough to usurp their doomed benefactors. The orange-barked madrones, with their smooth arching branches, shiny green leaves, and bright red berries that attracted flocks of band-tailed pigeons every fall, survived in places that could not sustain the conifers. So did the evergreen tan oaks, named for the tannic acid in their gray bark, which once made them the area's most commercially valuable trees. The big oaks had once established a niche among the conifers, but now, having grown too tall after the redwoods and firs were taken, they were dying, their tops rotten and leafless. Newer generations of hardy, crowded saplings stood in their shadows.

It was this mix of flora in various stages of growth and decline that provided us with our initial challenge, a virtual wall of green that we had to penetrate, to clear a trail through, in order to bring materials to the house site under the big fir. That task entailed more than clearing brush and taking out stumps, for we had to contend with the debris of the long-gone logging operation, the worst of which were those huge fir logs and stumps that lay in our path, oxidized and rotted into a vividly orange spongy material, termite- and scorpion-infested and girdled by shards of brittle black bark. Too heavy to move, too sodden to burn, and too mushy to chain-saw, we rolled, burned, and sawed them, devoting whole days to the removal of sections using all three methods. It didn't take us long to realize that cutting a narrow road to the house site by hand would take weeks; that opening up the area around the house site for gardens and pastures would take years; and that rehabilitating the land, sculpting it back into its original state, would take decades.

But on that first sunny morning after the rain, we weren't thinking about guiding principles or land-use philosophies. We had a job to do before we could get on with the real work of building a house: There was a quarter of a mile of road that had to cut across the length of the forty-seven acres. The boys had a rough idea of how we should do it. They'd crawled along the deer paths that tunneled under the manzanita and through the musk bush and roughed out the route we'd take as we wended our way down the ridge, skirting first one and then another of the impregnable redwood groves that stood between us and the house site. Our plan was to cut our way down from the Bench, where we first came onto the land with Lyle, cross the littered clearing that the boys had named Lizard Grove after spending a morning catching and comparing some of the hundreds of lizards that scurried about the big fir logs and stumps that we'd have to burn out, go through several acres of thick manzanita forest, chain-saw a trail through the couple of acres of big oaks and madrones, and come out on the rise under the big fir where we planned to put the house.

"Well, let's get going," Drew said impatiently as the rest of us reviewed the route. "We're not going to get anywhere talking about it." He burrowed in under a manzanita bush with a pair of long-handled nippers and emerged a few moments later, pulling a clump of cut-off branches behind him. "Move these out," he said imperiously as he crawled over to the next clump. "We need a saw in here."

"Who's he think he is, the boss?" Grant said incredulously.

"We'd better get working before we get in trouble," Micki said, laughing, as she dragged the branches off to the side. Grant picked up the gleaming new high-tensile Swedish bow saw and began working on the largest of a half dozen branches growing out of the partially exposed mahogany-colored root clump. Reed joined right in and began throwing small branches onto what was quickly becoming a glistening mass of dense, wet brush.

"It'll never burn," David said as he added an armload of branches to the pile.

"Sure it will," said Micki. "You just do the hauling and I'll get the fire going." She went over to the redwood grove where we had stacked the tools and returned with an armload of newspaper. She spent a few minutes crumbling the paper into balls, which she pushed back into the tangle of leaves and branches, then lighted. A thick column of dense white smoke curled up slowly out of the pile.

"I told you," said David. "You've smothered it."

"Just be patient," Micki said as she threw another branch on the pile. A moment later it erupted with a sizzling roar as a tight column of orange flame burst from the pile and cast hundreds of blackened leaf fragments skyward. The boys put down their tools and stood there watching, their eyes wide.

"Wow!" exclaimed Drew. "It looks like we're going to have some real fires here."

"This is only the beginning," said Micki.

"Well, we won't get anywhere if we just stand here looking at it," complained Drew as he bent over to pick up the nippers.

By noon we had advanced about twenty feet down the hill. We had been able to skirt the bigger trees—on the left, a redwood grove with its four tall dead-topped trees the boys immediately dubbed the "Ugly Brothers," and on the right some smaller, deformed firs that appeared to have been damaged by falling trees when the redwood grove was logged. But farther down there were five big fir stumps in our path that would have to be gotten out of the way if we were to proceed.

We had two of them ablaze by late afternoon when three men on horses appeared over the ridge. The oldest, who expertly guided his horse through the newly cut brush down toward us, was perhaps sixty, dark and mustached, wearing denims and a cowboy hat. The two who followed looked to be in their teens. The leader reined up his horse and studied us from its heights for a long moment—bearded David, Micki in the straw hat from Mali she'd bought on Telegraph Avenue, and three small boys, who had almost imperceptibly backed into the bushes and were staring back expectantly at him. "That your camper up there?" the leader asked laconically, unsmilingly. My God, thought Micki. Not only is he trying to *look* like the Marlboro man, he's trying to *talk* like him as well.

"That's right," said David, returning his gaze evenly. He was in no mood to be interrogated by these three; they had no business being on our land.

"Well, it's on the Flint property, and it doesn't belong there," said Marlboro.

"It's just until we can pull it up here," said Micki, stepping forward. "The realtor said it would be all right." Lyle had told us that the Flints, who owned a forty-acre parcel, part of which abutted our northwest property line, were an "older couple" from the Bay Area who hoped to build a retirement home up there someday.

"You didn't check with the Flints, though."

"We didn't think they'd mind," said Micki. "It's just on the edge of the road there." She could feel herself getting angry. They didn't owe this character any explanations. "They're not even up here," she added.

"You the new owners?"

"That's right," said David. No, he felt like saying, we're a bunch of gypsies who wander through the forest clearing brush and starting fires. Micki and the boys moved in closer to him.

Marlboro nodded, then shook his head as if to say "I was afraid so."

"Then we're neighbors," he said after a moment, with a look that indicated he didn't seem very happy about it. "The name's Mannix. We have the ranch up at the end of the road."

The realtor had mentioned an old homestead that was owned by somebody who lived in town. Mannix reined his horse around, and the others did the same.

"You ought to get that camper out of there," he said over his shoulder. "Putting it on somebody else's land just isn't neighborly." He paused. "You ought to be careful with those fires, too. The fire gets down in those dry fir roots and travels. You could set somebody else's place on fire." He turned and followed his companions, who had already started back up the hill.

"*Well!*" Micki exclaimed as they disappeared over the ridge. "That wasn't *too* friendly."

"I felt like telling them to get the hell out of here," fumed David. "Who do they think they are, anyhow?"

"I'm glad you didn't say anything," said Micki. "We can't afford to make any enemies. And the camper *is* on Flint's land."

"But Flint isn't complaining," said David. "What an arrogant son of a bitch."

Drew emerged from the bushes. "Let's get back to work. We have to keep these fires going."

* * *

"Look at that sky," Micki said as the four of us walked down to the fires after dinner. Reed had fallen asleep during dinner and was back in the camper. "The stars were never this bright in Connecticut. I remember it looking like this on my grandparents' farm back in Illinois when I was about your age, Grant."

"What's that sound?" David asked as we stood around the orange glow of one of the fir stumps. "Listen." The fires had cut smooth-walled baked-clay tunnels deep into the ground under the charred stumps. The cool night air was heavy with the sweet smell of camphor. A steady, mechanical-sounding beeping rose up out of the canyon.

"Quail, probably," said Grant. "We saw some down the hill when you and Mom were in the camper."

"I've got to sit down," Micki groaned as she sank onto a log. "I'm exhausted. You're going to have to carry me back to the camper."

"Not me," said David.

"Well, you didn't make dinner on top of everything. How long do you think it'll take us to get down to the house site?"

"At this rate? A couple of weeks."

"More than that, if we dig out the manzanita stumps," said Grant.

"We can't just leave them there," Drew said. "You or Dad will have to ax them out."

"I can do it," said Grant.

"Just as long as you're careful," said Micki, who stood up abruptly and poked at the fire. "We've got to get some sleep if we're going to get anything done tomorrow. Anybody going to walk me back?"

Later, in bed, the boys asleep on their side of the camper, Micki shook David's shoulder. "Are you asleep yet?" she said. He rolled over. "I just wondered where the gun is."

"It's right here," he said, "against the canvas. Why?" He reached over and touched the cold sweating barrel of the new shotgun. He had bought it in Berkeley, up on College Avenue, the week after they'd bought the land. Lyle had said there were wild pigs in the area and suggested they get a shotgun to chase them off. "Some of the old sows can get pretty aggressive," he said, then added, when he saw a look of alarm on Micki's face, "They're really nothing to worry about, but a gun just might be a good thing to have around in the country anyway. You never know." David had fired a .22 once or twice in his life, and Micki had never touched a gun.

"You're not worried about those characters who showed up here today, are you?"

"Well, we're still on Flint's land," Micki said sleepily, "whoever they are. I just want to make sure you know where it is."

A few minutes later she was asleep. David lay awake a little longer, listening to the beeping in the distance and the sound of something moving through the brush behind the camper. Probably a rabbit, he thought as he dozed off.

CHAPTER FIVE

Oh Shining Moon

We had been working nearly a month cutting the road through the woods when a big new Dodge four-wheel-drive pickup, complete with a heavy-duty winch bolted to its front bumper, came idling down the ridge, crunching branches and making its way past several of our smoldering brush fires. It stopped a few feet from where we were working around a clump of big oaks that sat squarely in the path of where the road had to go, and out climbed a tall thin man with a beard that hung halfway down the front of his bib overalls. He looked like a prophet out of a Thomas Hart Benton mural.

"I've been hearing some noise over here for a while and figured I ought to check it out," he said, walking toward us. "I'm Jim Gibson, and these here are Miles and Wyatt."

Two blond-haired boys about Drew's and Reed's ages came around from the passenger side of the truck. Jim nodded toward the road that he'd just come down. "Looks like you've been doing some heavy-duty work here. Not too bad for city folk, though I thought maybe I singed my tires back up there a way."

We introduced ourselves and told him that we were from St. Louis "by way of Africa, but that's another story," and Jim said he was "still city," living in "a banged-up old mobile home we hauled up there" and commuting for a few days every week to the Bay Area, where he worked as a drug program counselor. He and his family had moved up a year earlier.

"Looks like you got yourself a problem there," he said, gesturing toward the clump of oaks. Two of them leaned sharply first in one direction, then back up in the opposite direction, and David admitted that he couldn't figure out how they'd fall.

"Well, they're sure not worth dying for," said Jim. "Let's put a cable on that big one there." He went over to the Dodge, released the winch cable, and pulled it over to the tree, where he looped it around the trunk as high above him as he could reach. David walked over to the tree with the old Homelite.

"Where'd you get *that?*" Gibson exclaimed. "Old Sam saw you comin'," he said, laughing, when David told him. "That's okay. Some dude sold *me* a Sears. You ever try to sharpen one of *them?*" He checked the tension on the cable. "Maybe you'd better let me try this first one."

We stood back a respectable distance as he notched the tree on the side toward the truck, did a back cut a few inches higher on the other side, then returned to the truck and flicked on the winch rewind switch. The tree cracked and listed to one side for an instant, and then, as the cable tightened, it changed direction and fell neatly into the cleared area. Our boys, anxious to impress Miles and Wyatt, clambered over it with nippers and saws and began removing the smaller branches.

"We probably didn't need the cable," said Jim, unhooking and wrapping it around the tree next to the one he'd just taken down. "Gotta be careful of these twisted ones, though."

David, after making sure that everybody got back near the truck, cut a notch into the second oak, then did the back cut. Jim signaled to him to move back and engaged the winch. The tree lurched and crashed to the earth. Again, the boys were on it with saws and nippers almost before it stopped quivering.

"I don't know how we'd have done that one without a winch," David told Jim. "Thanks."

"You'd have figured out something," said Jim. "It just takes longer without the right tools."

We leaned against the front of the truck and watched the boys strip the tree. "Do you know Mannix?" asked Micki.

"He's your neighbor," Jim said. "He doesn't live up here, though.

Owns a bunch of buildings in town. That big old one across from the
fairgrounds? The Mannix Building?"

"He wasn't very friendly when he came by here a couple of weeks ago,"
said David.

"What do you expect from a judge?" said Gibson. "He owns the local
newspaper, too. You ever read it?" We'd glanced at the *Anderson Valley
Advertiser* when we were looking for property. A weekly, it contained
the usual small-town news, some vaguely reactionary editorial content,
and pages either so badly smeared with ink or so faintly registered as to
be unreadable.

"The paper's a joke," said Gibson. "People buy it only to see how bad
a job he does every week. That equipment he has down there ought to
be in a museum. But I'd keep my eye out for him."

"Why's that?" asked Micki.

"He's your neighbor. And a judge, and the owner of the local paper.
It'd probably be a good idea to try to get along with him." He waved at
his boys and shouted, "Let's go," then turned to us. "My old lady gets
bent out of shape if I'm gone for too long," he said. "She thinks I spend
too much time helping people with this baby." He pounded the fender
of the truck. "Does the job, though."

"He seems like a good person," Micki ventured as we watched them
back up the hill.

"I'd sure like to have that truck of his," said David. "It probably cost
about as much as we paid for the land."

"Not *that* much," Drew challenged.

"Well, *half* that much, at least."

"We'll make do with the Volvo, at least for a while," Micki said as
she gathered up an armload of oak branches and carried them over to a
fire. "Remember, *he's* got a job in the city."

We spent another week on the ridge above the prospective house site,
taking out dozens of oaks, slowed in our progress every time one of the
big, dead-topped trees became hung up against another tree as it fell.
Then we'd all stand back while David crept up under it and cut off
two-foot-long sections one after another until it dropped free. It was a
dangerously wrong way to go about it, of course: Sometimes a tree would
snap loose before David had finished the cut or lurch and fall in an
unanticipated direction. But as Jim had said, "All you really gotta worry
about are the widow makers," those big branches that sometimes snapped

off and came slamming down as the tree was being cut. A friend of his had been killed by one only months before. "He was wearing a goddamn *baseball* cap," said Jim. David donned a yellow Bakelite hard hat every time he assailed one of the big trees, but he wondered how much protection it would provide if one of the dead tops of the oaks broke off and hit him while he was working below. "You never know," said Jim. "A big one, and you probably won't have to worry about nothing ever again."

Micki's diary, May 1973: *Drew's definitely established himself as head of the road crew. Can't believe how easily he shimmies up the trees to try and sight how the road should cut through the brush. It makes me really nervous to see his blond head peering out of the high branches. We're both surprised at how useful the boys are, at least for short periods. Grant tends to drift off into his own world after about an hour, but Drew thrives on what is to him the most imperative of all categories, "hard work." Reed does his best to keep up.*

At last, after weeks of cutting, burning all sizes and varieties of brush, and axing out hundreds of manzanita stumps so they wouldn't puncture tires, our handcrafted road, narrow and ungraded, extended from the far end of the land to the rise where we were going to build the house. On a warm June morning we hooked the camper to the back of the Volvo, slowly towed it down the ridge, and backed it into a grove of redwoods just up the hill behind the house site, next to where we'd set up the summer kitchen that we planned to use until the house was built.

We'd gotten Jim to transport a banged-up, hundred-dollar gas stove and a bulky old three-hundred-dollar Servel gas refrigerator from the Home Town Store in Ukiah. After setting the stove and overpriced refrigerator (which the proprietor had assured us would "run forever") under a big oak tree, we hooked them up to a torpedo-shaped propane tank we'd brought up from town in the back of the Volvo. A few feet away, on a flat spot backed by a wall of huckleberry bushes, we arranged the heavy old oak laboratory table and the six navy-gray side chairs from a surplus store—and our summer kitchen, which looked out upon the spot where we would build our house, was in place.

Now the pop-top camper could be used exclusively for sleeping, and there was space enough for all of us to pitch in to help with meal preparation and cleanup. But with more space came dust, bugs, and wildlife.

"Bats won't hurt you," Grant said as we finished up a late dinner around the lab table after a day of widening the road down to the house site. "They're neat." The boys and David had come across one on an afternoon a few weeks before, when they were cutting their way through a dense, dark patch of firs. They had spent a half hour studying it as it clung upside down to the tree branch, exposed and fragile.

"I still don't like them," Micki said as one of several that we had been watching swooped past the refrigerator. "Yellow jackets during the day and bats at night."

"Yellow jackets don't sting."

"*You* don't have to deal with them. They were all over when I was making dinner tonight. And they *do* sting. I know that much."

"Any other complaints?" said David, pretending to be offended. "Here we put together this beautiful modern kitchen for you, and all we get are complaints."

"Well, for one thing, there's no place to store anything out here. Everything that isn't in the refrigerator is getting covered with dust. And can't we come up with a better water system? They might not be too heavy for you, but I hate having to haul those big containers around."

"What do you want? *All* the comforts of home?"

"Just a small kitchen with running water. I don't think that's asking *too* much, is it?"

"We're working on it," said David.

"And those damn bats," Micki said. "I don't care what you say, Grant. I just don't *like* them."

Baby skunks, though, were cute. A half dozen of them showed up one evening, bright-eyed, spotted little things the size of kittens. They'd crept out of the huckleberry bushes while we cleaned up the dinner dishes.

"Look at how fearless they are," Micki exclaimed as one of them scurried across the opening toward Reed. "Here, see if they'll eat peanut butter." She pulled a jar out of the refrigerator, spooned out a dollop, and handed it to Reed. The rest of us stayed back as he squatted on the ground before them. It took only a minute before one, and then the others, came up and nibbled daintily at the offering.

"They've never seen people before," said Micki. "But I wonder where the mother is?"

"Maybe we can have them as pets," Drew said hopefully.

"They eat chickens," Grant pointed out.

"Not these little fellas," said Micki. "Don't give them any more," she called to Reed. "We don't want their mother to come looking for them."

They came back every night for the next week for their spoonful of peanut butter, and then we never saw them again. It was probably just as well: Nobody had ever told us to be wary of friendly wild animals, the too-often carriers of rabies.

Micki's diary, July 1973: *The refrigerator and stove have made things easier. I've been baking all of our bread and making yogurt using the oven light to keep the temperature steady. Still, hauling water is a drag, hate it. Thought the Osh-Kosh coveralls were the perfect pants for the land, durable and comfortable, but poor Reed can't unbuckle his quickly enough for peeing. Back to blue jeans for him. Funny how we don't wear shorts here, hot as it is—too dirty, not enough protection. All took sprinkling can showers before dinner.*

"Well, you certainly have all the modern conveniences," Pat said sarcastically as she emerged from the bushes and came over to the table to wash her hands with water from one of the big green five-gallon containers. "What do you call it again?" she asked, laughing.

"The EDA," said Micki. "Ecological Disposal Area. Or Disaster Area, depending upon who used it last."

"Yes, well, all I can say is that it's a good thing we did our field work in the Solomons. At least there they wade out and shit in the ocean."

"Don't knock it," said David. "A few weeks ago we'd have just handed you a shovel and sent you off into the woods." The EDA was a slit trench halfway down the hill, a respectable distance from the kitchen area, and we'd taken considerable pains to instruct the boys on how to maintain it. At first we'd been a bit concerned about how Reed would manage it, for it was, after all, on a slope and required some balancing, but, like the rest of us, he'd learned to squat and handled our latest improvement with aplomb. We'd be "going to the EDA" for longer than any of us anticipated—for the next three years—while the house was being built, until we installed water lines, put in the appropriate bathroom fixtures, dug a septic tank hole, put in a five-thousand-gallon tank, and cut a leaching field. Not until then did we have a system that, when you came down to it, served essentially the same function in a very complicated fashion that the EDA had.

"I can't believe you're doing this," Pat said later as we sat around the table after lunch. The boys had gone off with Kristine and Neil to check out a spot that Grant was sure had been an Indian campsite. Pat and Eric, an anthropologist, had been our best friends at Connecticut, the ones who provided us with a place to stay the night we were driven out of our house. They had left Connecticut a year after we did, and Eric was teaching up in Washington. They were on their way south to visit Eric's mother in San Jose. They had been the first people we knew who had adopted racially mixed children, and Kristine and Grant had been the best of two-year-old friends back in Connecticut.

"Of all the people in the world, I can't see you doing this," said Pat. "I mean, to give up all that you were doing politically, then to come out here . . ." Her voice trailed off.

"It finally got to us," Micki said. "You can't imagine what we put up with in St. Louis. I don't know how we'll ever be able to go back to academia again. It's great to be up here away from all that."

"You took it too seriously," Eric said with a sympathetic smile. He was in his trademark shorts and sandals. The image of an aging surfer, Eric didn't let things bother him. He and Pat would go to demonstrations and would always be there when we needed them, but they knew when to back off. Pat had grown up in a family of labor organizers and civil rights pioneers that had been besieged during the McCarthy era and had firsthand knowledge of the toll that had taken. She had done her best to warn us. "They'll get you eventually," she'd say on those afternoons when we returned from political meetings to pick up Grant, meetings she refused to attend. We had spent several days hiding at their place after the Minutemen ran us out.

"I guess we did," said David. He always felt that Eric, laid-back and mellow, didn't do as much as he might have. "It's good, now, being out here and clearing the land, not having to worry about meetings, department heads, students, politics."

"But it's so, I don't know, raw, I guess," Pat said. "I couldn't ever live like this, and I honestly don't know how you can. It's okay now, but what happens when the rain comes? California isn't sunny all the time, you know."

"We'll manage," said Micki. "After Connecticut, after being run out of our house, nothing'll ever bother me again. You were there. You know that." She couldn't mention it without choking up.

"Yeah," said Pat, and for a minute nobody said anything.

We had inadvertently taped it. David was on the living room floor with Grant, showing him how to operate the tape recorder. A ringing telephone, and then, from a distance, Micki's voice: "David, it's for you."

A pause, and then, "Hello."

Another pause. "Who is this?"

David, closer now. "Micki, get the baby. Grant, get your jacket."

"What's the matter?"

"They're coming to burn the house."

"Oh, my God. Who? Why? I've got Drew. David, what's happening?"

The sounds of people moving around and some voices in the distance. A door slammed, and there was silence until the tape ran out.

The recorder was still on the floor when we returned to move out our belongings and sell the house a month later. We'd gotten threatening calls before, but this one was different. The voice was soft and even. "We've been watching you, Colfax. Your little boy was wearing a red, white, and blue mackinaw out there on the tire swing, all by himself for almost an hour." The swing behind the house, out of view from the road; they had been there in the woods. "We could have shot him any time we wanted. Teach you a lesson. But we're going to burn your house instead." A long pause. "You better get your little boy out of there now if you don't want something to happen to him, you commie son of a bitch."

We left the house and never went back. Three months later an attempt to burn out a Quaker community thirty miles away resulted in a shoot-out with the state police. Several longtime peace activists were seriously injured in the crossfire. The leader of the group that called itself the "Minutemen" was identified as "a well-spoken" man who lived a mile up the road from us.

From all the materials we'd collected, it seemed you couldn't consider yourself a real homesteader without some chickens and a goat or two. Jim, who didn't even have a dog at his place—"I just don't like having animals around," he said—told us to check out somebody named Theta. She'd been around for a couple of years and was trying to make a living by selling goat milk and cheese.

Theta lived in a cabin south of Boonville and had what appeared even to our untutored eyes to be a rather grungy-looking mixed herd of what she identified for us as Nubians, Saanens, and Alpines. Her stock, she assured us, was the very best, and it was only with great reluctance that she would part with any of her animals. Still, there was this Nubian milker and her month-old, hardy-looking black kid, which she might let us have for $75. It was what we'd paid for the chain saw, and it seemed like a good deal. We loaded the two of them into the back of the Volvo, sprawling them across the laps of the boys, and headed back to our place, where we named them Checouan and Essouria, after a couple of towns in Morocco.

We didn't think too much of it when Checouan, whom we'd tethered to a tree, gave less than a half cup of milk that evening: *Mother Earth News* said that production usually dropped until a goat got used to its new surroundings. We were certain that she would do better when we got her on some good alfalfa.

The next day we headed off to Ukiah to get some day-old, unsexed Rhode Island Red chicks. We'd had Leghorns in the carriage house back in St. Louis, but only for their eggs. "Rhodys" were a "mixed breed," which meant that they could be raised for meat or eggs. The idea was to feed them for a few months, butcher the roosters, and keep the hens for eggs.

The farm supply store at the north end of town was a busy place, where sour-faced old ranchers in town for the weekly truckload of feed contemptuously eyed hippie couples in granny dresses and tie-dyed shirts who were there for a sack or two of "guaranteed organic" feed. We carefully selected fifty chicks from the stacked brooders in the back of the store, had them load a bale of alfalfa and a sack of chick starter into the trunk of the Volvo, and, after several more stops, rushed home to set up a place for the chicks. David and the boys nailed some boards together for a pen and in the middle put a galvanized tub, inverted and with one end raised up off the ground a couple of inches with a couple of rocks. As evening approached, David lit a kerosene lantern and placed it under the tub. One by one, the chicks scurried for cover and warmth next to the lantern and, after a few minutes of vying noisily for position, were quiet.

"It looks like your washtub brooder works," Micki said as we climbed into the camper for the night.

"The chicks!" Micki cried early the next morning as she burst out of bed and leaped from the camper. We smelled the smoke and rushed out behind her. Oily black smoke wafted out from under the washtub, and there was no sign of the chicks. "We've killed them! What happened?"

"The lantern smoked up," explained David as he felt the tub. "It's not hot." He tipped it back slowly.

"I don't want to look," said Grant. "They're all fried under there. Ugh!"

"Nice going, Dad," said Drew, standing back alongside Reed.

The soot-blackened chicks were huddled in a pile against the smoking, carbon-encrusted lantern.

"They're dead, aren't they?" said Micki.

"I'm afraid so," David replied.

Suddenly one of the chicks broke away from the pile and began pecking vigorously at something on the ground. Another one joined it, and then another.

"They're alive!" exclaimed Micki. "I can't believe it."

They all survived, but not as the yellow fluff balls they'd been the evening before. For the next few weeks, until they feathered out, they looked as if they had been hatched in a coal chute. None of our books had told us that you had to trim the wick on a kerosene lantern in order to keep it burning evenly. Otherwise it would smoke up. Apparently it was one of those things you simply were supposed to *know*.

All, but one, of them survived.

It was a hot afternoon a week later when Grant stepped into the pen to get the mason jar waterer. It looked as though all of the chicks were lined up on the opposite side, in the shade, and he didn't glance down until he heard it cheep.

"I've killed it, I've killed it," Grant wailed as he sat on the ground, rocking back and forth, the dead chick in his hands, its intestines hanging from its crushed and lifeless body. "It's my fault. My life will never be the same," he cried, tears streaming down his face.

"It was an accident," said Micki, who had been in the camper when she heard him shout. "It wasn't your fault."

"Yes, it was. My life will never be the same."

"It's nothing to get upset about," said David, who had been down at the house site clearing brush and had come running up to the summer kitchen when he heard the commotion.

"You don't understand! I tramped on it. It's my fault. My life will never be the same."

Micki hustled off Drew and Reed. "Just let him be," she said. "It's pretty traumatic for him."

"If that's the worst thing you ever do, you'll be lucky," David told him, trying to console him. "Stop making such a big deal of it. It was probably a rooster that we'd have butchered in a few months anyway."

"But *I killed* it, Dad. My life will never be the same."

David headed back down to the house site. An hour later Grant got up and carried the dead chick into the woods. At dinner he told us how he had buried it and decorated its grave with twigs. Micki elbowed Drew and gave him a warning look when he snickered.

Micki's diary, July 1973: *Today Grant saw a buck deer, a three-pointer, that he thinks might be a different species from the does we've been seeing. Yesterday the boys discovered some all-year-water ferns down in the canyon. Saturday night Drew had an alarmingly high fever, so high that I drove him to Ukiah in the middle of the night; just didn't want to take a chance with no telephone and no doctor in Boonville. Nothing serious, he's okay now.*

"I *knew* I heard something out there last night," Micki said at breakfast one morning after we'd begun to clear the house site. "It looks like some deer came by and got into the alfalfa." About a quarter of the bale was gone. At ten dollars a bale, it had to last a month if we were to break even on the milk we expected to get from Checouan. It was bad enough that she wasn't producing; we certainly couldn't afford to feed the deer.

We were ready for them the next night. The boys had fallen asleep quickly after another hard day of clearing, and we were in bed with what had become our main reading materials in recent weeks—how-to-do-it manuals on house construction and animal husbandry. "Listen," Micki whispered. "They're out there again."

David sat up and pulled the shotgun from its place between the mattress and the canvas camper wall. "What are you going to do with that?" asked Micki.

He signaled for her to be quiet. "I'm going to scare them off," he said as he pumped a waxy yellow shell into the chamber. Buckshot was the best, the man in the gun shop had said. It would "take care of pigs, deer, raccoons, and almost anything else, up close."

They ran off into the brush as he opened the camper door. He pointed the gun in the direction they'd gone and fired, the blast shattering the steady, rhythmic sounds of the nighttime forest. For a moment everything was still, then Micki called out, "Is everything okay?"

"Bring me a flashlight," David said tersely as he pumped the empty shell out of the chamber. Something was moving in the brush.

The shot had awakened Grant. "What's the matter?" he cried. "I heard a shot."

"Nothing," Micki said as she joined David outside and handed him the flashlight. "Go back to sleep. Dad just scared off some deer." David flashed a light in the direction of the sound.

"Oh, my God," he whispered. For a moment he thought he'd be sick. A big buck lay there on its side in the manzanita, its head a bloody mass, its legs flailing wildly in a desperate, blind effort to get up. It must have been standing guard there in the dark, looking right at David when he fired.

"What are we going to do?"

"Get the butcher knife," said David, his voice shaking. He'd never killed anything before. Nothing. Micki returned with a knife and the Coleman lantern.

"Something's the matter," Grant called out. "I know it."

"I'm going in with the kids. We can't let them know what's happened. They'd never forgive us." She hurried back to the camper. "It's all right," she said as she entered, and the camper door slammed behind her.

David stood there for a moment in the glow of the lantern, took a deep breath, bent over the animal, and grasped one of its antlers. The buck's strength startled him as it jerked its head back and pulled free of his grip. This was worse than he could have ever imagined. He took another deep breath and now, holding on to the antler more firmly, twisted the animal's head back and, with one movement, drew the knife across its throat. The buck convulsed violently as its lifeblood gushed into the shadows. After a few minutes it was still. David returned to the camper, feeling numb.

"What are you going to do with it?" Micki whispered as he wiped off the knife.

"You'll have to help me drag it," he said. "We have to bury it."

It took us a couple of hours to dig a shallow grave, drag the animal down, bury it, and cover the spot where it had died with leaves, twigs, and branches.

"What was all that banging around about last night?" Grant asked suspiciously at breakfast the next morning.

"Nothing," Micki assured him. "Nothing at all. Dad just chased off some deer, that's all. You heard the shot."

Years later, when hunting and butchering had become, out of necessity, a part of our daily lives, we eventually confessed what had happened that night. "I always wondered why the grass was always greener there," said Grant. "And that's why you dumped a wheelbarrow load of dirt on it that time when I started digging up those antlers, isn't it?"

"Of course," said Micki. "We really panicked when it started *bloating* up on us."

Drew was incredulous. "You didn't even *think* about eating it? What a waste."

"Yeah," admitted David. "But we didn't know the first thing about gutting or skinning an animal back then."

"Boy," exclaimed Reed, who had been too young to remember the earliest days on the homestead and grew up thinking that *everybody* knew how to do such things. "You guys were *really* out of it."

David had finished reading the chapter on foundations in the U.S. Department of Agriculture manual *Wood Frame House Construction*, and he turned out the Coleman light. As he rolled over and faced the screened-in canvas window of the camper, the light caught his eyes. Somebody was out there in the forest. He could see their shadowy forms as they moved around a lantern.

"Micki," he said, shaking her. She had been asleep for at least an hour. He reached for the shotgun and grabbed a handful of shells from the box he kept in a corner of the bed near his head.

"What is it?" she said irritably.

"Wake up. There's somebody out there."

Micki sat up suddenly as she heard him pump a shell into the chamber. "Where?" she said. "You mean *people?*"

"Go to the door, and ask who it is." David had shifted into a prone position on the bed and had trained the shotgun on the light. "I'll keep you covered."

Micki stumbled out of bed, lurched unsteadily toward the door, and opened it a few inches. "Who's out there?" she called in a thin, wavering voice.

There was no answer. She turned to David, who was peering intently out the window. "Should I call again?"

David didn't answer.

"What do you want me to do?"

"Wait a minute," said David. The urgency in his voice had disappeared. "It's okay. Everything's okay."

Micki stood at the door, her hand on the knob, wide awake now. "David, what's going *on?*"

"It's okay," he said, pumping a shell out of the chamber and putting the gun down. "It was only the moon."

"The *moon?*"

"I thought I saw somebody out there with a lantern. It was only the moon." He rolled the canvas flap up higher. "Look at how low it is down there in the trees."

"And you wanted me to draw their fire?"

"I only wanted to see how many were out there."

"And what was supposed to happen to me?" Micki climbed back into bed. "You really wanted me to draw their fire?" she exclaimed. "I can't believe it."

"It was only the moon," David said sheepishly.

"Thank God," said Micki. She rolled over, her back to him. "I can't believe it," she said. "The *moon*."

The boys got the full story from Micki the next morning. David didn't want to talk about it. "Can you believe it?" she repeated for about the fourth time as they sat around the table eating breakfast. "He wanted me to draw their fire! I'm half-asleep and he sends me to the door to get shot at. And you kids think it's funny!"

"Well, it *was* only the moon," said Grant. "It *is* pretty funny."

"What were you going to do if there really were people out there, Dad?" asked Drew. "Shoot them?"

"I don't know," said David. "Maybe scare them off."

"After they killed your mother," Micki said ruefully.

"It seemed like a good idea at the time," said David. "Can't we just drop it?"

"That's what we ought to call our place," proclaimed Grant. "Shining Moon Ranch." We'd been trying to come up with a name for the land ever since we'd bought it. There was Tsi Fang, after the Chinese program in which troublesome intellectuals would be sent into rural areas to acquire humility; Cold Comfort Farm after the English satire; and No Slack Ranch. But nothing sounded quite right.

"Shining Moon? It's too hippie-sounding to me," growled David, who would have preferred to drop the whole subject. It *was* a pretty stupid thing to have done, but he wasn't going to admit that now.

"That's even better," said Micki. "People'll think it's very mellow, but we'll know it came from the night you mistook the moon for a gang of rednecks."

"I didn't *say* they were rednecks."

"Yes, but that's what you thought," Micki persisted. She didn't mention Connecticut, but she knew that was what both of them were thinking about.

By the end of the week the night was enshrined in song. Grant claimed that David was responsible for it; David attributed it to Grant. Micki, after hearing it sung a thousand times over the years, blamed it on both.

I saw a light, I saw a light
A-coming through the woods
I thought it was a burglarman
A-coming for my goods

Oh Shining Moon
Oh Shining Moon
Why are you fooling me?
I'm up here on the mountaintop
With my poor family

I got my gun, I woke my wife
And sent her to the door
I said if they were coming here
That they would be no more

Oh Shining Moon, etc. . . .

It went on for a half dozen verses, only a couple of which—mercifully—survived over the years.

PART THREE

Shelter

CHAPTER SIX

Foundations

From Micki's diary, July 1973: *One year ago yesterday we left St. Louis en route to Uganda. Instead, we find ourselves leveling a house site in Mendocino.*

For some reason, we thought it would be easy—so easy, in fact, that only a few months before, we had seriously entertained the idea of putting up a "spec" house, then selling it at a profit, as a way of supporting ourselves in the country. Building a house couldn't be *that* difficult, we reasoned. After all, we did have *some* building experience—we'd spent hours painting and remodeling most of the dozen places we'd lived in before. And we didn't plan to put up anything very *complicated*. Our first house, the one back in Connecticut, the one we'd been driven out of, had been that. We'd designed it, had it custom-built, and saved a few thousand dollars doing most of the finish work ourselves, while holding down two jobs, caring for a couple of infants, and being up to our necks in political work. Then there was our second house, in St. Louis, which was half again as large. We'd already built our "dream house," only to see it become the setting for our worst nightmares. And nobody needed a house the size of the St. Louis place. All we wanted was a small plain house on the edge of the ridge.

We were bolstered by the knowledge that what we were planning to do had been done by dozens of other folks out in the hills of Mendocino, and from what we'd heard, they hadn't found it *that* overwhelming. It bothered us a little when Jim said it was something *he'd* never try, but then Jim didn't like animals, either, and his place was no homestead. In those early days of summer, as we drew up plans and cleared the building site, we were supremely confident that we would have our house framed up and occupied before the rains arrived in November.

Closer in, on the ridge opposite us and down by the river, a dozen recently built structures were scattered among the trees, ranging from tepees and yurts to redwood-shingled sheds on the backs of old pickups and battered, forever-immobilized old buses. What these lacked in size and durability they more than made up for in their inspired use of recycled junk and decoration—psychedelic, Indian, and Far Eastern motifs, banners, bells, stained-glass windows, totem poles, barn wood, bottle caps, kewpie dolls, concert posters, peace symbols, unbarked posts, hand-hewn beams and shingles, slabwood, beads, tinware, stoneware, macramé and woven hangings, all combined in a style known as "Mendocino Funk."

It was a style we were too old and too jaded to find anything more than passingly amusing. For all of our political activities we had always remained, deliberately and critically, on the fringes of the so-called counterculture of the sixties and were more than occasionally put off by its excesses, its celebrities, and its self-indulgent shenanigans when, from where we stood in the antiwar and community organizing movements, there was *important* work to be done. We certainly were not about to embrace its styles and values now and felt no need for our house to serve as an expression of our creativity or alienation. We'd leave it to our neighbors, to other owner–builders, to carve their massive redwood lintels for their entranceways, to install broad expanses of stained glass, to build large fireplaces out of hand-picked river rocks, and to panel their walls in elaborately patterned strips of redwood, pepperwood, and madrone. All we needed and wanted was shelter—plain, solid, and inexpensive.

But before we could draw up any plans for such a place, we had to get rid of three big clumps of towering oaks that sat squarely in the middle of our building site. It was not enough merely to get them down and burn the stumps out to ground level, as we did with similar oak clumps while we were cutting the road. Here we had to burn out the massive root systems as well as the stumps so that we could level the site. Oblivious of the fact that the wet spring had evolved into a hot, tinder-dry summer, and that we could very well have set the entire county ablaze, we blithely piled tons of brush and foot-long sections of wet oak around the stump masses and set them afire, tending to the fires from early in the morning to late at night, maintaining the kind of blast-furnace infernos that were necessary to dry and consume the green root systems that penetrated deep into the hard orange-clay soil. For two weeks, as the forest and brushland around us baked in the June sun, we fed the roaring fires, sweating and singed, without ever considering the possibility that our plans might be utterly undone by a spark that fell unnoticed into a pile of dry leaves up or down the ridge. It was probably only because most of what we were burning was wet, or "green," and threw off few sparks in what was an unusually calm and windless summer, that we didn't end up being remembered as the idiot newcomers who set the county on fire that spring.

From Micki's diary, July 1973: *David's parents are here and helping us with the fires. Grandpap apparently outdid Drew after three days of Drew's pushing him: Drew pretty much gave up on work by midafternoon by saying that Grandpap needed to stay out of the sun. After lunch David's mother said, "You're doing the same thing your grandparents did," and obviously did not mean it as a compliment. Homer had the access road graded on Saturday. We're glad we didn't have a bulldozer do the road because it sure made a mess of things.*

Once the tree roots had been burned out we were able to begin work on leveling the building site. A cat—in local parlance, the big yellow Caterpillar bulldozers that cut the logging roads through the woods—could have done it all in a matter of hours. But just getting one onto the land would have torn up the place, and we would have been left with the inevitable slash of raw earth and piles of tangled brush that would still have had to be cleaned up and burned. Besides, hiring a cat would have cost a couple of hundred dollars and was not something we'd budgeted for when we calculated costs of putting up a house. Aesthetics and economics dictated that we do it ourselves, level the site with pick, shovels, ax, and wheelbarrows.

Like the cutting of the road—and, we were soon to realize, most of our projects—it took longer and was harder than we'd anticipated. Indeed, for a few hours it looked as if we weren't even going to be able to *begin* the job.

"I don't understand what we're doing now," scowled Micki, standing by as David hacked a sharp point on a redwood two-by-two.

"These are for the batter boards," he said. "They're used to square up the site. We make these H's and put two at each corner of the place where we're going to put the house. Then we run lines from one side to the other and can adjust them on the crosspiece of the H's until the diagonals are equal in length. That tells us the corners are square." He picked up a hammer and one of the stakes.

"I don't have the slightest idea of what you said. Is that what that book you've been reading says to do?"

"Well, yeah, why?"

"Just so *you* know what you're doing."

David peered across the site and held the stake in place. He hit it firmly with the hammer, but the stake point barely nicked the dry, hard-baked earth. He smacked it again, with the same result.

"How far do you have to get them in?" asked Micki.

"So they'll stand up so that we can put a crossbar on them," David snapped. "This is a hell of a way to start." He hit the stake harder this time, and it split. "Give me another one," he said.

"How many of these do we have to do?" asked Micki, handing one to him.

"Sixteen." He positioned the second stake.

"It's going to take forever at this rate," said Micki. "Are you sure you're doing it the right way?"

The second stake split with the first blow.

"If we can't even get the goddamn batter boards in, maybe we ought to call it quits right now," David snarled as he tossed the stake into the pile.

"Do we need them?" asked Micki. "Maybe if we just have a rough idea of where to level it, we can worry about squaring it later."

"No," David said as he stood there, smacking the head of the hammer into the palm of his left hand and glaring at the ground. "We have to square it up now."

Micki waited a moment. "David."

"What?"

"It's just an idea, but maybe if you started a hole with a pick, they'd go in better?" If David got so upset over this now, what was he going to be like later on? she wondered.

"See if you can find it."

Two hours later the stakes were in place, all sixteen of them, set back a couple of feet from what was to be the perimeter of the house. With Grant "bucking"—holding a hammer against the backside of each stake as David nailed in the crossbar from the opposite side—the H's went in without any trouble. Drew and Reed strung lengths of cord from each H to the one opposite and looped them over the horizontals. "If you think you can manage without me, I'm going up to start dinner," said Micki.

"Okay," said David. "I'm just going to show the boys how to square things up." He squatted down next to one of the H's and scratched a parallelogram into the ground with the claw end of the hammer as the boys gathered around him. "Now how do we keep from building a house that looks like this?" he asked, pointing to the drawing on the ground.

"That's cockeyed," Drew observed.

"Right," said David. "Now I'm going to show you how to make sure it's not cockeyed."

It was almost dark when David and the boys came up from the house site.

"Did you get it laid out?" Micki said apprehensively.

"Everything's in place," said David. He was in a good mood now. "Right, boys?"

"Yeah, we sure learned a lot today," Drew said brightly. "Geometry."

"Geometry?" said Micki, setting a hot bowl of brown rice on the table.

"The Pythagorean theorem," said Grant. "You use it to square up a house."

"That's great," said Micki.

"Yeah, but Reed didn't understand much, though," said Drew.

"I did so," Reed said indignantly. "I held the tape for Grant."

"I'm sure that Drew didn't know any geometry when he was only three and a half," said Micki, giving Drew a sharp look. "So we start digging tomorrow?"

"After we get the lines level," said David.

From Micki's diary, August 1973: *As much as we've talked about it, I can't visualize what the house is going to look like, much less how we're actually going to build it. The dust is getting worse as it gets drier and is frustrating to live in, cook in, and breathe. Need some new cupboards for food and dishes; everything on the open shelves is covered*

with dust, so we end up washing dishes after each meal and then,
again, before the meal. I'm finding it really exhausting to be at the
house site all day, then having to prepare dinner under such primitive
conditions. Actually, tonight Grant cooked dinner—flour tortillas and
beans—and it was quite good.

"Wow," David said as he held the line above one of the H's and peered
at the small aluminum level he'd attached to it. "Look at this." The site,
which *looked* almost flat, was actually two feet higher at one end than at
the other.

"What do we do about that?" said Drew.

"We dig," David said, wincing. "We'll have to go down about three
feet on this end."

"That's going to be a lot of digging," said Grant.

"We're going to have to work our asses off," Drew said.

"What'd you say?" Micki said sharply.

"I said it's sure going to be a lot of work," he replied with a mischievous
grin.

From Micki's diary: August 1973: *Twelve loads today. Total: 310.*
August 9. *Eight more loads, total, 486, and we finished the footer*
trench. **August 10.** *Poured footers.*

We stopped counting at five hundred and thirty wheelbarrow loads.
We'd set fifteen loads a day as our quota, which, if we started early
enough, we could get done before the sun was too hot. David's job was
to loosen the hard-packed clay with a shovel and mattock, the boys filled
the wheelbarrow, and Micki took it down and emptied it in the dip
behind the house site that we wanted to level out for a garden. After
lunch, if we met our quota and were not too tired, we'd drive down to
the river and, if nobody was around, strip down for a bath and swim in
the pristinely clear, slowly moving river.

The swimming hole—all of six feet deep and perhaps four times as
long—was the gathering place for our neighbors, people with names like
Rainbow, Crazy John, Betty Boop, Pogo, and Little Richard. Some of
them had settled on the ridge above the river when "Compost College"
was up there, a short-lived experiment in "simple living" founded by a

dropout college president who had since gone on to other things. The fact that we were older, had children, and were obviously not as self-consciously mellow as they set us off from them immediately. The differences in our "life-styles"—the term had just entered the language—made our attempts to "relate" to our new age neighbors somewhat difficult, but we did our best to be cordial even as we limited our riverside social life to perfunctory exchanges of greetings—"far outs" and "outta sights"—before moving upstream to wash off the day's grime.

Reed, though, too small to be of any help in the digging and hauling and content to sit under the big fir looking at picture books while the rest of us worked, didn't like the water and saw no reason to have his hair washed that afternoon when Micki decided the job could be put off no longer.

"Reed, your hair is filthy," she said, advancing upon him, bottle of shampoo in hand, as he sat on the embankment, digging in the gravel.

"No!" he screamed as she picked him up and carried him over to a knee-high pool, set him down, and began splashing water into his hair. "No, no, no!"

"Come on, Reed," Micki said disgustedly as she worked the shampoo into his thick, curly hair. "You're acting like a baby."

Suddenly a dark figure leaped out of the trees and came charging up the river. It was Crazy John, big and bearded, his eyes wide, his face contorted.

"Stop hurting that child!" he screamed as he came at us. Reed was stunned into silence.

"It's okay, John," said Micki, backing away and pulling Reed with her as David waded into the pool alongside her. "I'm just washing his hair."

"You're hurting him," shouted Crazy John. "Stop it now."

"It's okay, John," Micki said soothingly. "It's okay."

"Don't you *ever* hurt him again," ordered John. "Do . . . you . . . hear?"

"Yes, John, we hear," Micki said as she led Reed up out of the river.

"Okay, then," said John. He turned and, a moment later, had disappeared back into the woods.

"He really *is* crazy," Micki said as we headed home, Reed's hair still unwashed.

"There are a lot of crazy people living out in these hills if you ask me," said David. "Of course it doesn't help when your four-year-old has a fit about having his hair washed." He cast an accusing look back at Reed, who was slumped down in the backseat between his brothers.

"I bet you never try to wash Reed's hair again when John's around," said Drew. "He's really lucky."

"It isn't funny," Micki said. "It isn't very funny at all. He scared me half to death, the way he came charging up there. It's nothing to be proud of, young man."

From Micki's diary, August 1973: *Last week we discovered a marvelous warm river, the Rancheria, where we can bathe, wash our hair, and have privacy. No more sprinkling can showers!*

David—who had gone to art school and once considered becoming an architect—had spent the first two weeks in July in the air-conditioned comfort of the new county library in Ukiah, where he drew the plans for the house. Simple as we wanted it, it had to have lots of glass, for without electricity we hoped to use natural light as much as possible. We had come across what appeared to be a straightforward layout in a how-to magazine and adapted it to our needs. It would have an open-beamed ceiling, a pine decking roof, clerestory windows above a big living-dining room space, two bedrooms, a small kitchen and bath, and sliding glass doors all around, all of this enclosed in a twenty-eight-by-forty-foot rectangle. A bit unconventional, but only a bit, and certainly nothing fancy.

We'd build it "according to code," of course, for we had heard too many horror stories about the county building department's campaign against noncode "owner-built" houses, a campaign that was generally and openly billed as a semiofficial effort to stem the influx of troublemaking sex-and-drugs-crazed hippie newcomers who were settling in the hills and living in all manner of unapproved dwellings.

"They're mean sons of bitches," one of Jim's friends had told us. "A bunch of ex-contractors who couldn't make it in the construction business and are taking it out on hippies." If you lived far enough out or planned to move on before too long, you probably could ignore them. But otherwise it was best to play along with them or run the risk of being "red-tagged" and having your place demolished. Only a couple of places had been bulldozed, but a few dozen families out in the hills were spending most of their time, it seemed, fending off agents from the building department. The last thing we wanted was confrontation. We had been involved in too many of those for far worthier causes over the past ten years and were not about to take on some petty bureaucrat who had the power to slow or halt construction on our house. It would be worth paying the two or three hundred dollars for a building permit and putting up with the paperwork if it would keep them off our backs.

"Here he comes," Drew shouted as the roar of the truck out on the access road became louder.

We ran up to the Bench, where the driver was maneuvering the big bright yellow lumber truck, loaded with cement and two-by-sixes for the foundation, back and forth into position so he could drive up the narrow ramp. Three days before, we'd sat in a Ukiah office of the one lumber company that made deliveries while the owner looked at our plans and calculated what we would need and when, in order to build the house.

"Do you think you can make it?" David shouted.

"If you kids got anything that looks like a road, I'll make it," said the driver. He put the truck in neutral and climbed out of the cab.

"I'm Will Minkler," he said with an engaging smile. "These your boys?" He poked at Grant. "I have three myself. A bit older than you young fellers, though." He started up the rise, and we followed. "Let's see what you kids have here," he said. We exchanged glances. Kids? David was probably older than he.

"No overhanging trees all the way down?" We were looking down at Lizard Grove, where the road was the narrowest.

David shook his head.

"No problem, then," said Will. "We wouldn't want to scratch up Mr. Mayfield's new truck, now, would we?"

"He helped us figure out what we needed," Micki said. "He's a pretty nice guy."

"If you don't work for him, maybe," said Will, swinging back up into the cab.

The truck lurched slowly down the road, tipping precariously in several narrow spots where Will had to edge it past the redwoods and over oak stumps that it hadn't been necessary to burn out for the Volvo and camper to get by. He pulled up below the house site between the big grove of redwoods to the west and the half dozen six-foot-tall scraggly firs we'd left behind the dug-out area, got out and looked around, then got back in and turned off the engine. "You kids didn't leave a whole lot of space here, did you?" He grinned as he hopped down and proceeded to the back of the truck, where he began undoing the cables that fastened the load in place. "Looks like I'm gonna have to back out of here when

I'm done," he said as the last cable broke free. "But we can worry about that later, huh, Grant?"

He reached up and with one hand pulled a ninety-pound red-and-tan bag of cement off a pallet and pitched it casually into David's arms. "There're sure a lot of these here," he said as David staggered a few steps backward and dropped the sack on the ground. "You kids aren't going to mix your own concrete, are you?"

"Yeah, we are," said Micki. "Why?"

"Oh, I don't know," Will said. "It's just that I never heard of anybody doing it themselves, that's all." He laughed. "Hey, don't look so worried. It's okay with me, you guys."

We unloaded the hundred bags of cement in a matter of minutes, as Will moved nonstop, up and down, jumping onto the truck bed, where he'd toss the sacks to where David could reach them, hop down to help him stack them for a minute or two, and then climb back up to move some more.

"I think you little guys there can handle these," he said as he snapped through one of the three metal bands that held together the stack of sixteen-foot-long two-by-sixes that extended over the back of the truck. He effortlessly pulled three of them off the top and slid them over the edge until one end rested on the ground.

"Just move one at a time, one guy on each end," he said as Drew and Grant, who had been anxiously standing by waiting for an opportunity to help, charged over to them.

"You can help, too, little fella," Will said to Reed, who had been standing off by himself, and broke into a big grin. "Give him a hand, Mama. You gotta start these guys *young* if they're gonna work in the woods!"

An hour later the truck was nearly unloaded, with stacks of two-by-fours, two-by-sixes, and sacks of cement lined up beside it. Thirty-five sheets of plywood, the big four-by-six beams, some specially treated pieces of redwood that would be bolted to the foundation after it had been poured, and a couple dozen precast concrete pier blocks remained.

"Don't let the little guys touch this," Will said as he handed down three long pieces of redwood. "They got some bad stuff in them."

David took one of the boards and began another stack. "I can't keep up with him," he said as he passed Micki, who was straightening an adjacent stack of two-by-fours. "I thought we were in pretty good shape until now. This guy is *strong*."

"How can you keep doing that?" Micki called over to Will, who was working a beam to the edge of the flatbed as if it were a two-by-four. "You're wearing us out."

"Hey, I went to work in the woods when I was thirteen." Will laughed. "Wasn't much bigger than Grant there, really. You toughen up fast that way. Not that I'd recommend it. I never got much of a formal education," he said half-apologetically, then abruptly changed the subject. "Now, do you kids really plan to build this house up here all by yourselves?"

We nodded.

"Without any help?"

"We hope so."

"Well, there's enough on this load to bring it up to floor level. I sure wish you luck. My wife—my third, just got married a few months ago— would never let me try something like this. I'm tired of living in the woods, though. Got a nice little house in Ukiah that keeps me busy."

After moving the wet and heavy sixteen-foot-long fir four-by-sixes, which we'd use to support the floor joists, the sheets of plywood were easy. We stacked them in a neat pile, resting on some two-by-fours, behind the redwood grove. It would be a while before we'd get to them.

"At last," Micki said to nobody in particular as Will gathered up the metal bands that were scattered across the bed of the now empty truck, and David and the boys sat slumped together against a tree. "I'm exhausted. You didn't even work up a sweat, Will."

"Hey, that was nothing," said Will. "We load and unload three or four of these a day—sometimes five, if the deliveries are close by and we get back to the yard too early. This is only my third one today. I *could* use a beer, though, if you have one."

We sat in the shade of the redwoods, surrounded by the sweet-smelling, freshly milled wood, and drank beer. "It's too late to get back for another delivery, anyway," said Will, who told us how he'd operated his father's logging equipment for years, doing jobs in Oregon and California, until they'd had a falling-out a few years ago and he went to work as a driver for the lumber company. It didn't pay very well, he said, but at least it was easier than logging. His legs were giving him some trouble, though. We told him how we'd left St. Louis and moved to Morocco, and then, for some reason, perhaps because we liked him and needed to see how he'd handle it, we told him about our civil rights and antiwar activism before we'd moved to the land. We were sure that he had not been involved in anything even remotely similar, and this was, after all, the summer in which Nixon assured America that he was "not a crook."

"Hey," he said. "It's good you did that, you know? People gotta understand that it's the big boys who run this country that gotta be stopped. You think the timber companies give a damn about anything but making a fast buck? Let me tell you, I remember a lot of times when we couldn't get a halfway decent price for our logs just because they knew they could screw us. They'd stockpile more than they needed, then tell us to take or leave it. Shoot, whatever you kids were doing was all right." He grinned and saluted us with a half-empty bottle of Burgie beer, sixty-four cents a quart at the Anderson Valley Market. It was a better tribute than we had gotten from most of our fair-weather friends in academia.

We had just completed the trenches for the footers, the concrete base on which the foundation would rest, and David and the boys were fixing the reinforcing bars in place, when Smokey came by.

"What're ya gonna do for water?" he growled as he stood next to his dump truck, surveying the scene. He'd just delivered a load of what they called "aggregate"—the sand and gravel mix used to make concrete. Grizzled, middle-aged, and cantankerous, Smokey was the town's jack-of-all-trades: road grader, gravel hauler, backhoe operator, water witcher, pump repairer, septic system expert, mechanic, and woodsman. We'd met him shortly after we'd bought the land—the realtors always let him know who was new in town—and he'd come by to let us know that he'd be available to put in our water and sewage systems and seemed offended when we said that we planned to do that ourselves but would need his sand and gravel when we started work on our foundation. Jim had warned us that Smokey was notoriously unreliable when it came to making deliveries—"You gotta call three times before he even writes it down"—but he had responded so quickly to our request when we'd seen him in town a few days earlier that it was obvious he'd come up mainly to see how far we'd progressed in the months since his first visit. Clearly, he was unimpressed.

"We're going to haul it up from Faulkner Park," said Micki, referring to the ten-acre county-owned stand of virgin redwoods at the bottom of our access road.

"In what?" asked Smokey.

"In the Volvo, in five-gallon containers," she answered. "We've been doing it all summer."

"That's gonna take a lot of trips," Smokey harrumphed.

"We'll manage," said Micki.

"Yeah, well, people do a lot of stupid things," he commented as he climbed into his truck.

"I guess he's mad he didn't get the job," David said after he'd gone. "We will manage, won't we?"

It took us a week to mix and pour the concrete for the six-inch-deep, ten-inch-wide foundation footers. We set up a work area next to the pile of river-bottom aggregate, and we took turns mixing concrete with a shovel in the big blue contractor's wheelbarrow, four buckets of cement, twenty of aggregate, and a few buckets of water for each load, the boys taking turns filling the buckets and double-checking the count. Every third or fourth load, while David wheeled the mix over to the trenches and rough-troweled the concrete into place, Micki went down to Faulkner Park and filled the two five-gallon green poly water carriers.

"That's the easy part," David said one hot Sunday evening as we stood at the edge of the site, proudly surveying our work, the finished footers. "Getting the foundation wall forms built and into position is going to be a bitch."

He was right. We knew we were doing it the hard way, but the lumber yard owner said we could save money by nailing two-by-sixes together to make the forms, then disassembling them and using them for floor joists. "They'll be a little bit concrete-stained," he said, "but nobody's going to see them under your house anyway."

The trouble was that a half dozen sixteen-foot-long two-by-sixes, when nailed together, resulted in a heavy and unwieldy half-form, and it took at least a couple of hours to plumb, level, and join them end to end, secured firmly and precisely in place above the footers. We worked together side by side for a week, leveling the forms with bits of rock and stones that Reed and Drew collected and ordered according to size so they'd be on hand when we needed them, coating the forms with used motor oil so they could be removed easily after the concrete had set, driving stakes, twisting wire into place, and lining up twenty-foot lengths of reinforcement bar. At last we were ready for our first inspection, our first visit from the building department.

"He's here," one of the boys shouted as a car stopped out on the access road. A few minutes later a tall, craggy-faced man appeared.

"The name's Clark," he called up to us as he approached the house site. "Just another damn bureaucrat here to give folks like you trouble." He glanced at the forms and nodded his head approvingly. "Just kidding.

You got nothin' to worry about from me. I'm here to help, believe it or not."

He walked around the perimeter of the foundation, squatted down, and tested the tautness of the reinforcing wiring in a few places, and pushed at a couple of stakes. "Looks like you're ready to go," he said. "I'll see you next week or so."

The next day we hauled over a small gasoline-powered mixer from a rental place in Ukiah—after doing the footers we knew we'd never be able to do all of our mixing in a wheelbarrow—and, on an unseasonably cloudy August afternoon, began work on the foundation walls. We took turns feeding the mixer, and the boys were standing next to the forms, where their job was to work the concrete down into the forms through the reinforcing wire.

"I think something's wrong, Dad," said Grant, squinting up through his oversize plastic safety glasses as David pulled up beside the form with his sixth load. "See how it's kind of bulging out here?"

"It'll be okay," David said as he tipped the wheelbarrow forward and poured the concrete into the form. "We've got it braced strongly enough." It *did* look as if it were bulging a bit, but we'd reinforced them exactly as the book directed, and the inspector had given us the go-ahead; of course they'd hold. He was opening a new bag of cement when Drew let out a shout.

"Dad! The forms are collapsing!"

David bolted across the house site to the corner where the three boys stood staring at the mass of concrete that had pushed through the buckled forms and was oozing down the hill like a menacing gray lava flow.

"Dig!" shouted David. "We've got to get it out of here before it sets up, or we'll never get it out. Everybody! Use your hands!"

An hour later the five of us sat side by side on the forms, concrete-splattered, our hands wrinkled, sore, and alkaline-burned, exhausted and dejected, staring silently at the pile of concrete that sat there rebukingly before us.

"Well, at least we got it all out before it hardened," said Grant.

"Great," David said tonelessly.

"What happened?" said Micki. "I thought you said they were strong enough."

"How the hell should I know?"

"We'll just have to have somebody else do it," Micki said. "Obviously this is too much for us."

David stood up and wiped his hands on his pants. "I'm going to skip dinner," he said. "We can't give up now."

"I don't need anything to eat tonight," seconded Grant.

"I'm not hungry, either," Drew concluded.

"Good," said Micki. "Then I don't have to cook. You guys can have some fruit, and there's plenty of milk."

We worked together, barely speaking to each other, until dark. As David cut new stakes, Micki drilled new holes for additional reinforcing wire and the boys twisted it into place. The next morning David was up and on the site at sunrise, driving the new stakes into the ground and nailing them into place against the forms. "We're ready to go," he said as he joined the rest of us a couple of hours later at the breakfast table.

"Are you sure they'll hold this time?" asked Micki, rubbing her concrete-bleached hands together. "I don't want to have to do that again."

"They'll hold," David said tersely. If they didn't, he was calling it quits.

By nightfall we had poured the entire south stem wall. The forms held.

From Micki's diary, August 1973: *Think I might have permanently damaged my hands from hauling water for the foundation. Don't want to tell David, since I'm the only one besides him who can lift the water containers in and out of the Volvo. Tried doing laundry on a washboard but gave up; doesn't get things clean enough. Laundromat in town is filthy, but that's the only option.*

We didn't pay much attention—other than to note how big and heavy they were—to the beams that afternoon when Will delivered them; we had a truck to unload, and it would be weeks before we'd be using them. But now, with the foundation walls poured and the pier blocks in place, we were discovering why it was important to check out materials when they were being delivered, as the five of us, grunting and groaning, using sledges, fir poles, crowbars, and sacks of cement as weights, pushed, wedged, and pounded the warped and twisted timbers into position where they'd serve as supports for the floor joists. Our efforts weren't motivated by aesthetics, but rather in the hope of coming up with a floor that was reasonably free of bows, waves, sags, or bulges. An experienced builder would have merely planed down the high spots and shimmed up the lows, but we persisted over a couple of days and eventually succeeded in wrestling all but one of the troublesome four-by-sixes into submission. The one that resisted all our misdirected efforts left us the legacy of a warped floor and an inoperable sliding glass door in the corner of the living room.

But if the collapsing forms and the time spent on the twisted beams raised some doubts about just how good we were at this sort of thing, we were heartened by the quality of the foundation walls when we removed the forms. If it wasn't exactly a professional job—there were a few rough spots here and there where we hadn't worked the concrete down into place—it was, as Drew declared as we pulled off the first of the oil-blackened forms, "pretty darned good."

Exhilarated, we set about completing the foundation work. There were redwood sills that had to be leveled carefully in a slurry of cement spread on the tops of the walls like the icing on a cake. The two of us bolted them into place while the boys disassembled foundation forms and scraped off the encrusted concrete and oil.

"Hey, Dad," called Reed, his faced streaked with oil and dust, as he stood there in his Osh-Kosh coveralls, hammer in one hand and a length of two-by-six in the other. "This is *fun!*"

"More fun than clearing brush?"

"A lot more," he said. "We're really learning to do things here, aren't we?"

"I guess we are," said David, laughing. "Well, now that the foundation's in, I guess the really hard part is over."

There in the late summer sunlight, with our painstakingly handcrafted, starkly gleaming foundation in place, we were too busy congratulating ourselves to consider the possibility that the *really* hard parts lay ahead of us.

Micki's diary, September 1973: *Today the box of* World Books *arrived back from Uganda. The boys remembered them from St. Louis and dug right in. Reed found pictures of redwoods and skunks and was asking about words. He likes to pretend he's reading. Hope they survive the dust and grime.*

CHAPTER SEVEN

With a Little Help
from Our Friends

The first rain of the season—a light drizzle—came just as we were begin-ning work on the stud walls, but, intent upon building corner pieces, getting the two-by-fours braced and plumb, we barely noticed it. It had been a warm and balmy September, and things had been going smoothly for a few weeks. After our bout with the floor beams, getting the joists in seemed easy, and even the plywood flooring went down without a hitch. Thanks to the U.S. Department of Agriculture and its *Woodframe House Construction* manual, we'd learned about "cripples," "headers," "sills," "let-in braces," and corner posts, how they were used and how to make them. We'd painstakingly assembled eight-foot-long sections of the wall flat on the floor and then, one by one, all of us pushing and pulling together, raised them up into position and fixed them in place with temporary bracing.

"It's beginning to look like a house now," Micki said after we'd finished the last perimeter wall section. "Now how do we get the roof on? And what about *rooms*?"

It was a simple enough design. A high "bearing wall" would divide the house in half lengthwise, and on it we'd rest the roof beams, the big four-by-eight twenty-footers.

"How in the world are we going to get those big beams way up there?" Micki asked.

"I haven't figured that out," confessed David. "We'll worry about that after we get the room dividers and the bearing wall up."

"How much time are they going to take?"

"A week or two. Maybe three."

But by now Micki had become well aware of David's tendency to underestimate how long each job would take.

"Will that give us enough time to get the roof on before the end of October?" she asked.

"Sure," said David. That was a month away.

It had been a long summer and autumn, during which we had left the land only when we had to go over to Ukiah for groceries or the odd piece of building material. So when Micki's parents, whom we hadn't seen since going off to Uganda, wrote that they'd be flying out from Florida to San Jose, two hundred miles to the south of us, to attend a family reunion, Micki decided to take a well-deserved break from work on the house. And when she returned a few days later with the news that her cousin's son, who had been at the reunion, had volunteered to come up with a friend and give us a hand, David was wary.

"They're going to work for free?"

"Jeff—that's Midge's boy—said he's got until January, when he's going to graduate school. And this friend of his, who's a carpenter, is waiting to take some kind of government test. He said they'd work in exchange for meals and a chance to do some hunting after I told him I was a good cook and that there were deer all over the place."

"Are you sure we won't end up with another Wayne?"

"God, I hope not," said Micki.

Wayne had been among the first wave of visitors who'd descended upon us early that first summer. It wasn't that we didn't welcome good company or couldn't use all the help we could get. Part of the "visitor problem," as we came to call it, was that most of them just weren't very good company, were more of a hindrance than a help, and at least one was a certified psychotic. Part of our problem was cultural. Self-styled citizens of the Woodstock nation were on the move, and northern California had become a must-visit stop on the counterculture circuit. Since the "Summer of Love" a half dozen years before, communes and collectives had been endlessly forming and dissolving in the hills up and down the coast, and not too far south of us hundreds of hippies, freaks, and assorted flower children had descended upon the thousand-acre Wheeler Ranch and turned it into a hippie mecca. But our place, Shining Moon Ranch, was not the Wheeler Ranch. To the disappointment of many who somehow found their way to our place, we were a *family* with a clear idea of what we were going to do together, and we were not looking for recruits. We weren't admirers of the counterculture with its tawdry icons and shallow enthusiasms. We didn't revere the writings of Carlos Castaneda or Richard Brautigan. We didn't think that *Even Cowgirls Get the Blues* was one of the best books ever written, that the *I Ching* contained the answers to the world's problems, or that meditation cleansed the soul. We didn't smoke marijuana, drop acid, chant, or go on vision quests. Clearly we were not there, in the language of the day, "to mellow out on the land." Our concerns were at once more mundane and more profound: we had a house to build, land to clear, gardens to put in, and the future of three young children to worry about. We'd paid our political dues and were now having to play catch-up, with neither the time nor the inclination to discuss psychology or the cosmos with the earnest, self-absorbed, and sometimes stoned strangers who'd managed to find us.

From Micki's diary, September 1973: *Can't seem to keep the goats enclosed in anything, hate to keep them tethered, though. Chicks are thriving, feathered out and getting big, lost only two. Visitors! We've had nineteen different people here in two weeks, and the other night was the first time in fifteen days that we were here alone. I'm sick and tired of cooking their meals in return for their "help." They're all so oblivious to what we're doing and are not in the least bit helpful.*

Still, we indulged them. Even after Wayne. A few years younger than we, he had come up from Los Angeles with a social worker friend when we were digging the foundation and put in a good couple of days with the shovel. We saw no reason not to let him stay on and live in a tent back in the woods when our friend left. "It would be good for my head if I could help you get your place together," he had said. And for a few days he did just that. He worked alongside us on the house site, regaling us with tales of his days as an aspiring actor and part-time animal trainer in Hollywood. Toward the end of the week he even arranged for his six-year-old son, Scott, to come up on the bus and stay with us. It was just a matter of days, though, before Wayne began disappearing in the evenings and not showing up until midafternoon of the next day.

By the end of the second week we were taking care of Scott on a full-time basis. When Wayne showed up at all, it was only to raid the refrigerator, and then he'd disappear back into the woods. We realized that he'd connected with some of the heavy drug users who were camped down by the river, but it took us several days to get up the courage to tell him that if we were to continue to baby-sit Scott and feed the two of them, he'd have to put in at least a few hours of work every day. David told him, as carefully and gently as he could, one afternoon at the kitchen site when Wayne returned, sweating and glassy-eyed, from one of his overnight forays.

"I knew it!" he exploded. "I knew it. You're just like everybody else. Just like my goddamn wife. I don't need to take this shit from you." He charged at David, stopping just inches away. "I don't need to take this shit, you hear? You know what? You give my kid nightmares. We don't need to take this shit. We're leaving. You're gonna be sorry you did this to me and my family." He stormed off into the woods, toward his tent.

"*We* give *his* kid nightmares?" exclaimed Micki. "For a moment there I thought he was going to hit you. He's about twice your size. Do you think we have anything to worry about? He said he was going to make us sorry for what we did."

"What'd we do? He knows he was ripping us off, and we called him on it, that's all."

Later in the day Grant and Drew sneaked up to where Wayne and Scott had pitched their tent and found that they were gone. But they hadn't gone far enough to put us at ease. That afternoon on the way to town we saw them standing by their tent, which they had set up down in Faulkner Park. On our way back Wayne stepped into the road in front of the car, shouted what seemed to be some sort of threat, and glared ominously at us as we passed.

"He looks scary," said Micki. "What if he comes up after us or something like that?"

"He heard the Shining Moon story. He knows we have a gun. He won't bother us."

"Even if he's on drugs?"

"He looks like he couldn't carry off much of anything in his condition," said David.

"I don't know. He might be some sort of Charlie Manson."

We were relieved a few days later to hear that Wayne and some of the people from the river had moved out to the coast, and it wasn't until the end of the summer, when our social worker friend returned to spend some time before setting off on his own personal vision quest, that we learned anything more about him.

"Oh, I wish you had handled him better," said the social worker. "I really thought that with all your experience you'd be good for him."

"Good for him?" Micki exclaimed. "He was wiping out our food, all of our cheese and fruit, and leaving his kid with us while he went out and got high. What were we supposed to do?"

"Well, I assumed that you would have been more supportive of somebody who had spent a lot of time in and out of mental hospitals."

"Mental hospitals?" we shouted almost simultaneously.

"He was one of my clients," said the social worker. "It's really a shame you couldn't handle it. I really thought you could."

"Wait a minute," said David, his voice rising. "Maybe you'd better tell us some more about your client that we 'couldn't handle.' "

The social worker blithely proceeded to tell us that Wayne was a member of the social workers' "mental patients' liberation group." Diagnosed as a schizophrenic, he lived on the disability payments he received and had a long history of violence. "But I didn't think anything up here would upset him, least of all you two," he said.

Micki spun around at him, her eyes blazing. "Why in the world didn't you tell us that when you left him up here?" she demanded.

"It wouldn't have been fair to him," the social worker said in a soft, calculatedly soothing voice.

"And what about us?" continued Micki. "We have tools, shovels, chain saws, guns all over the place, and you put a psycho up here with us? My God!"

The next morning our friend came down to the camper and announced that he was leaving. "I've been picking up some really bad vibes," he told us. "Some really bad vibes."

Jeff, Micki's second cousin, and Michael arrived in an old pickup a week after Micki returned from the reunion. Jeff, a recent graduate of Berkeley, was dark and curly-haired, with an infectious grin. He told us that Michael had a degree in art from Santa Cruz but had given up trying to make a living as a potter and had been working as a carpenter after helping his parents build their home in the Santa Cruz mountains. "He knows a heck of a lot about building," said Jeff. Micki had told him about Wayne and some of the others who'd come by to "help us."

*   *   *

"They've got really good tools," Drew announced after he and the boys helped them unload. "A grinder and a planer and a six-foot-long level that we really could have used when we were doing the foundation."

"Well, they're real carpenters," said David, a bit too defensively, Micki thought. In an effort to be frugal we had been trying to get by with as few tools as possible, and some of our bargain shovels and hammers had turned out to be anything but bargains.

"They're really nice," said Grant. "Not like Wayne."

"Wayne was okay at the beginning, too," Micki warned. "Let's just wait and see."

Michael and Jeff ambled up to the camper a half hour later after walking around the building and checking out what we'd done so far.

"It looks real good," said Michael.

"Do you think we can start working on those beams, then?" David asked. "I'm not looking forward to cutting those angles. One mistake and we'll wipe out a fifty-dollar piece."

"Yeah, those guys are expensive," said Michael, nodding his head. "Ah, I don't want to tell you what to do, but maybe we should get your pony walls in before we, ah, put the beams up."

David glanced at Micki. He'd been in charge so far, and things had gone along reasonably well. Still, we needed help, and besides, he wasn't sure he knew what a "pony wall" was. "You mean the end walls that run up to the roof?"

"Right," said Michael, breaking open a six-pack that Micki had set out on the table. "We can wait if you want, though. It was just a suggestion."

"No," decided David. "Let's go with the pony walls first." Already he liked Michael's low-keyed, tentative manner. And over the weeks that followed we all came to appreciate it. As Jeff said, he knew a lot about construction but went out of his way to avoid making it uncomfortably obvious. "What if," he would say when one of us ran into trouble—figuring out how to nail in a piece in a tight corner or working out a combination of angles—"what if we, ah, if we moved this piece over here, and worked it across sorta like this? Do you think it would, ah, work?"

Jeff, experienced as he was, paid him his due—in his own way. "You're the *carpenter*," he'd declare loudly whenever Michael made a suggestion. "I just *work* here. It sounds *good* to me, boss. Whatever you say, boss. Whatever you say."

Our main task, after the pony walls and the top plate were in place, was to get the fir roof beams notched and up. David left to Jeff and Michael the job of figuring out the angles of the cuts and worked at the less demanding task of fitting blocks between the bearing wall studs while they climbed up and down the ladders, beams on their shoulders, meticulously measuring, chiseling, and rasping each one until it fit tightly in place where the "birds-mouth" notch crossed the top plate. We'd managed to get the first three beams up over the kitchen area and attached to the plates with perforated little metal angle pieces they called "strong-ties" when the October weather suddenly turned dark and cold.

"Let's get these guys covered," shouted Michael, who was sitting on one of the beams that we'd just worked into place. He pointed to a cluster of dark clouds that had formed above Goat Peak.

The boys jumped down from the house and began rooting behind a stack of lumber for the rolls of black plastic we'd gotten earlier in anticipation of rain. "There's a real gully washer on the way," Michael called as we climbed up on the adjacent beams. It hit just as we finished covering them and were weighing down the plastic with two-by-four blocks.

"Get the tools covered," shouted David, jumping down as the first wave of wind-driven rain swept across the canyon, drenching us in seconds.

"Cover that roof decking *good*," Michael yelled to the boys as he pulled the generator under a corner of a plastic tarpaulin. "If that gets wet, it's all over." Micki ran over to help Grant and Drew, who were struggling to pull a sheet of windblown plastic over the stack of knotty pine.

A few minutes later we were jammed together in the camper, stripping off our wet clothes and taking turns standing next to the stove.

"This storm's coming from the south," David said as he moved out of the way and on to one of the foam rubber mats where Grant, Drew, and Reed huddled together.

"Most of them do, this time of the year," said Jeff, drawing his hand across his forehead and shaking it above the sink.

"Out here on the coast all of them do," Michael said.

"And we've got all those sliding glass doors on that side," said Micki. "For the sun. We just assumed that the north would get the weather, didn't we, David?"

"I noticed that on the, ah, plans," said Michael. "I didn't want to say anything, but I kinda wondered about it. It's going to be hard to, ah, keep the rain out when it gets going."

"Well, this is a bad one, isn't it?" asked David.

"This is just a little shower," Jeff said ominously. "Wait until the rains *really* hit."

"Great," Micki said as she turned down the stove. "Well, where's everybody going to sleep, now that the rains are here?" It was going to be hard enough putting together the kinds of meals Jeff and Michael had come to expect—and certainly had earned—on the little camper stove, in such a cramped space, much less come up with sleeping arrangements. Jeff and Michael had been sleeping outside, on the house site.

"We can sleep in the truck tonight," Michael said. "We'll figure out something else in the morning."

"Maybe it'll stop raining by then," Micki said as she poured some water into the pot. The rain pounded noisily on the fiberglass roof of the camper.

It was still pouring when Michael and Jeff came into the camper the next morning, grumbling about their aching backs and sore limbs.

"You can't sleep in the truck another night," Micki said as she stirred some cheese into a skilletful of scrambled eggs. "Don't feel you have to stay up here to help us, you know."

"Ah, well, we gotta stay until we get the roof on," said Michael, perched precariously on the edge of the cot and sipping a cup of steaming coffee. "There's no way you're going to get it up yourselves."

"That's for sure," said Jeff. "But we gotta wait for the rain to stop and for things to dry out. That might take a week or more."

"Maybe we could stay down at Bear Wallow for a couple of days," said Micki. "We'll never dry out in here if it keeps raining."

"It's worth checking out," David said.

From Micki's diary, October 1973: *Writing this under a line strung with dripping clothes. Rain is making life difficult. Can't drive car down our road, have to carry everything in from access road—water, groceries, lumber, feed. Made six trips back and forth today in pouring rain. Boys are spending most of their time in camper; they can't help with the beams, and Michael and Jeff have more or less replaced them. Michael is really good with the kids. He and Grant stalked a wild boar for a couple of hours the other day but didn't get close enough to see it. Had tacos for dinner. Hard to keep coming up with good meals with no oven—the summer kitchen's been washed out. Have been simmering lots of soups and beans on the camper stove. Gave up on shelter for the*

chickens and set them free. Goats huddled in redwood grove. Everything
soaked.

Michael and Jeff were right: There was no way the two of us would be
able to get the beams in place and the roof on by ourselves. The beams
were too heavy, and putting on a few thousand square feet of pine decking
required more muscle power than we'd be able to muster. It would be
worth moving down to Bear Wallow to keep Jeff and Michael around.

Bear Wallow, we'd discovered, was directly below us in the canyon,
hidden on the other side of the first of the ridges we looked out upon. It
was a resort that derived its name from a clearing nearby, where, according to some some old-timers, families of black bears used to gather
to wallow in the dust. A nephew had inherited the property sometime
in the sixties, put up an A-frame lodge, and scattered a half dozen cabins
with names such as "Alpine" and "Hideaway" about the place. His plan
had been to rent them out to hunters and their families, a concept that
neglected to take into account the brevity of the hunting season, the
relative scarcity of game, and the tendency of most men to leave their
families at home when they went hunting. As a result, the resort and its
carpeted cabins with fully equipped kitchens sat empty for most of the
year, while the nephew, undaunted, used the once productive eight-
hundred-acre sheep ranch as collateral to finance a variety of what eventually proved to be similarly ill-fated real estate ventures in the area.

Gary, the nephew, was happy to rent us a cabin for $250 for the month
of November. It was furnished straight out of the Ukiah Montgomery
Ward Discount Outlet, but with its hot water, electric heat and lights,
and kitchen facilities, it seemed like the height of luxury after six months
of camper and summer kitchen living. Jeff and Michael took one of the
bedrooms and the rest of us the other, stringing the living room with
clotheslines and turning it into a much needed drying room. We hadn't
planned on the expense of renting a cabin—a month earlier, when it
was warm and sunny, we would have found the idea preposterous. But
now, as the rain continued to come down in sheets, seemingly intermina-
bly, day after day, it was clear that for once we had made the right move.
If we couldn't work on the house, at least we'd be warm and comfortable.

It turned out to be the rainiest month in county history. Surely, we
would tell each other, it couldn't continue for very long at this rate—
but, just as surely, it did. We quickly learned to take advantage of any
break in the weather. Any sign of a clearing would precipitate a frenzied

rush for coats, boots, and notebooks in which angles and measurements had been calculated and recalculated while we'd been waiting, and we'd pile into the cars and loop our way back up the ridge to the house site. Invariably, it seemed, we'd encounter a new disaster—a stack of wood that had been rain-soaked when a tarp had blown off, a power tool that had been left uncovered. Undaunted, one of us would begin sweeping the slurry of water, sawdust, fir needles, and twigs off the floor, while another undid the latest damage. Once the floor was reasonably free of water we were able to start up the generator without worrying about electrocuting ourselves, and then begin cutting and drilling. If we were lucky, we'd get in an hour or two, and occasionally even an entire afternoon, of work. Some days we'd have the floor just about dry when the rains would descend upon us again and we'd have to retreat to Bear Wallow to dry out—and curse the weather. Sometimes the sun came out and, perversely, we thought, the temperature would drop twenty degrees in a matter of hours. Then the clouds would roll in, it would warm up, and the rains would begin again.

Instead of turkey that Thanksgiving, we had three of our Rhode Island Red roosters. We weren't surprised when they turned out to be tough and stringy, since they should have been butchered months before. But we'd never killed anything before and had put off learning how until Michael, a longtime hunter, showed us how.

"You, ah, eat meat, don't you?" he asked. We stood apprehensively in the rain on the deck of the cabin as he lifted one of the birds out of the box in which we'd transported it from Shining Moon. "Then you, ah, ought to appreciate where it, ah, comes from." With a quick motion he snapped its neck, the bird's wings flapped wildly for a few seconds as he held it out at arm's length, and then it was still.

"Argg," said Grant, recoiling in horror. "I'm never going to eat chicken again."

"Well, ah, that's okay, too," said Michael, reaching for a knife. "Now some folks would *pluck* this fella, but I think we ought to skin him." Reed and Drew, fascinated, stood close to him, watching intently as he administered a few expert cuts, then, holding the carcass out in front of him, pulled off the feathers and skin in one piece.

"That's really neat," exclaimed Drew.

"I think it's *gross*," Grant said from across the deck.

"Well, you don't have to eat it," said Micki.

From Micki's diary, November 1973: *My mother would be proud of me. Eviscerated three chickens. Entrails were awfully smelly, but the tricky part is getting out the lungs. Set out all the guts for the boys to identify. They liked the idea of finally eating something we produced ourselves; after the garden was such a disaster last summer I think they thought we were hopeless homesteaders. Still raining. . . .*

A few days later—it was still raining—Michael, who had been out hunting for a couple of hours, backed his truck up close to the deck and told us to come outside. "You want to, ah, *really* learn how to butcher, don't you?" he said as we approached the truck. One evening when the boys were asleep we'd told him and Jeff about the buck David had accidentally shot, and now Micki flashed him a look of warning not to reveal our secret. "Well, here's your chance," he said with a nod. He pulled a big buck—a "three-pointer," he called it—out over the tailgate and onto the deck.

"I just couldn't let it go on by," he said almost apologetically. "It was just *asking* to be, ah, harvested." And over the next several hours we learned how to hang, gut, skin, and cut up a carcass. It was a revolting process, we all agreed—much worse than doing a chicken—but something we'd become very good at doing in the years ahead.

It had rained every day that November, and now, in December, it didn't show any sign of letting up. Michael and Jeff couldn't stay much longer—Michael had to take park service exams, and Jeff needed to get ready to go to school. "But we've *got* to get that roof decking up and protected," Michael insisted. "Those beams are going to start twisting on us if they get much more rain. All we need are a couple of good days."

Finally we got the break we needed. "Let's *hit* it!" shouted Michael as we piled out of the pickup and Volvo on what was the first clear morning in nearly six weeks. "Let's get that roof *on!*"

It was an all-or-nothing effort, for it would be all but impossible to protect the pine roof decking from the rain if we didn't get everything in place and covered before the next onslaught. We set up an assembly line, with Grant, Drew, and Reed pulling out the twelve-foot-long tongue-and-groove knotty pine boards from under the layers of wind-tattered plastic sheets and hauling them over to where David cut them to length and passed them to Micki, who pushed them up between the beams to Michael and Jeff. They were perched on the beams, armed with crowbars and hand sledges that they used to force them into line, as most of the boards had become warped and twisted in the wet weather. At the end of that, and the next four days, we carefully covered the roof with sheets of plastic and held it in place with long wooden strips tacked into position every three feet or so. "Just two more days and we'll have it," Jeff declared as we returned to Bear Wallow. It was a crisply clear and starry night.

Early the next morning we awoke with a start to the familiar sound of rain. "Forget about coffee," shouted David, pulling on his jacket. "Let's get up to the house."

It was worse than we'd feared. There, billowing in the wind like a huge black sail of a pirate ship, was the plastic sheeting, the wet, rain-soaked raw pine roof exposed and glistening wetly in the gray morning light.

"Micki," David said in a dull, tired voice as we stood there in the wind, listening to the plastic snap and crackle in the wind, "maybe we ought to just call it quits now, before things get any worse." It was just a matter of time before the roof would begin to swell and buckle and we'd have to rip it all out.

"David, we can't." Micki stood firm. "Not now."

Michael was the first one in the house. "It's not leaking in here," he shouted as he grabbed for a ladder and slammed it against the bearing wall. "Let's get up there. We can save this mother yet!"

Jeff scrambled up to the roof behind Michael, where, after a few desperate lunges, they managed to get hold of the plastic sheeting, gather it in, and smooth it over the pine decking.

"Get those battens that blew off up here *fast*," Michael yelled down at us. "And we're going to need a lot more. This time we're going to cover it *good*."

An hour later, soaking wet, their faces flushed, Michael and Jeff climbed down and stood with us in the living room area, looking up and examining the ceiling. "We lucked out on this one," said Michael. "Another half hour of that rain and we'd have had a nice pile of fire-wood—when it finally dried out."

"There'll still be a few water stains," said Jeff. "There's a bad spot over by that beam." He pointed.

"That's, ah, *your* work," said Michael. "You *know* my sections were *tight*."

* * *

It was a clear and cold night. The moon had just risen above the ridge to the east and was shining through the tops of the redwoods. Grant and Drew were on the roof with us, each with a rope around his waist, the other end thrown over the peak and lashed to the stud walls below. They were nailing in the last sheet of insulation.

"It's just like nailing in plywood," Drew said when they began the job early in the day.

"The only difference is that you'll kill yourself if you're not careful," said Grant. "It's a long way down."

Michael had gone back to San Francisco to take his park ranger exam. Jeff was below us, rolling the final section of felt paper into place. The moonlight began to fade as David helped Drew toward the ladder and he climbed down, the rope still around his waist. Grant followed him. Micki held the flashlight as Jeff and David nailed down the last half dozen battens. No sign of rain. The roof was on and covered. We'd made it.

We were in the house by Christmas Eve. Not that it was *habitable* in any conventional sense of the term. But there was a roof, and it was *enclosed*. And before they had packed up and headed back to the Bay Area, Michael and Jeff had helped us install the 8 six-foot-wide sliding glass doors, nail heavy-duty translucent plastic sheeting over the bathroom and clerestory window openings, and wrap the entire house in black felt paper. Jim had come over with his truck, and we'd moved the rain-splattered refrigerator, stove, table, and chairs from our long-abandoned summer kitchen into what would be our new kitchen. We set up sleeping quarters in the northeast corner of the house, surrounded by stacks of lumber, rolls of insulation, wood scraps, and tools that seemed to be everywhere. The boys slept on one side of the new Ashley woodstove, the two of us on the other, on mats from the camper. We propped our pillows against the skeletal stud walls, balanced our kerosene lights on stacks of books and wood scraps, and hung our clothes on nails driven into convenient two-by-fours.

It had taken us less than six months to get it together. Six long, outrageously hard months, we agreed, but we'd done it. We were in our house, the house we'd built from the ground up, sitting around the surplus-store table on surplus-store chairs, surrounded by stacks of redwood siding and fir two-by-fours, eating our first real meal in it as moisture from the green lumber fogged over the windows and trickled down into small puddles on the floor. We didn't have electricity, plumbing, a telephone, or even walls, but we were together, and, as we were to remind ourselves again and again in the years to come, we had much more than most people—thanks to more than a little help from our friends.

From Micki's diary, Christmas 1973: *All day yesterday out in the rain, looking for the biggest and best-looking Christmas tree that would fit into the house. Came up with a sixteen-footer, touched the ceiling at its highest point. Boys spent the day decorating it with strings of manzanita and madrone berries, and Drew climbed up the stud walls and capped it with a big paper star. Didn't matter that there were no lights on it, although Reed rather wistfully observed that we could use the generator to power them. Stayed up late assembling Schwinn bikes we'd gotten them; hope they can learn to ride up here in the woods. Gave each other Aladdin lamps. Went to town to call grandparents but couldn't get through. Had turkey and made a pie from a couple of pumpkins we'd grown ourselves. Boys said it was the best Christmas ever.*

CHAPTER EIGHT

A Tar-Paper Winter

The glaring light that poured through the sliding glass doors woke us early. There was at least a foot of snow on the ground, and it was still coming down in big, lazy flakes.

"So it never snows in Mendocino?" Micki joked later, after the boys had gone outside to play in the snow. She was standing at the stove, scrambling eggs for breakfast. It was Grant's ninth birthday, and we'd celebrated it the night before by going over to Ukiah to see *Charlotte's Web* and *Willy Wonka and the Chocolate Factory*. It had been our first evening out together since moving on the land. On the way home we noticed that it was getting unusually cold.

"I hope it snows on my birthday," Grant had said as we came up the access road.

"It never snows in Mendocino," David had said authoritatively.

"Okay, so I was wrong," David said to Micki's back. "It's not *supposed* to snow in Mendocino County. That's why we moved here, remember?" He was standing next to one of the sliding glass doors, watching the boys pelt each other with snowballs.

"This looks more like Connecticut than California, doesn't it?" said Micki.

David didn't answer. "Look at that," he said in a strangely flat voice.

"Look at that." She turned. David was pointing to the far end of the house.

It took a second for it to register. "Oh, my God," she exclaimed. "The wall's collapsed!" There, beyond the stud walls, sparkling in all their snow-covered splendor, were the redwoods and firs, and beyond them the slate-gray sky. "What happened?"

We quickly discovered that the weight of the wet snow that had collected in the ripples of the tar-paper wall had pulled it down into a crumbled heap that lay next to the boys' mats and bedding.

We spent the morning stapling the stiffened black paper back in place, and attaching a few dozen batten boards to the studs to strengthen it. It was something we'd find ourselves doing over and over again, all around the house, as the winter wore on—tacking and patching and fitting pieces of tar paper into place—as the driving winds and pounding rains took their toll of a humble building material that was never meant to serve as the only barrier between the elements and a family huddled in their stud-wall skeleton of a house.

"Do you think we're snowbound?" Grant asked excitedly as the snow continued to come down and we sat around the roaring Ashley stove, surrounded by the boys' dripping jackets and pants.

"Well, we can't get out," said Micki.

"What's 'snowbound' mean?" Reed asked.

"It means that you're trapped by the snow," Drew told him. "You can't get out because it's too deep."

"We could *walk out* if we wanted to," said Reed.

"*You* can walk out if you want," Grant said. "But I bet you couldn't make it all the way to town."

"Dad and Mom could," said Reed. "So that means we aren't snowbound, right, Mom?"

Jim made his way up in the Dodge a couple of days later.

"We figured you might have frozen to death or something," he said as he stood in the kitchen, his beard glistening with snowflakes, while we brewed up some coffee. " 'Course I'd be a little late to do anything about it if you were. Ain't this a hell of a thing? I had to cut through a half dozen little firs on my way over here."

"Oh, we've been keeping nice and warm and have plenty of food," Micki assured him. There was plenty of firewood from the snags and windfalls that we'd stacked along the road last summer. And with all the snow we didn't have to worry—for the first time in six months—about hauling water. Only the Rhode Island Reds seemed to be having a hard time of it. When the rains came we'd left the hens huddling together under a sheet of plywood in a hastily constructed pole and chicken-wire pen. Now they were providing us with comic relief as they tumbled about in snow up to their heads, flapping and cackling indignantly.

"I wouldn't worry about them," said Jim. "If they managed to live through those rains, they'll survive any kind of weather." He sipped his coffee. "But, hey, have you seen any coons up here recently? There're all kind of tracks on the road coming up. Some of the big ones look like they might be mountain lion."

"Wow," said Grant. "Maybe that's the one I saw when I was out hunting with Michael. Remember, Mom?"

"You didn't see one," Drew said. "Michael said you heard something that might have been one."

"Well, I *thought* I saw one," said Grant.

"They won't attack people, will they?" Micki asked.

"Hell, I don't know," said Jim. "But I bet they'll go after your chickens or one of those goats of yours. They just haven't smelled them yet. It doesn't make much difference, though. If a mountain lion don't get them, the skunks or possums will. That's why we don't have any animals. They're not worth the hassle."

"Skunks and possums won't bother goats, will they?" asked Grant, his brow furrowing.

"Maybe the little ones," said Jim.

"Well, we don't have to worry," Micki stated, turning back to Jim. "We're down to only one goat now, you know. Checouan, our milker, died right in the middle of all that rain in November. I guess it was our fault." She flipped over a ball of dough she was working and smacked it hard on the breadboard, as if to make her point. "We knew she was sick, and when we finally got around to taking her over to Ukiah she was half-dead. The vet kept her alive overnight and then charged us fifty dollars to have her buried."

"You should have just pitched her over the ridge on the way back," said Jim. "The vultures would have finished up the job. That's what they're out there for."

"She was a miserable goat," said David. "The best she ever gave us was a cup of milk—once."

Jim grinned knowingly. "That's what happens when you get involved with livestock." He took a last mouthful of coffee. "But what the hell, I don't even go near our garden."

It was still snowing the next day when Micki finished baking, and the sweet aroma of fresh bread filled the house. Right before Christmas Micki had promised Gary, the caretaker down at Bear Wallow, that she'd provide the bread for the wedding they were having down there that afternoon. He'd come over for dinner one night when we were staying in the cabin and raved about the Cuban bread she'd been baking for years. "We owe him a favor or two," she told David when he asked why she'd agreed to do it. "He never once complained about the mess we made with all of us living there. Our dripping clothes probably ruined his rugs."

"At two dollars a loaf, six loaves a day," Micki said as she pulled the last one out of the oven, reached around the stud wall, and set it on the old workbench next to the table saw, "maybe we can make a living baking bread."

"It'd take a lot of bread," said David.

"Arggh," groaned Micki. "Bad pun. Now what am I going to put these in?"

"How about that basket from Morocco?" Drew suggested.

"Are you really going to walk down there?" asked David. "It's at least three miles."

"They're counting on me. Maybe I can find somebody with a four-wheel-drive to bring me back."

She packed the still warm loaves into the basket, pulled on a couple of sweaters, put on her Mali hat, slung the basket over her shoulder, and headed off into the snow. She stopped and turned a few yards from the house. "Send out a search team if I'm not back by dark," she shouted.

"Funny," said David. "Very funny." He slid the glass door shut.

"Yeah, Dad," said Grant. "What about the mountain lion?"

"Maybe they like bread," Reed said quietly.

"This is serious," said Grant. He sat next to the sliding glass door, paging through books and looking up every few minutes for the next three hours until we heard the sound of a truck coming up the access road. Micki appeared at the door a few minutes later.

"Homer came along just as I started up the access road," she said as she brushed off the snow, her face flushed. "He said he hadn't been up to feed his animals since it started to snow.

"Actually, it's a good thing he came along. Going down wasn't so bad, but it's pretty steep coming back. I was afraid it might be dark before I got home." She took off her outer sweater and hung it on a nail. "Old

Homer was pretty friendly. He wanted to know if we needed anything. Did you know he had a Jeep?"

"Did you get your twelve dollars from Gary?"

"Yes. And he even gave me a three-dollar tip."

"Wow," David exclaimed.

"It's a hard way to make fifteen dollars. I'd hate to try to make a living at it."

We drove the Volvo to the bottom of the access road when the snow began to melt, figuring that it would be better to have a car available at the bottom of the access road a mile away than snowbound at the top. But we hadn't anticipated the freeze-up that followed. For the next couple of weeks, after the snow had disappeared from sight and all roads were clear except for ours, we spent our days breaking up the layers of dirty black ice that covered the access road, which, being on the north slope and shaded by overhanging trees from the low winter sun, stayed cold and forbidding. We'd hike down to the Volvo, go to town to fill the green containers with water, drive the car back as far as we could take it, then work our way back home, breaking up the gravel-encrusted ice a few inches at a time with picks and shovels.

"I thought that we were supposed to be getting away from winter when we moved out here," Micki said as she methodically hacked at the ice with a mattock, while the boys, following along behind, shoveled the broken shards into the brush and dragged the five-gallon water carriers up the road a few feet at a time. "This isn't like Connecticut. In Connecticut at least we'd be able to take hot baths when we got home."

"You can take a bath if you want to," said David.

"Oh, sure. With melted snow, maybe. In about three inches of water. I mean a real bath, in a real tub. The kind where you turn a tap and you can have all the hot water you want. *That's* a hot bath."

From Micki's diary, January 1974: *Trouble with the Volvo, kept stalling, so we closed up the house and drove to Berkeley to get it fixed. Made it halfway back up the access road, then parked and walked in the rest of the way by the light of the moon. Light on the snow on the mountains was spectacular. Somebody had left a door open and the goat had gotten in and made a real mess of things; spent the first hour back cleaning up.*

When we got the access road open again, we were able to resume our weekly baths. It still wasn't easy. We'd have to haul the five-gallon containers, two at a time, in from where we'd parked the Volvo, down into and back out of a ravine, down past the summer kitchen, and up to the house. Once inside, we'd empty them into two big stockpots and a teakettle and put them on the woodstove to heat while we cleared an area for the galvanized tub—our former chicken brooder—near the Ashley stove. We'd go through the cycle several times, heating the water, filling the tub, bathing, and emptying the water out the door, once for the boys, then for us. But there was nothing unusual about all of this, we reminded the boys, who found it all very amusing. This was the way Americans had been doing it for generations before indoor plumbing became commonplace. Still, cramped in the tub, as the precious hot water cooled too quickly, we were glad that we didn't have to look forward to doing this for very long.

There were a few warm and sunny days before we were hit by the kinds of storms Michael had warned us about. The first one drove us to the back of the house, where we hunkered down as far away as we could get from the exposed southern wall, which shuddered and flapped noisily as sheet after sheet of wind and rain beat against it. The wind, we quickly discovered, came in waves and seemed to pick up speed as it swirled down into and up out of the canyon. We came to dread it: the sound of an express train speeding through a subway station, followed by a moment of silence, and then the inevitable loud bang, as if someone had fired a shotgun in the house, as the plastic sheeting that covered the clerestory windows above us snapped back into place.

"David, come look at this," Micki shouted over the noise of the storm the next morning as she stumbled sleepily into the kitchen to put on some coffee. The front half of the house was an inch deep in water that had leaked in through the three sliding glass doors as they were being buffeted about by the wind.

"How's the roof?" David asked as he came into the room.

"It looks like we've got some leaks up there, too," Micki said wearily. "I never thought I'd miss the ice and snow. This is going to be a real mess."

"Well, if we'd had another month, we could have gotten the shingles on. This is just too much for the tar paper to handle."

It seemed that we devoted most of the next couple of months to getting water off the floor inside and keeping the tar paper from blowing off the roof outside. The boys took turns using a hand brush and dustpan to sweep up the water, which they'd dump into plastic buckets, which, in turn, had to be emptied out the back door every half hour or so. Some evenings, when the storms were especially ferocious, when the leaks and seepage got too bad, we'd all have to pitch in to mop up the encroaching water, which threatened to turn the living area into a pond. Once the inside water was under control, the two of us would turn the job back over to the boys and get working on the roof, which was increasingly coming to resemble a patchwork quilt of tar paper and crazily aligned batten boards as the winds and rain took their toll, first on one section and then on another. Most of the damage seemed to be done at night, and we quickly became accustomed to pulling on our hats and coats and going out into the night, flashlights in hand, and crawling up on the roof with staple gun, more batten boards, felt paper, hammer, and nails to deal with the most recently discovered leaks. It was dangerous—the front roof was especially steep, and wet tar paper was slippery—and often as not repairs made under these conditions didn't last the life of the storm. Eventually, after a particularly bad storm during which we worked nonstop for hours, bailing bucket after bucket of water out the back door, and had gone up on the roof a half dozen times trying to plug leaks with new sheets of tar paper and battens, we gave in and drilled a half dozen holes in the plywood floor. From that point on all the boys were able to forget about their buckets and dustpans and simply sweep the water toward the holes, where it drained into the dust of the crawlspace below.

From Micki's diary, February 1974: *Reeling from the work and the rain. Rearranged lumber piles so we have more space in living room. Put up several pieces of siding on north exposure. Drew lost his shoe in the EDA, charged into the house furiously, indignant. Ashley stove eats a lot of wood and is a bit cantankerous. Been keeping it going full blast because of all the leaks.*

Then, as if signaling a truce, the weather turned spectacularly beautiful. Beneath a warm and forgiving March sun, we climbed onto the roof, stripped off all the mosaic remnants of what we'd so desperately stapled into place just days and weeks before, and began stapling down a fresh layer of sun-warmed tar paper.

"I know we'll be up here again after the next storm," Micki said as we climbed down. "That's going to tear up just like the other stuff did."

"Do you want to make a run for it?" asked David. "If the weather holds, we can get the shingles on in a week."

"I don't see how things can get much worse. Let's get going. I don't want another month of sloshing through water in the house."

And so, after dutifully consulting yet another how-to-do-it book that specified precisely the length to which the starting shingle of each row needed to be cut in order to ensure maximum weather protection, we began a job that, like almost every one we undertook, ended up taking more than twice as long as we'd originally calculated. Still, we managed to get the southern exposure shingled before the next storm hit. That took care of the leaking roof but didn't make the storms any quieter or the living room floor much drier. The plastic sheeting still crackled and snapped, and we still had to shout to be heard over the roar of the wind. And we knew that the south-facing glass doors would have to come out if we were ever going to use the living room as more than a woodshop, as we were currently doing. We still had to move stacks of wood out of the pools of water and sweep water into the drainage holes during every storm. But at least we no longer had to crawl out on the roof or dedicate *all* our time to bailing and mopping on those stormy nights.

On those long quiet evenings after an early dinner we'd gather around the table to play games and listen to the ancient leather-bound portable radio that one of our summer visitors had left behind to keep us from "*completely* losing touch with the rest of the world." For some reason— it could have been the weather that year or the peculiarities of the radio—all we could pick up was a static-ridden San Francisco all-news station and, with crystal clarity, a Portland station six hundred miles to the north that featured old-time radio classics. So our sense of being isolated and out of touch was further compounded as we found ourselves in a kind of audio time warp. While most children across America were sitting in front of television sets watching "All in the Family," "Sanford and Son," and "Kojak," our boys tuned in to programs the two of us, in the days before television, had listened to as children—episodes of "The Great Gildersleeve," "Henry Aldridge," and "The Shadow." One series, though, was new to all of us, and it quickly became our favorite. "Lum and Abner," in the Jot 'm Down Store, and characters such as Caleb Weehunk, president of the school board, were fictional backwoods types from a different time and place, yet their adventures and concerns in rural Arkansas in the thirties and forties seemed uncannily similar to ours in the hills of California so many years later.

Later, if we weren't studying one of our how-to books in anticipation of some forthcoming project, we'd play games. Grant and Drew would lobby for Monopoly or Scrabble but, after some ritualistic grousing, usually settled for simpler games that Reed could play. "It's no fun for Reed to play games he doesn't stand a chance of winning," Micki would admonish them when they complained.

"Why not?" Grant would counter. "He's got to get better at them, that's all."

And he did. Tired of being blamed for another dull night of Parcheesi, he set himself down in a corner of the house with Mille Bornes, "the French road marker game," playing four hands simultaneously and inventing imaginary companions with whom he conversed hour after hour. Before long he was beating all of us—Grant and Drew rationalized their defeats by agreeing that their little brother was a "game freak"—and night after night we'd huddle together around the table, the flickering kerosene lights casting long shadows on the stacks of lumber and insulation, as shouts of "Flat tire!" and *"Coupe fouré!"* rang through the house.

From Micki's diary, March 1974: *A gang of river hippies stopped by on the solstice after one of them saw our stump fires from the opposite ridge and thought we were having a celebration. Ended up with Crazy Wolf, Rainbow, and Dulcimer sitting in the living room chanting and singing with the boys, who loved it. I made tostadas.*

Micki baked a cake and the boys spent the morning decorating their bikes with crepe paper in preparation for a "first-year-on-the-land parade." The "shell"—a contractor's term for what we'd managed to put up—was pretty much finished. Our tar-paper winter was behind us: We'd covered it with redwood siding on the outside and gleaming bats of foil-backed Johns Manville insulation on the inside. It had been an unbelievably full and exhausting year in which, more than once, we had pushed ourselves to the limit, and one in which we had learned more than we thought we would ever have to know. But what we didn't realize, as we stood in our crude, unplumbed kitchen, watching the boys roaring up and down the road, singing at the top of their lungs, "Oh Shining

Moon," was how much more we'd have to learn and how much more remained to be done.

From Micki's diary, May 1974: *First-year tally: Twenty-three ducklings, forty-nine broilers, twenty layers, pregnant goat, dog, cat, and two peacocks down from Homer's, noisy as hell. House with no water, no plumbing, plastic windows, no partitions, but roof, outside walls, and floor. An unbelievably satisfying, hard year.*

David, Micki and the boys.
Armed with shovels we work on the land.

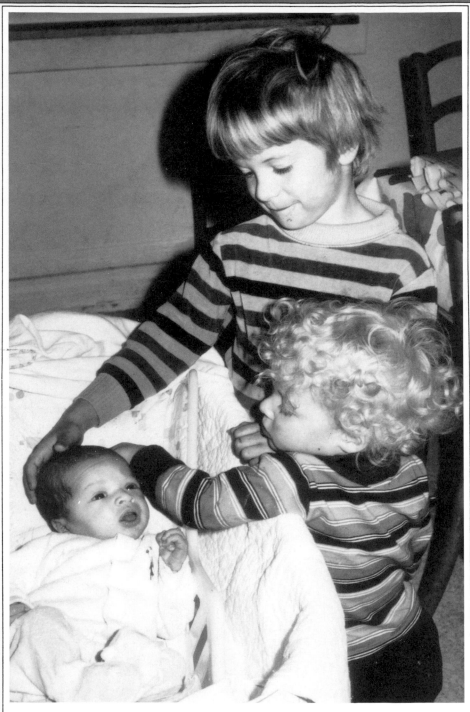

Grant, age 5, Drew, age 2, and Reed, 3 months old,
make one another's acquaintance.

Christmas 1970:
one tree, numerous
book shelves
and three sons.

By 1972, our garden
is growing—
and so, it appears,
is our hair!

David raises high the roof beams.

Garth, the newest member of the family,
helps out with a pick and a smile.

We always got by with a little help from our friends.

Garth with friends. (*Paul Miller*)

Home, at last.

PART FOUR

Learning
Together

CHAPTER NINE

The Forty-Seven-Acre Classroom

"Well," Peggy drawled as Micki handed her the yellow card that she had put in our mailbox, "did you get the boys enrolled in school?"

"Not yet," Micki said warily, caught off-guard.

Peggy Bates—Post*master* Bates, as she slyly insisted on being called— had moved to Boonville twenty years before as part of the post–World War II migration of "Arkies," "Okies," and "North Dakotans" into the valley during its timber boom. Chili, her husband, had made a fortune buying and selling land, and Peggy had become postmaster. She was a briskly efficient woman in her early forties, who, as Micki quickly discovered, recorded everything that went on in Anderson Valley and, if she trusted and liked you, did not let her carefully cultivated aura of discretion keep her from sharing a particularly good piece of gossip or a sharp-edged observation.

"You folks sure are going to have a lot of reading material up there on your place," she'd said to Micki as she handed her another battered carton of books, one of many that had arrived in Boonville that summer after having taken more than a year to make the trip to Africa and back. "And all the way from Uganda."

Micki had felt obliged to respond with a brief account of our ill-fated odyssey, as Peggy nodded sympathetically. "Well, I suppose you could have done a lot worse than end up in Boonville," she said. "And you're going to build a house up there on Homer's road?"

Micki told her she didn't know that our access road was known as "Homer's road."

"Well, that's just what some of us *newcomers* call it. Even Homer's a newcomer. He was born in North Dakota. Actually, it used to be called Fat Clow's Bark Road. The Clows, now, they're real old-timers. They say that Fat Clow used to go up there—probably to your place—to collect tan oak bark and ship it down to San Francisco to treat the fishing nets."

"You're an old-timer, aren't you?"

Peggy snorted. "My Lord, no. Chili and I have been here more than twenty years and we're still considered newcomers. Always will be, I suppose." She leaned out over the counter to make sure nobody was on the other side of the partition where the mailboxes were. "Some of these old-timers here won't accept you unless your grandparents were born here. And some of them, I can tell you, shouldn't be talking too much about their ancestors."

And now Peggy knew that we hadn't enrolled the boys in school, Micki reflected uncomfortably.

"Well, I don't blame you," replied Peggy. "Keep them out of school as long as you can, that's what I say. My boy went all through the schools here and I was a homeroom mother and all that, and I can tell you, I think he'd have done just as well if we'd kept him at home."

"Well, we'll probably be sending them off before too long," said Micki, more than a bit taken aback by Peggy's candor. "It's just that they're learning so much up there, helping us get the place together."

"I'll bet they are," said Peggy. "And I say good for you."

It wasn't that we'd *planned* to keep the boys out of school. Micki had visited the local elementary school immediately after we'd made an offer on the land, and she'd returned with a thumbs-down verdict. The first-grade teacher seemed burned out and the fourth-grade teacher more concerned with maintaining discipline than anything else. "A typical grade school," she'd reported, and not very different from the many we'd visited while conducting our school segregation research back in Connecticut in the middle sixties. We didn't give it much more thought in the months of clearing, digging, and building that followed: The boys were learning too much, there beside us, even to think of sending them off to school when September rolled around.

We weren't concerned that Grant, who was almost nine, hadn't learned to read, for it was clear that there was little incentive for him to waste time on Dick and Jane stories when the ensuing discussions as we traveled, looked for land, and prepared the house site were so much more interesting. He and, to a somewhat lesser extent, Drew were learning in much the same way that children have for centuries—by listening and by doing. There were days in which discussions would go on nonstop— days when we'd talk about the destruction of the poverty program while clearing brush, explain the significance of Watergate while nailing down the floor of the house, and rail at the latest atrocity in Vietnam while eating dinner. Since leaving St. Louis and being together most of the time for so long, we'd developed our own oral traditions. It wasn't as unequal an exchange as we might have assumed. We certainly knew more about politics and world affairs, and art and geography, but when it came to putting together a homestead, the boys could see that we were as much the novices at it as they were. So we figured out things together— the best place to fell a tree, how to position the house, what was wrong with the generator, where to put the garden. We had the advantage of being able to draw upon the stack of how-to books we'd accumulated, but when it came right down to getting things done, the boys' perspectives generally proved to be every bit as valuable as ours.

It wasn't until late that autumn, when we were worrying with Michael and Jeff about how we were going to put up the roof beams, that Grant found a reason for learning to read. He'd been off that afternoon, over on the neighboring parcel looking for arrowheads with Drew and Reed, and returned breathless with the news that he'd discovered "an Indian camping ground." We were engrossed in laying out the cuts on the beams and greeted the news rather perfunctorily.

"But, Dad, this is a real Indian camp. There're all kinds of flint pieces, and you can see where they had this big circle. What would that be for?"

"I don't know, Grant," David said distractedly. "I don't know anything about the Indians around here." He turned back to Michael, who was checking our calculations.

"Mom, the Pomos used to be around here, right?"

"Right. But I don't know anything about them, either. What about you, Michael?"

"Nope," grunted Michael.

"Nope," Jeff echoed without having been asked.

"Well, how am I going to know what I've found if nobody knows anything?" Grant complained.

"You could check it out in some of those books under the camper," said Micki. We had gotten a dozen cartons of them back from Uganda.

"You *know* I can't read," he said plaintively.

"There are a bunch of programmed readers in there somewhere," said Micki. "From the New City School." She had sent them over to Uganda just in case there was a problem with the schools there. A friend had recommended them, a series of a dozen workbooks originally developed by a maverick educator for use in adult literacy programs. We'd looked through them and found them to be unlike any learn-to-read materials that we'd ever encountered. Well illustrated and featuring a wide range of engaging characters of all races in a variety of settings, they were, best of all, *witty*, and we could imagine an adult using them without feeling that he or she was being treated condescendingly.

Grant went through them in a matter of weeks, and on our next trip to Ukiah he checked out all of the library books on Native Americans. And a few months later, on one of our rare trips to the Bay Area for building materials—brass screws for the siding and trim—we spent the afternoon in the anthropology section of the University of California library selecting college-level monographs on Indians.

If we were a bit taken aback by the speed with which Grant learned to read, we were even more surprised by how readily Drew and Reed took to it. They didn't progress as rapidly—Grant seemed hell-bent on making up for lost time now that he was literate—but the results were such that later, when we'd find ourselves talking to other parents about education, we could in truth say that Grant, Drew, and Reed all learned to read at the same time—at ages nine, six, and four.

Grant's diary, June 1974: *I have found more mounds. They have shells around them. The shells are of abalone. The mounds might be burials. Also I found some pottery and a scraper. The pottery is plain, but it looks fired and is different colors. The scraper is sandstone. I still don't know why those things are in the mounds.*

There was never any doubt in our minds that the boys were *learning*, right alongside us much of the time, questioning, exploring alternatives, working out solutions as we worked on one and then another project and confronted one challenge after another. The *World Book Encyclopedia* was there when, in the process of working on a clogged carburetor on the generator, one of the boys asked what, exactly, a carburetor did, and when, as we were thinning out redwood groves for poles for the garden, somebody asked if redwoods grew only in this part of California. Now that all three of them could read, and as their questions became more difficult, the encyclopedia and dozens of science and nature reference books came to occupy a central place in our lives. And they soon had their favorite authors—Richard Scarry, Dr. Seuss, Maurice Sendak, Laura Ingalls Wilder, Madeleine L'Engle, Roald Dahl.

Once the house was up we turned our attention to the next item on our agenda: growing our own food. We didn't have water, room partitions, or indoor plumbing, and the windows might be covered in plastic sheeting, but that was of little consequence compared to the importance of getting in a garden and an orchard. We'd made something of a stab at growing tomatoes that first summer, bringing up leggy plants from Berkeley that spring and watering them by hand from the five-gallon water carriers, only to see them shrivel up in the sun as the summer wore on. And we'd even ordered several dozen strawberry bushes in response to a "one-time special offer" in *Organic Gardening* and planted them up near the summer kitchen, where those that weren't eaten by the deer burned out not too long after our tomato plants.

From the very beginning we suspected that our soil was better suited to growing trees than vegetables, and our first summer's efforts had confirmed that. Now, as the second summer approached, we set about the job of improving it. We pored over how-to-grow-it manuals and bought a soil-testing kit that confirmed not only that our soil was bad, but that it was going to take a lot of pricey soil "amendments"—greensand, oyster shell, rice hulls, blood meal—to make it productive. And we all learned what a pH—alkalinity/acidity—reading meant, and the functions of nitrogen, potassium, potash, and trace minerals.

"I hate the way this looks," Grant said that afternoon as we were installing the garden fencing behind the house. "It's ugly."

"We've got to have it," said Micki, looking up at him. "How else are we going to keep the deer out?" She and the three boys were pulling hard on the wire, straining to keep it taut while David nailed staples into the redwood post. He drove in the last staple, and we moved down to the next post.

"We could make a fence out of twigs and branches," said Grant. "That would look better than this ugly wire."

"And it would take us forever to put up," David pointed out.

"Well, I'm going to use branches and poles for my garden."

"Your garden?"

"I've got a place picked out, down past the house there."

"And you're going to clear the area?"

"Yes."

"And dig it up? And haul water for it?"

"Yes."

"But, Grant, that's going to be a huge amount of work."

"Not if you do it the way the Indians did."

The two of us exchanged glances. Grant certainly knew more about Indians by now than we did, and we had no idea what he may have gleaned about gardening from his reading. Earlier that spring, following directions he'd found in one of his books, he had hand-ground some dried manzanita into a flour, which he put in a bread that we all very dutifully ate but agreed that it did not noticeably enhance the flavor. And then there was the acorn flour that served as a staple of the Pomos who'd lived in the area and which, we agreed after tasting it, required a better source of water than we had to leach out the bitterness. "Go ahead and try it," said Micki. "But let's get this fencing in first."

When we finished up a few days later, Grant disappeared into the woods with Drew and Reed. A week later they invited us down to see "Grant's garden," and we followed them through the brush into a clearing. They had built a seven-foot-tall fence out of poles and branches woven together, which enclosed a thousand-square-foot patch. Inside, carefully laid out, neatly mulched mounds and pits had been planted in squash and corn—"Only Indian foods," Grant informed us.

Grant tended his garden for hours on end throughout the summer, carefully hand-watering his plants one by one. One afternoon in August he proudly presented us with a half dozen "perfectly formed" ears of corn and, several dozen ears later, was ecstatic when his squash placed third ("Out of twelve entries, Dad, that's pretty good, isn't it?") at the county fair in September.

"We're *almost* living on the land, aren't we," he said, beaming, the white third-place ribbon in his hand as we headed back up the hill.

"Well, it's a *start*," Micki said with a laugh. If we had tried to live off *our* garden that summer, we'd have starved.

Micki's diary, August 1974: *Yesterday the first cucumbers; some more of Grant's corn. Today to Ukiah after asking road crew to deliver us mulch (a truckload now sits near the garden). Picked 92 pounds of*

*plums, 45 pounds of apples, and 20 pounds of pears at the Butler
Ranch. Beans producing, tomatoes not quite ready. Slaughtered twenty-
four ducklings in the last week. Never again: plucking took hours.
Thought we could make a pillow with the down but ended up with only
a handful.*

It took us longer than we'd expected to master the art of mountain
gardening—to learn how to cope with bad soil, too hot days, cold nights,
afternoon winds, and not enough water. But eventually we did manage
to develop a productive garden, which, thanks to our generally mild
winters, provided us with most of our food year-round—greens, cauliflower, broccoli, and carrots in the winter, and everything from artichokes to melons in the summer. But we didn't do so well with our
orchard. In fact, it was something of a disaster.

We agreed that we couldn't really call our place a homestead until we
got an orchard in. Every self-respecting homesteader had to have a goat,
chickens, a garden—and some fruit trees. And since it would take a
couple of years for the dwarf trees and five or six years for the full-size
trees to start producing—we'd learned that in our how-to books—we
wanted to get on with the project as soon as possible. Fruit trees were
expensive, though, at least from our no-income, nickel-and-diming it
perspective.

"I know what!" exclaimed Drew one evening when we were talking
about whether we could afford the fencing and ten or twelve dollars each
for the trees. "We'll get all of our friends and relatives to buy a tree.
Then they can have half the fruit when they start producing!"

Micki laughed. "And we'll ship them bushels of apples a couple of
years from now?"

"No," said Drew. "If they don't want them, we'll sell it and send them
the money. It'll be a good deal for them."

"And who's going to present this idea to them?" said Micki, wondering
where Drew had come up with the notion. It was a little bit too clever
to suit her.

"We can write to them," said Grant, "if you'll help us with spelling
and all that."

"Just to relatives," said Micki. "Not our friends."

Grandpa Nash, Micki's father, was the first to respond. He wanted a
Delicious apple tree and enclosed the exact amount Drew had requested:
$12.95 for a Stark's Nursery Special. Grandpa Colfax wanted apricots

but got a plum tree instead when Grant, after checking the growing charts, decided that apricots wouldn't do well in our area. Aunt Grace bought in with two peach trees, and Aunt Irene, characteristically, sent a note saying she knew she'd never see any of the fruit and what were we doing raising our kids to be capitalists but enclosed a check for fifty dollars "to plant whatever you want."

We quickly cleared and fenced in a half acre up on the ridge and put in several dozen bare-root stock trees—apples, pears, plums, cherries— blithely unaware of how much water they'd need to get growing. Somehow, in our reading, we'd assumed that once we got them in they'd flourish like the firs and the redwoods around them, never once giving much thought to how much water they'd need over those hot summers until they managed to put roots down deep into that hard-packed clay soil. We watered them as often as we could, but it was not enough. Most of the trees survived, but barely, and over the years they stood as stunted evidence of our failure to do things in the right order, that we'd done it backward, putting in the orchard and only then worrying about water. We didn't have the heart to pull them out—they were, after all, the grandparents' and uncles' and aunts' trees. Fortunately, they all forgot about their investments and never asked what happened to their fruit, which was a good thing, because most of the trees survived only to pass through their productive years without yielding more than a few baskets of undersize apples, or pears, or plums. We agreed that it hadn't been a bad idea, but we probably would have done better to invest in grapes— or, better still, an adequate water system.

Grant's diary, August 1974: *Worked on my strawberry pyramid. Mom canned some jam from huckleberries we picked two days ago. Drew, Reed, and I gathered pinecones, which we hope to roast and then eat the seeds inside them. This is the most exciting event of the day—six little zuchinies (is that how you spell it?).*

CHAPTER TEN

Water Music

From Micki's diary, October 1974: *Am really bone-tired. Always used to laugh when my mother said Grandma died from hard work. Maybe it's possible. Can't believe we're still lugging those water carriers.*

Even as we hauled it, month after month, first for cooking and bathing, then to mix concrete, and later for our gardens, we knew that it was just a matter of time until we'd have the water situation under control. After all, there was a creek several hundred feet below us, and the boys had discovered a tiny year-round spring in the canyon between the house and the access road. All we had to do was collect the water, get it up to a point where we could store it, and gravity-feed it back down to the house and the gardens. It seemed simple enough.

The spring made the most sense. It was only a hundred feet down and, according to the boys' calculations, was turning out about five hundred gallons a day, even in August after nearly three months of no rain. It wasn't much, but it was enough to get by on until we came up with something better. So, after cutting a ledge into the rocky hillside and chiseling an opening into which we could insert a pipe, we headed over to Ukiah for the materials we'd need and ran smack up against yet another vocabulary we'd have to master.

"How much head do you want?" asked the clerk at the pump shop.

"Head?" said David. "It's about a hundred feet down."

"Well, a centrifugal pump might do it, then. You got a foot valve there now or what?"

"No," said David. "What else do we need?"

The man lifted a pump down from the shelf. "You got power?"

"No," said David.

"Then we'll put a five-horsepower Briggs on this," he said. "What kind of pipe are you using?"

"What *should* I use?"

"One-inch ABS, I guess, and you'll need clamps."

"Oh," said David.

The clerk threw a few boxes of stainless-steel pipe clamps on the counter and proceeded, without giving David another glance, to pull another half dozen odd-looking pieces out of various bins behind him.

We returned with the car trunk filled with a few coils of black plastic— "ABS"—pipe, assorted plumbing, and a shiny new pump. Balanced precariously on the roof of the Volvo, like a swollen, rounded-end aluminum canoe, was a five-hundred-gallon stock watering trough. It took us all afternoon to maneuver the trough down the cliff and onto the ledge, where we connected the intake pipe, the foot valve, pump, and the line that ran up to the vinyl wading pool that sat where our summer kitchen had been. We gave a cheer as the first trickle of water arched into the gleaming new trough, watched it cover the bottom, and then climbed back up the hill to wait until morning, when we'd have enough to pump.

"Here goes," David shouted as we stood beside the trough full of shimmering, crystal clear spring water, and he snapped the starter cord of the Briggs and Stratton. The engine roared to life, and then there was a loud bang, a cloud of blue smoke, and the clanging and crunching sound of broken metal as it ground to a halt.

"Looks like something went wrong, Dad," said Grant.

"That's brilliant, Grant," David said. "Just brilliant." Now he'd have to disconnect everything, haul the pump back up out of the canyon, and take it back to Ukiah. But, as we were soon to learn, when it came to water, nothing was that simple. It took several days before another pump could be located, which meant yet another trip over and back, and then the connections didn't fit, which meant still another trip over and back. It was another week before we gathered again around the trough deep in the canyon and held our breath as David snapped the cord. This time the engine didn't fail, and the water level in the trough slowly began to drop. After waiting a couple of minutes, Drew and Reed had raced up the cliff and come charging back down with the news that we'd succeeded in getting water to the top of the ridge.

It was a makeshift system at best and required constant trips up and down the cliff, David and Grant starting and Drew and Reed stopping the engine as we alternately filled and emptied the hundred-gallon kiddie pool. But it allowed us to gravity-feed water down to the kitchen and provided just enough pressure to activate a sprinkler in our garden. Best of all, it meant that our water-hauling days were behind us. Or at least until the pigs got into the act.

They weren't wild pigs, exactly. In fact, one day Homer had met us in town and warned us against shooting any pigs that came our way. They'd be all his, he said. "You be sure to let me know if they come down to your place. Sometimes they get through the fence."

It seemed that it had long been his practice to keep some domesticated sows running loose up on his place, where they'd be bred to the big wild boars that roamed the hills. Not only was this illegal—feral pigs had become a major problem in northern California—but he infuriated local pig hunters by staking claim to any and all offspring that, with their aggressively protective parents, roamed in bands across the ridges, rooting and digging up pasture and woodlands with the destructive efficiency of a chisel-plow operator run amok. It didn't take too long for the pigs to discover the low-sided kiddie pool; within a week it became a regular water stop. We never actually caught them *in* it. Rather, we'd discover we were out of water—they'd crush the sides in—and David would charge up the hill, shotgun in hand, only to see them disappear over the ridge, snorting and grunting as the dog chased off after them, yipping hysterically.

Micki insisted that it always happened just when she was in the middle of washing her hair or rinsing dishes. "I *hate* this," she'd fume, "I just *hate* this. If we don't get a better water system, those pigs are going to drive me *mad!*"

From Micki's diary, December 1974: *Working on bathroom. Got a good deal on a used tub (weighed a ton) that we now fill with water carried in from the kitchen. Put quarry tile floor in bathroom; took three trips back and forth to Ukiah to have them cut. Awful stuff. Seems that* *everything in the place at this stage is so interdependent that every project becomes a colossal undertaking. Kitchen organized now, after ten days of utter chaos on the food front; now everything that was in bathroom is at the foot of our bed—toilet, sink, pipe, tools. Sick of moving messes from one corner of the place to another. Moral: Never try to live in a place while you're building it.*

But the five hundred gallons a day we managed to collect—and lose most of to the pigs at least once a week—wasn't enough to justify investing in a sturdier, more permanent setup. What we needed was *more* water. We spent hundreds of hours in the dank canyon, laboriously chiseling a channel back into the black basalt rock in an effort to increase the pencil-thin flow. But it all came to nothing.

"I have a friend who can dynamite it for you," Jim said one afternoon when he climbed down into the canyon with us to check out the system. "Hell, you can pound that rock for a year and not get any more water."

"Dynamite it?" David asked him.

"Yeah. The only trouble is that sometimes he knocks out the whole damn spring. It's happened a few times. The folks he was doing it for weren't too happy about it."

The obvious solution, of course, was to get somebody to come in with a big rig, drill a well, and put in a submersible pump and some big redwood water tanks. But we couldn't consider any such extravagance, no matter how much sense it made. We'd already spent more than we'd anticipated and were running out of money. We didn't have the couple thousand dollars to invest in what could turn out to be a dry hole. And we learned that what we'd thought was our ace in the hole, our year-round creek way down in the canyon, wasn't going to save us: to get water out of there would cost us a fortune in pumps and fuel. It began to look as though we were going to have to live with the pig-battered kiddie pool and the daily ration of five hundred gallons until, somehow, we could have a well dug.

But, according to Bud Sloan, we'd have no trouble finding water if we used his brand-new hand-held water-drilling rig. Micki had introduced herself to him one afternoon when she'd stopped to ask if he'd be interested in selling any of the weathered redwood siding he was ripping off a decrepit shack on the edge of town that a faded sign identified as the "Boonville Social Center."

"It used to be a bar," Sloan, a balding, middle-aged high school teacher, told her. "They say there used to be fifty of them here in the valley during the boom." He wasn't interested in selling the wood, which he was getting in exchange for tearing down the building. He had just bought a piece of land north of Boonville and planned to use it to build a new house.

"Do you have pretty good water out there?" Micki asked him. We'd looked at the piece with Lyle back when we gave barely a passing thought to the availability of water.

Sloan said he expected to have it soon. He'd just bought one of those drilling setups that was advertised in *Organic Gardening*, and he planned to use it as soon as he finished tearing down the social center.

"I could use some help setting it up and all that," he said. "If you're interested, I could let you use it after I'm done with it in exchange for some help over at my place."

It was an offer we couldn't refuse. A couple of weeks later David and the boys joined him out on his piece. Bud said he expected to find water in a matter of hours. He'd even brought a movie camera with him so he could record the moment when the water came gushing to the surface. The setup consisted of a heavy-duty vertical shaft engine, a couple of connections, a dozen ten-foot-long pieces of three-quarter-inch metal pipe, a carbide bit, and a water pump. The water was pumped down the pipe to cool the bit as it cut through the earth and sent its tailings back up to the surface in a muddy slurry. Every so often it would be necessary to pull the pipe out of the ground to add new sections or to repack the bearings.

Sloan handled the engine for the first hour or so as it noisily, roughly, and with excruciating slowness cut its way down, a micromillimeter at a time, into the earth. When nothing happened after getting down to fifteen feet, he passed it over to David. For the rest of that day, and all of the next, and the day after that, they took turns. Every time a new ten-foot length was added, we agreed that it would be the one that hit water. But one week and a half dozen sixty-five-foot-deep dry holes later, after the movie camera had long since disappeared, and after Bud had invested another $200 in a "professional," special diamond-tipped bit that the manufacturer guaranteed would do the job—but didn't—Sloan agreed that we had logged enough hours to try it out at our place.

We knew exactly where we'd drill. On one of his visits when he was trying to stoke up some business, Smokey, the sand and gravel man, had offered to "water-witch" our place and, after solemnly exploring some "promising" spots on the ridge with his oak witching stick, had declared that there was "lots of water" near a redwood grove just below Lizard Grove. And by counting the pulsations of the witching stick, he was even able to tell us exactly how far down it was: "sixty-seven feet, no question about it."

We hadn't given his efforts any credence back then. Water witching was one of those quaint practices we'd heard about but certainly couldn't take seriously. But now, after spending so many months trying to find a reliable source of water, we were ready to believe almost anything. We set up the pump, dug a small pit to hold the recirculating water, and began to drill. The first ten feet were easy—a day's work. Then we hit stone and for the next two weeks hung on to the rig as it ground endlessly and imperceptibly through solid rock. Hour after hour we took turns slumping over the sputtering and increasingly smoky and smelly engine, clutching the handlebars on either side as it kicked and vibrated, as the droning pump engine a few feet away added to the cacophony. For diversion, we'd peer across the top of the engine and line it up with first one and then another of the branches of a small fir tree just below us in an effort to obtain some discernible indication of our progress, hour after hour. The tedium was broken only by the need to repack the bearings, or to pull out the sections and wrench them apart and reassemble them after clearing the core, or when the drill, edging into a harder stratum of rock, would kick back and all but pull the rig out of our hands. But the tedium was offset by the prospect of water: a lot of it; and accessible. At the end of the second week, we hit Smokey's sixty-seven feet. No water. By now Micki's hands and arms were too sore to handle the rig, and David was left to do the job with one of the boys, who took turns reading in the shade of the redwood grove, until he was needed to help pull out the pipe to add another length or to clean the bit.

"Anything?" Micki asked as she brought up lunch the day after we passed seventy feet. David shook his head.

"We'll try another five feet," he said. "That'll take a couple more days at the rate we've been going."

"Do you think this was a mistake?"

"Well, at least we don't have two or three thousand dollars invested in the equipment, like Sloan does."

"But what a terrible waste of time."

Seventy-five feet. Still no water.

"Might as well keep going," said David. "Maybe the water table is down this time of the year."

Another week.

"We'll quit on Sunday night, no matter what," said David. For nearly a month now almost everything else around the homestead had been put on hold while we were drilling, and there was just too much else that needed attention.

Sunday night, at eighty-seven feet, David pulled out the pipe and called it quits.

"It was stupid, really," said Micki. "To think that Smokey could pinpoint the water like that. It might be a hundred or even two hundred feet down—if it's there at all."

"Well, we should have realized that it wasn't going to work for us when Sloan couldn't get anything down in the valley, where there's plenty of water," said David. "At least we gave it a good try."

Bud, meanwhile, continued to keep trying—on his own. He never did manage to find water and ended up mounting a water tank on a trailer and hauling water from the school grounds to his new house for several years until, shortly before giving up on country living and moving to Ukiah, he hired a commercial outfit to do the job. Prospective buyers, he'd been told, were not interested in a place supplied with water from a faucet behind the high school gym some fifteen miles down the highway.

Eventually, though, we came up with a solution. For years we'd thought about all those springs on that ridge to the west, a quarter of a mile away. Joe Cervetto, who played Columbus in San Francisco's annual parade, had a small cabin there where he spent a half dozen weekends a year. He had established a successful janitorial business in the city back in the thirties after emigrating from Italy, had become a luminary in the Italian wing of the Republican party, and had bought the property—"Refugio Cervetto"—for his children, who, he was quick to tell us, had grown up and couldn't care less about it. We'd meet him on the access road a couple of times a year. Often as not, the oversize generator he used to power his pump and cabin lights would be protruding from the trunk of his latest Mercedes, back from yet another trip to the repair shop.

"Nobody around here knows how to fix these things, Colfax," he'd declare indignantly. "How come?" We'd always know when Joe arrived for a weekend, for the nervous hum of the generator carried across the canyon.

Joe found us perplexing. One afternoon, not too long after we moved onto the land, when we were butchering chickens, he stopped by with two of his nephews from Milan whom he'd hoped to interest in the janitorial business. When they saw what we were doing, they hurried back to their car for their cameras and proceeded to photograph us at work. We laughingly imagined ourselves being featured in a future slide show in Milan, where we'd be described as "American peasants," for hadn't we ourselves taken similar photos in Italy a dozen years before?

"What do you do this for, Colfax?" Cervetto asked with a frown after his nephews had returned to the car with their cameras. "My brother and me, we do this when we come from Italy." Joe had cultivated his accent over the years. "We raise pigs, sell them, in Oregon. But you? You are an educated man. Why you do this?" He gestured toward the half-built house, the burned-out garden, the old Volvo.

We resisted the impulse to enter into a political discussion with this longtime Reagan appointee to the California Ports and Harbors Commission. There was a lot of water on his ridge.

"For the kids, Joe," said David.

"Ah," Joe said, his face brightening as he nodded approvingly. "You do it like me. For the kids."

Joe said he wouldn't mind if we ran a water line from one of his springs over to our place. He had plenty of water, lots of springs, and a well. The problem was getting through the woods from Refugio Cervetto to Shining Moon. Two deep canyons separated our places, and the woods were so dense it was impossible to sight a route. Still, by now we'd lived with collapsing water tanks (we were on our third, $12.95 on sale at K mart), marauding pigs, and water-starved gardens for so long that it was worth it. We could see the big tree in front of our house from a spring just below Joe's cabin, and we set our bearings with a compass. We headed back into the woods from a place below the Bench with chain saw, nippers, and bow saws, cutting our way through, checking the compass every dozen feet or so, never quite sure that we were going to come out anywhere near the spring, until, after a week of nonstop labor, we emerged into a clearing directly opposite, right on target.

We'd bought nearly a half mile of three-quarter-inch polyvinyl chloride—"PVC"—pipe and began snaking it across the ridge, welding together the twenty-foot-long sections with a strong-smelling, tapiocalike glue.

"I don't know what we're going to do here," Drew said on the middle of the third day, after we'd brought the line up out of the canyon and into the clearing on Cervetto's land. We had to get the line along the face of a steep cliff, and there was nothing accessible to which we could attach it.

"We could wire it to those trees down there," said Grant, pointing to some scrub oaks that grew out of the rock halfway down the escarpment.

"Yeah, if we could get down there," returned Drew. "You want to try it?"

"Not me," Grant said. "There's no way to do it. We'll have to run the line way down there and back up again."

"I know how we can do it," Reed piped up.

"Oh, sure," said Grant.

"Just lower me down with a rope."

"And you're going to glue the sections together and wire them in place?" Grant asked.

"Sure," said Reed.

"I don't know," Micki said. "What if you slipped or something?"

"Two of us can hold on to him," said Drew. "He doesn't weigh anything."

"He's so skinny he won't even bounce," said Grant.

"Very funny," Micki said.

"I can do it," Reed insisted. He turned and headed back up to the house for a rope.

When he returned we tied it around his waist and slowly lowered him down the face of the embankment. He held a can of glue in one hand and a clump of rags for cleaning off the pipes in the other, a roll of wire and linesmen pliers in his back pocket. As we held him there, dangling, Grant lowered down the end of the pipeline with another line, and Drew, on the other side of us, let down another section of pipe.

Reed pulled in the floating two pieces, wiped the ends clean, applied the glue, and jammed them together. "It's easy," he called up to us as he stuffed the glue and rags into the front of his shirt, twisted around, and took the wire and pliers out of his pocket. It took him only a few minutes to wire the suspended pipe to the base of one of the trees. "Okay," he called. We pulled him up, moved twenty feet farther along, and lowered him again.

"I knew he could do it," Drew said as he lowered another section. "I always knew he might be good for *something*." We knew that for once he wasn't being sarcastic, that he actually was proud of his little brother.

After we reached Cervetto's spring and boxed it in with scrap pieces of plywood, we moved the horse watering trough and pump up out of the canyon at the other end of our land and abandoned forever the spot where we had spent so many hours working so futilely to increase the flow of water. Just below Lizard Grove we cut a ledge into the embankment and put the trough in a place where, according to our calculations, the water, rising up out of the canyon to the same level as the spring, would fill it.

It worked. There would be plenty of water, provided we managed to collect it all, pumped twice a day, and kept the pigs out of both the kiddie pool at one end of the line and the spring box at the other. But of course the pigs continued to collapse the kiddie pool and root in the spring box, and it wasn't always possible to coordinate pumping and watering the garden. And worse, we soon discovered that the centrifugal pump, factory specifications to the contrary, simply wasn't up to the task of lifting the water another twenty feet higher than it had during that first year in the other canyon. As a consequence, we burned out an engine every year or so—almost always, it seemed, during the hottest week of summer. Clearly our water problems were far from being solved. Still, the new system was a major improvement, and like most of the low-tech, low-cost systems we improvised over the years, it worked well enough to allow us to get on with other, more pressing tasks until we could afford the time and money to get back to it. Eventually we replaced the pump, built two pig-proof ferro-cement water tanks, and enclosed the spring box. It took years—a dozen of them—over which the boys took turns starting and stopping the pump, repaired breaks in the water line, hunted down marauding pigs, cleaned out the spring box, and hauled burned-out and replacement engines in and out of the canyon. Over those years the collection, conservation, and use of water was a persistent and often all-consuming concern.

PART FIVE

Facing Reality

CHAPTER ELEVEN

Killer Bees and Carpentry

"Something's bothering the goat," Micki shouted from the kitchen. "It looks like she's dug up a nest of yellow jackets." She ran out past the garden to the black oak where Essy was tethered.

"That stupid goat," fumed David. He and the boys had left the lunch table and stood in the doorway. Micki was next to the tree, working frantically to untie the rope as the braying goat lurched and pulled away from her. Suddenly Micki turned and ran back toward the house, beating her head and shoulders.

"They're all over me!" she screamed.

David ran out and brushed a half dozen wasps out of her hair as hundreds of them swarmed around us, diving into our faces and hair, buzzing angrily. Waving our arms wildly, we ran into the house, where the boys fell upon us, swatting with rolled-up newspapers the dozens of yellow jackets that had managed to come inside with us.

"Mom, are you okay?" Grant asked as Micki collapsed on the sofa.

"They stung me on the neck, up under my hair," Micki gasped, hunching her shoulders. "I'm all right. I should have known better than to go out there without some protection. David, you've got to get her loose. They'll kill her."

"Who cares about her? Are you okay?"

"No, really, help her. I'm all right."

David pulled on a heavy winter jacket and wrapped a bath towel around his head and neck. Essy was down on the ground now, braying piteously as a black cloud of wasps swirled around her. David circled up behind the oak tree, then, charging past it, slashed the rope with his knife. Jumping up, Essy ran into the woods, the swarm in pursuit, as David sprinted back to the house, where the boys were waiting with their rolled-up newspapers.

"Did they get you?" asked Micki, still on the couch.

"They went after Essy." Big red welts were beginning to form on his arms and hands.

"David?" Micki's voice was fading. "I . . . I feel faint." Suddenly her head fell back, and she slumped sideways.

"Micki!" cried David, shaking her. "Micki!" He slapped her. There was no response.

"Don't hurt my mother!" screamed Drew, pounding on his back. "Don't hurt her!"

"I've got to get her to a doctor." David picked her up—Micki's head hung lifelessly to the side—carried her out to the truck, and pulled her up onto the seat.

He roared down the access road and onto the country road without stopping, horn blowing, tires squealing. The nearest doctor was in Ukiah, forty-five minutes away. Micki sprawled beside him, rolling from side to side as he negotiated the curves. Through town, horn blaring, passing cars, forcing them onto the shoulder, turning into the Ukiah-Boonville Road. Twenty-one miles.

"Micki," he pleaded. No response. "Micki!"

She'd been unconscious for fifteen minutes now. He blew his horn frantically and flashed his lights, and the logging truck pulled off to let him pass. He was going too fast—the road dropped off hundreds of feet on both sides and was treacherous enough under ordinary circumstances. At the top of the ridge now, the gray-green Ukiah valley shimmered in the midafternoon heat far below them. He reached over to feel for her pulse and nearly lost control of the truck on a switchback curve. Was she . . . dead? He slowed down and took her hand. He couldn't feel anything. She couldn't be dead; it was impossible. But maybe . . . no, they'd be in time. They had to be. Down the mountain, through curve after curve. The logger he'd passed back there must have recognized him and radioed ahead, for all the other trucks were pulling off as he came up behind them. He almost rammed a dusty, slow-moving pickup as he came around a curve, its driver gesturing angrily as they passed. Five more miles now. He'd need a police escort through town. The Highway Patrol barracks were at this end of town, so they'd spot him right away. Just so they didn't try to stop him. As soon as he got through these curves—a car had gone over the edge here last year—it was mostly straight.

"David?" Micki, dazed, was trying to sit up. She sat up unsteadily and braced herself against the dashboard. "David, slow down. Please. I'm okay."

He reached over and took her arm. "You fainted. I thought you were dead."

She nodded and rubbed her hand over the back of her neck. "The yellow jackets. How long was I out?"

David glanced at his watch. "At least a half hour."

"The boys must be really upset. We'll have to call Jim and have him go up and tell them I'm okay. Now please slow down. I'm all right."

It took another five minutes to get to the hospital.

"This is epinephrine, just to be safe," said the emergency room doctor as he filled the syringe. "How many times do you think they stung you?"

"Six or eight times, maybe more," said Micki. "But I didn't swell up. I just felt myself growing faint."

"Anaphylactic shock," the doctor said as he injected the stimulant. "Your whole system overreacts. That's why you didn't have a local reaction." He discarded the syringe. "You were lucky. It can be fatal. You were out for a long time."

"It could have killed me, then? What about the next time? What if I get stung again?"

"You never know. You said you never had an allergic reaction before, and maybe this had something to do with their swarming, or what they'd been feeding on. But our bodies change, and you could have developed this allergy fairly recently. It's more common than people think. In fact, there's evidence that some deaths attributed to heart attacks are the result of allergic reactions to bee stings. You'll have to get a bee sting kit and learn how to use it."

"Great. Now I won't even be able to go outside without worrying about dying."

"You're going to have to take care of yourself," said the doctor.

The boys greeted us, wide-eyed, at the driveway.

"Jim came over," said Grant, taking Micki's hand. "He said you were okay. Drew was really upset. He started hitting Dad when you passed out. He thought he was hurting you."

"I'm okay now," said Micki, putting her arm around Reed.

"We're going to pour kerosene on the nest when it gets dark," Drew told her.

That night after dinner Micki showed us how to use the bee sting kit we had picked up at the pharmacy before leaving Ukiah.

"One of you will have to inject me in case I get stung again," she instructed. She took a syringe out of the red plastic case. "You push the plunger down to here. If that doesn't bring me around, you give me the rest of it five minutes later. Do you think you can do that?"

The boys all nodded solemnly.

"You still have to get to the hospital, though," said Grant.

"Right away," Micki said.

"So Dad always has to be around to drive," Drew pointed out.

"He has to be within hollering distance," said Micki. "Dad or someone else. Until you're old enough to drive. Let's just hope I don't get stung again."

Without a phone, far from neighbors, and an hour from the nearest doctor: We couldn't have chosen a worst-case scenario. One thing was clear, though: Micki couldn't be left on the mountain without another driver nearby. But the way things were going, it was beginning to look as if we'd all be leaving Shining Moon before too long anyhow.

The house looked a bit more civilized after David returned from St. Louis with a pickup and a trailer filled with our belongings. We had a sofa now, and a couple of end tables that replaced the boards and boxes in the living room, and in the corner of what would be our bedroom, once we got the interior walls up, we'd put our big brass bed and a couple of antique dressers. There was even the washer and dryer.

"Why in the world did you haul them all the way out here?" Micki had exclaimed as the boys unloaded them. "You knew we'd never use them."

David shrugged. He just couldn't bring himself to leave them behind.

"Yeah," said Drew. "When we get enough water *and* electricity."

Micki was right. After storing them under tarps for three winters, we finally hauled them off to the dump.

David's trip out to St. Louis and back had been an expensive undertaking. We had written to Rob, an old friend and amateur mechanic there, asking him to keep on the lookout for a good truck, since we knew nothing about such things. Shortly afterward he wrote that he'd found a "fantastic" ten-year-old three-quarter-ton Chevy that needed only a bit of work. David hitchhiked east and loaded up. On his way back he spent a couple of days in a Kansas junkyard replacing the rear end, a weekend in a Fort Collins service station replacing a piston with the help of a sympathetic mechanic, who sent him on his way with a cheery, "Good luck, you'll need it," and an afternoon on the edge of the Great Salt Lake Desert replacing the radiator.

"So how much do we have into it now?" Micki asked after the truck was unloaded.

"About three thousand. And it's burning a quart of oil every hundred miles."

"What's that mean?"

"It means the engine's just about shot," said David. "I knew that back in Colorado. I was lucky to get home."

"And Peggy Bates said we could have bought Chili's old pickup for two thousand—and it was newer."

"Yeah, but we didn't know anything about trucks. We trusted Rob, remember?"

"He did us a real favor, didn't he? Now we've got a broken-down truck, a worn-out car, and only a couple thousand dollars left. And no matter how we cut back, that's not going to last us very long."

"We can start doing firewood," said David.

We'd learned that it was what some of the locals did when logging prices were down. You could get a hundred and twenty dollars for a load of wood in San Francisco. Since it took a day to cut, split, and load, a day down and back, and thirty dollars for gas, it was a hard way to make a living. But for the past couple of months we'd been going to the city every two weeks anyhow. Three years before, several specialists back in St. Louis had told us there was nothing we could do about Reed's "lazy eye," and that he—and we—would simply have to learn to live with it. But we'd always suspected that given our reputation and the fact that Reed was black, we hadn't been taken as seriously there as we should have been. Now, in California, as the eye worsened, we'd contacted some of our old friends in the health rights movement, who had helped us locate a San Francisco specialist who said that it might be corrected if the eye were patched and checked every couple of weeks.

A two-dollar ad in a Bay Area flyer—"Mixed oak and madrone firewood, $45 a half cord. Box 246, Boonville"—got us into the business. Since we had no telephone, we had set the price low enough to make it worth writing to us to arrange for delivery, and we soon had several dozen orders lined up. The job would have been considerably easier if we'd had a good chain saw or a four-wheel-drive truck that could get us in closer to the trees. But those were unthinkable luxuries, and we had to compensate for the crudeness of our equipment with what the boys proudly referred to as "Colfax muscle power." David would take down the trees— we selected them with an eye to how their removal would improve the remaining stands as much as to their accessibility—and cut them into sixteen- or twenty-inch-long rounds. Together, Drew and Reed, wearing glasses now, his eye covered by a patch, would wrestle the heavy, wet pieces to where Grant could upend and split them, as Micki would dip in between blows to gather the pieces and pitch them into the truck.

Any of the old-timers could have told us we shouldn't have been so accommodating. "You pull up, you dump it," one of them said years later at one of the fairs, when we were talking about our firewood days. "They want it stacked, you charge. They want it behind the house, you charge." But we offered custom service at wholesale prices to what turned out to be an unusually demanding lot. ("Anybody who'd order firewood by *mail* has got to be pretty weird," said the old-timer.) There was the Berkeley professor—"Who else?" muttered Micki—who stood watching, his hands folded across his chest, as we lugged a few pieces at a time up his too-narrow-for-the-truck driveway and around to the back of the house, where, as he'd directed us, we fit it all into a tiny crawlspace. There was the elderly gentleman in a blazer who had us hand each piece to him to be examined for dirt or sawdust before handing it back to be stacked in a corner of his immaculate garage next to his Mercedes. And there was the occasional small windfall—the executive who insisted on being told how "a nice family like yours finds itself in the firewood business," who gave Reed a five-dollar tip ("It was because of his eye," groused an envious Drew), and the time a homeowner paid us ten dollars to haul away some old kitchen cabinets from a remodeling job, which we refinished and installed in our kitchen.

If we were lucky, we'd clear twenty dollars, only because the physician, after Reed once mentioned how we were financing our trips down and back, refused to charge for the visits, saying it was all part of his "research." But often as not, the truck would break down, and we'd end up canceling the appointment, spending the day in yet another strange garage, or hitchhiking home and adding one more spot to our list of memorable places such as those "where the fuel pump broke," "where the U-joint snapped and we spent all day in the downtown Novoto

garage," and "where the hippies in the padded van picked us up." Fortunately, Peggy—Postmaster Bates—spread the word that we were selling
firewood at pretty good prices and generated some local business for us.
By the time Reed's eye improved and we didn't have to go to San
Francisco as often, we were able to narrow our delivery area to Boonville
and Ukiah and managed to do better than just break even in the firewood
business.

From Micki's diary, January 1975: *Reed doesn't seem to be minding*
his eyepatch and is taking it all with considerable élan. Good thing he's
not in school—might be hard for a five-year-old to handle.

The firewood business, if we kept at it full-time, generated just enough
money to cover our basic expenses. As long as nothing went wrong, we
didn't need that much money. There was the hundred dollars a month
that we owed on the land, and we needed gasoline for the pumps and
vehicles. Micki had become adept at turning out good meals based largely
on beans, rice, eggs, and whatever the garden and the chickens produced.
But we couldn't expect the truck to last much longer without repairs,
and our clothes—we were all down to our last few pairs of jeans—were
beginning to look a bit bedraggled. And we didn't clear enough to buy
materials to do any inside finish work on the house, even if we could
have somehow found the time to do it. It was obvious that if we were
ever going to do anything more than merely scrape by, we'd have to
upgrade the firewood operation with a new chain saw and a winch so
that we could be a bit more efficient at what we were doing, find a job
in town, or start looking for a job back in academia.

From Micki's diary, February 1975: *Tired of scrimping. No meat, no*
movies, no dinners out, no baby-sitters, no new books, no concerts.
Living on nothing, an incredible drag, worrying about money all the
time. Ironic. The trouble with being poor is that it takes up all your
time.

It looked as if our friend Bud had come up with what we needed when
he stopped by one afternoon to propose that David build a house for him.

"Why you?" Micki said after he'd left. The valley was filled with self-taught "hippie carpenters" who were fighting for jobs at four dollars an hour.

"He likes my work?"

"Oh, sure." Micki laughed. "I hate to say it, but you're not that good."

"Well, I'm not very good, but I *am* slow," said David, slightly offended.

We could only surmise that Bud, who was a bit of a snob, liked the idea of having a former college professor working for him. Not that he was paying a lot for it: He'd pay David five dollars an hour to take charge of the whole project.

It proceeded in sharp contrast with the way we had built our house, mainly because David was able to subcontract the hard jobs that we had done ourselves. He hired a bulldozer to level the site, rented prefabricated forms for the foundation, and had concrete trucked in from Ukiah. He hired a couple of hippie carpenters to help with the framing and immediately scandalized them by insisting that they be paid the same hourly rate as he was getting. It was okay with Bud. He was making more than twice that at the high school.

But as the house—a simple rectangle with a lot of glass and a decidedly less complex roof design than ours—took shape, David was surprised to realize just how much he disliked building a place for someone else. For all the problems we'd encountered, he'd enjoyed working on our house and found it to have been an immensely satisfying experience. But there was little satisfaction and no future in building houses for others at five dollars an hour. And it wasn't without its risks, as he was reminded that cold and rainy afternoon when one of his helpers slipped while on the roof and was saved from a couple of broken legs, at best, by a section of scaffolding that had no reason to be where it was. Then there was the conversation about how a friend, another carpenter, was getting along after falling from a ladder and all but castrating himself on a beam and was in the hospital with no insurance, no worker's compensation, and no prospect of ever working as a carpenter again. Meanwhile, there was Sloan, his friend—a *teacher* no less—warm and comfortable down at the high school, making twice the money he was, with all the benefits. If this was what it took to stay on the land, it wasn't worth it. He didn't see the kids all day, came home exhausted, and hadn't done any real work on our house since he'd begun the job. This was what old Scott Nearing had warned against: You either survived by living on the land or you made compromises that undid everything that made it worthwhile.

David cut another shingle and fit it in place. It was time to consider some other options. Maybe it was time to head back into academia. From the peak of a half-finished roof in a near freezing drizzle, it was an idea that was looking better and better every moment.

From Micki's diary, February 1975: *David came home tonight edgy and tired. Said building a house is one of the dullest things anyone can do. Says by midmorning he's thinking, Well, that's $12.50 so far. I don't like being here alone with the kids. Nothing's been done on our house for months. Grant's into Indians, has done a bunch of short stories called "Boys and Girls of Mayan Days," and is intent upon publishing them. Reed and Drew are building a treehouse in an oak grove up near the old summer kitchen.*

CHAPTER TWELVE

Turning Point

"I don't know if I'm going to be able to handle this," David said as the red-brick high-rise dormitories of the state university rose into view out of the freshly plowed cornfields. It was spring, Sloan's house was finished, and we'd made it across country to Illinois in the pickup without, to our surprise and relief, breaking down.

"Don't be silly," said Micki. "You'll do just fine."

David was scheduled to give a seminar the next day on the Hungarian social theorist Georg Lukacs, based on some research he'd done at Washington University four years before.

"I'll bet half the department hasn't even heard of him," Micki said. "I'm sure they'll be impressed."

"Hah!" said David. "I doubt it. Look at that soil there. It'd sure make things a bit easier if we had several dozen acres of that stuff back in California."

David had sent out numerous letters to colleges early in the spring, expressing his interest in a teaching job. Three of them had eventually invited him for an interview. They were an odd mix—a midwestern state university, an eastern women's college, and a big-city university—and David was wary.

"Why only three? And these three?" he said as we prepared for the trip. Since the colleges were paying David's expenses, we'd all be able to drive out and back as cheaply as he could fly, and after three years of nearly nonstop work on the mountain, we were looking forward to it as a kind of family vacation. The pickup was in pretty good shape at the moment, and it took only a day to put together a plywood camper shell so the kids could ride in back.

"I'm too well-known. It has to be that. The word's out."

"Don't worry about it," Micki said impatiently. "At least you got the interviews. And they really aren't *bad* schools."

The boys took turns riding in the front with us, one at a time, and spent most of the trip bundled up in the back, playing games and reading.

Micki was half-right: *none* of the members of the sociology department seemed to have ever heard of Lukacs, but they *were* impressed. The next afternoon the chairman offered David a visiting professorship that paid half again as much as his last teaching job, and we celebrated with a couple of large pizzas that we had delivered to our motel room.

"That wasn't as bad as you thought it would be, was it?" Micki asked the next day as we headed on to New York. It was unlikely that either of the schools there would make a better offer, but it would be a chance for the boys to see the city.

"It's only a visiting professorship," said David. "Hardly a ringing endorsement."

"I'm sure they'll keep you on if you want to stay. It might even be better this way. We won't be obligated to stay if we don't like it there. Anyway, it'll be good for the boys to spend some time in a midwestern town and see how the rest of America lives."

Both the women's college and the city university offered David a job, but it didn't take long for us to calculate that it would be all but impossible to live in New York on what they'd pay. We headed back to Illinois, lined up a house for the fall, a Dutch colonial on the village square, and David telephoned the department chairman to check out some details of the contract.

"Oh, this is very awkward," said the chairman. "I'm afraid the dean has decided that we won't be able to offer you a position in sociology this fall."

David exploded. "What are you talking about?" They'd written him, paid his way out to give a seminar, and made a firm offer. He'd even rented a house for the fall.

"It's very awkward," he mumbled. "Very awkward."

"I knew it!" David exclaimed as he slammed down the phone.

"Well, kids," Micki said as the boys gathered around us, wide-eyed and alarmed. "It looks as if we won't be moving to Illinois after all. The bastards." She turned to David. "It's a good thing you did those other interviews."

David called the city university the next morning. The chairman said he was waiting to "firm up" the offer—some papers had to go through channels, and then he'd be in touch. The department head of the women's college wasn't in. After a half dozen more calls from roadside telephone booths and being told that she was "unavailable," David gave up on trying to reach her.

"Let's face it," he said. "Washington University got to them."

"They probably just called Washington University and were told to stay away from you," said Micki. "The city university job might come through. Whatever happens, at least we got a free trip to New York."

The kids talked us into stopping in Boomtown, a casino complex outside of Reno. They had advertised an all-you-can-eat buffet, and we were all tired of the cheese, bread, and fruit diet that had sustained us across the country and back. "Steal all the fried chicken you can, kids," joked David. "This might be the last time you'll see meat for a long time."

Back in the truck Micki opened up her purse and unwrapped a napkin. She had taken enough fried chicken to last us until we got home.

"Look!" Micki shouted as she hopped out of the truck a few weeks later, waving a letter. "City university sent your course assignments and wants your book orders and a note that says: 'We're all looking forward to having you here with us this fall.' "

"Now all we have to do is figure out how we can afford to live there," David said with a sigh.

"We'll manage," said Micki. "But first we have to get the house in shape so somebody can take care of it while we're gone. Nobody's going to put up with it the way it is."

We spent our last few dollars on bathroom fixtures, put up Sheetrock in the boys' room, ordered glass for the battered, plastic-sheeted clerestory windows, and installed a flush toilet. The place still looked like a warehouse, but now that it at least had the amenities of a cold-water flat, we could look for somebody to house-sit it over the winter.

A month later Homer came by with a telegram.

"That's it," David said as he handed the yellow envelope to Micki. "Strike three."

" 'Please call the City University of New York,' " she read. "They can't back out on us now, can they?"

We rode into town without speaking. David called from the pay phone in front of the fairgrounds. "I'm afraid we won't be able to offer that job to you," David was informed.

"But I've got my room assignments, my book orders; the chairman made me a firm offer."

"Sorry, Professor Colfax. It's been nice talking with you." He hung up.

David crossed over to the truck in front of the market, his head pounding. "That's it," he said. "Just like that. No job." The bastards must have gotten to him, too, he thought.

"What are we going to do? After we spent all that money getting the place fixed up . . ." Micki's voice trailed off.

David climbed into the truck and sat down beside her. The boys, in the back, were silent. "There's still one place," he said slowly. "I never followed up on their letter. It's in some godforsaken part of Canada. North of Lake Superior. They were always advertising for people. They might be desperate."

They were. "Are you sure you'll come?" asked the chairman. "I don't want to ask the president to make a formal offer if you're going to turn us down." It sounded as if it happened all the time. David had spent most of the week going back and forth to town to pick up telegrams and place calls. It was their fifth telephone conversation since he had first contacted the chairman and sent his résumé. "And you're sure you can teach ethnomethodology?"

"Yes," David told him. He'd teach nuclear physics if it would get him the job. Ethnomethodology was theoretical nonsense, but it wouldn't be any worse than the statistics he had been talked into teaching in order to get the job in St. Louis.

"You're sure now?"

"What?" A logging truck roared past.

"You're sure you'll take the job? And be here on September first?"

"Yes," said David. We'd be there. Wherever it was.

A few days later David signed the contract.

"Thunder Bay," Micki mused. "It might be nice."

* * *

Michael had come up to do a little hunting and to help us install the clerestory windows. It was our last remaining job before we headed to Canada the next week. "I, ah, really don't like this kind of work," he admitted as we hauled the wooden crate containing one of the four-by-four-foot sheets of plate glass onto the back roof. "Glass, I mean. A guy on a job I was on was putting in big windows like this last year and one of them broke on him. Cut his jugular. He bled to death right there. Fortunately, I wasn't, ah, there that day."

"That's a happy story," said David. "Pull up your end a little more."

Micki pulled into the driveway, back from her daily trip to town. "Put the glass down," she shouted. "I don't want you to hurt yourself when I tell you the news."

"What's the matter?" said David, alarmed.

"You're a *father*. We got a telegram from Portland, from the adoption agency. They want us to call them right away. They have a boy, born yesterday. An Indian-Eskimo."

"Hey, congratulations, Pop." Michael grinned. "Just what you need. Another kid."

Ever since we'd brought Reed home back in St. Louis five years before, we'd planned to adopt another child. But in the intervening time, a national association of black social workers had publicly declared its objections to the placement of racially mixed children in white homes, asserting the dubious proposition that it was better for such children to grow up in group homes and foster families than to experience the psychological hardships of growing up in white families. We had been bluntly discouraged from proceeding further when, shortly before moving to the land, we'd inquired about adopting another child through several Bay Area agencies. There were no white children available, and racially mixed children would not be placed in white homes. But now, even as the race issue faded, we were faced with another problem: having gone through the process once before, we were sure no social worker would approve our home.

"You ought to try the agency we went through," Pat Larson had suggested the summer before. She and Eric and the kids had stopped by again on one of their semiannual trips to visit his mother farther south. We were talking about our fear that we probably wouldn't be able to adopt another child as we had always planned. "The one up in Portland.

They were really open to us back when interracial adoption was pretty rare."

"Do you think we could get away with it?" David asked.

"Get away with what? This is a great place for kids," said Eric.

"Well, it's a little more civilized than it was the last time you were through," said Micki. "But you know it would never get past a social worker."

"Portland's several hundred miles away," said Pat. "They wouldn't do a home visit. You write to them and then we'll do the same."

We did as Pat suggested, submitted a batch of forms, and within a matter of weeks found ourselves being invited to Portland for an interview. We dug what remained of our best clothes out of the bottom of a trunk and headed north with the boys, carefully rehearsing them en route for their interview. Social workers, we explained, sometimes had a hard time dealing with people who were *different*, so we'd all have to be careful about what we said. We probably shouldn't say much about politics or selling firewood or Dad building Sloan's house, and we should pretend that we had fun on the mountaintop all the time.

"So what are you going to say if the social worker wants to know what you like most about school, Grant?"

"My parents teach us at home," he recited. "The local school is far away and not very good. We do a lot of reading and math."

"Be sure to add that last part," said Micki. "Why do you want a new brother or sister, Drew?"

"So we can have more help on the land." He laughed.

"No, seriously."

"I *know*," he said, offended.

"Well?"

"Because we could provide them with a good home."

"Right," said Micki. "Do you hear that, Reed?"

"Yep," he said brightly. Reed loved games.

The interviews went as expected. The boys were taken off to play, while the two of us put on the same blandly pleasant faces that had served us so well when we'd gone through the process of adopting Reed. There was nothing unusual about us: just a well-off, comfortably middle-class academic couple spending their sabbatical building a cabin in the woods. A few hours later the beaming social worker reunited us with the boys and told us we'd be hearing from her soon.

"Did we pass?" Grant inquired anxiously as we went out the door.

"I think so," said David. "How'd it go with you guys?"

"Reed and Drew were perfect," Grant said proudly. There was no question but that *he'd* done as well. "It was really funny. They asked us all the questions you said they would."

We celebrated the event by having lunch at a deli, where we all ordered exotic fare such as pastrami sandwiches and fancy pastries. Reed startled us with the comment that he didn't remember ever having eaten in a restaurant before.

And now, as we were preparing to head off to Canada, they had a baby for us.

"I don't know how we're going to work it," Micki said. She had set a bag of groceries next to the kitchen door and was facing David and Michael, who had climbed down from the roof and were sitting on stack of redwood boards. "There's no way I can drive two thousand miles and take care of a newborn baby at the same time." We'd planned to drive both the car and the truck to Thunder Bay, Micki and the boys in the Volvo and David and household goods and clothing in the pickup.

"It's not two thousand miles from Portland," David pointed out.

"Well, whatever it is, I'm *not* going to drive *and* be responsible for the baby."

"What about Raj?" suggested Michael. "He should have plenty of free time now that he's done with his course work."

Raj Singh was a Trinidadian, a former "scholarship boy" who lived in San Francisco with his wife, Toby, a flight attendant. A student at San Francisco State, he'd been drafted, spent a year in Vietnam, and returned to become active in Vietnam Veterans Against the War. An old friend had introduced us, and he and Toby, who was active in the flight attendants' union, drove up to visit us every month or so. Unlike most weekend visitors, they always pitched in immediately upon arrival to help us with whatever we were doing and they brought us up-to-date on political life in the metropolis. Irrepressible and charming, Raj had only one fault: before leaving, he would always insist on preparing a goat curry "the way they do it in Trinidad"—an undertaking that left the kitchen in a shambles for the rest of us to clean up.

Michael was right. Raj said he'd be happy to drive the Volvo to Duluth. He could catch a plane back to San Francisco, using the pass airlines provided flight attendants' spouses. The boys would ride with him, and the two of us would keep the baby with us in the pickup.

Three days later we closed up the house as best as we could, leaving it empty at the last moment when the woman who was to house-sit it backed out when she found a place closer to town that came complete with running hot water, a telephone, and electricity. Homer promised to keep an eye on the place, and Michael said he'd be coming up once a month to hunt and check things out.

We left with something of the same sense of exhilaration and apprehension with which we'd headed off from St. Louis to Uganda three years before. This time, though, we knew we had a place to come back to, a place we'd hold on to even if we stayed in academia. We'd been on the land for less than three years, yet it seemed as if we'd been there for decades. We'd come close to going broke and had had more than a taste of what it felt like to live on the edge. If nothing else, it made us feel as if we were prepared to handle anything. It was disconcerting to think about reentering that world of steady paychecks, electric lights, central heating, hot water, television, shopping malls, and all those comforts that we had so mindlessly taken for granted until we found ourselves without them up there on the mountain.

"Well, I declare, a new baby *and* a new job way up there in Canada?" exclaimed Postmaster Bates as we stopped by the post office on our way out of town. "You folks sure like to keep busy, don't you?" She handed us a batch of change-of-address forms. "And Homer's keeping his eye on your place?" She raised a skeptical eyebrow. "Well, you get up there and get that baby and get back here soon, you hear?"

"I can't believe it," David said as he sprawled out on the bed. "Two thousand miles for *this*? It's like a bad joke."

We were in a one-room log cabin in a park on Lake Superior, just outside Thunder Bay. The weather was cold and bleak, with the wind off the lake slicing through the campground. We had to remind ourselves that it was only early September. Back in Boonville the temperature was in the nineties.

"It's actually a good construction job," said David, critically observing the carefully notched and fitted logs. "It's a shame they painted it, though. Powder blue, for God's sake."

"How long do you think it'll be before we find an apartment?" asked Micki as she bent over the baby, who was wrapped in blankets at the foot of one of the beds in the crowded room. Garth cooed contentedly, his black hair jutting forward like the outstretched fingers of a hand, an infectious smile lighting up his dark round face. A stop at the adoption agency and an hour with a lawyer, and he'd been made irrevocably ours.

He'd slept on the seat of the pickup between us as we made our way along the Columbia River, across the northern plains of Montana and North Dakota and into the rolling hills of Minnesota and northern Ontario, Raj and the boys following behind us, hour after uneventful hour, in the Volvo. We'd arrived in Thunder Bay two days before, leaving Raj in Duluth to catch a flight back to California.

Professor Cecil French, the department head, had come by the motel to meet us before we'd unpacked. He was a nervous, dapper sort who resembled Thomas Dewey—Truman's "man on the wedding cake"—and who within minutes after introducing himself informed us in rapid-fire order that he was "a reformed boozer," that he and his wife "didn't get along," that Thunder Bay was "a dump," and, most disconcertingly, that the university would pay for only one night in the motel "now that you've arrived." Oblivious of the fact that we had just traveled a couple of thousand miles with a new baby and were anxious to get to bed, he spent another half hour impressing upon us the importance of submitting receipts for all our travel expenses to the business office the next day, then another half hour on what a difficult man the dean was and how fortunate the department was to have been allowed to hire David. "Don't expect too much," he said as he stood in the doorway, about to leave. "This is the kind of place where the faculty goes down to *Duluth* 'for a big weekend.' "

"My God," Micki said after he left. "*He's* going to be fun to work with. Welcome back to academia."

Thunder Bay was hardly the "dump" that Cecil had called it. A dreary grain-shipping port and a hard-rock mining center, it didn't have anything resembling the slums in which we'd spent so much time organizing in Hartford and St. Louis. At worst, it resembled a depressed New England mill town, with its unpaved and potholed streets, tar-board-sheathed houses, weatherbeaten stores and shops, and unkempt neighborhoods. It had never crossed our minds that we might have trouble finding a place to live once we arrived, and we were shocked to discover that the town suffered from a serious housing shortage. "I'm afraid you'll be lucky to find anything in less than a month or two," the first realtor we visited told us, and we heard much the same over the next two days as we scoured the town.

"This is great," David said as we returned to the motel at the end of the second day. "We come up here to make some money and we're going to piss it away in this crummy motel."

"You might be able to stay over at the park for a few weeks if they're still open," the manager suggested when David inquired about weekly rates.

"Log cabins," Micki said dully as we pulled up to a row of tiny neat buildings that backed up on Lake Superior. "How nice. A new experience. A chance to rough it. With an infant."

"At least it has electricity," David said as we settled in. "All the comforts of home."

"We don't have electricity at home, Dad," Reed reminded him.

"He's only kidding," said Grant. "He's being facetious."

"Oh," Reed said as he flicked the light switch on and off.

We didn't have to stay there as long as we'd feared. Apparently a number of other new faculty members were having the same trouble finding a place to live and had complained about it, with the result that we were informed about the availability of several apartments in a new townhouse complex adjacent to the campus and were able to move in within the week.

We hadn't brought any furniture with us—there was no room for it in the pickup, and besides, we'd managed to get along without it during those months back on the land. Instead we'd packed a box of tools and a book on how to make plywood furniture and set to work building it.

Within a week we had our dining room table and six chairs, a cradle for Garth, bed frames, a sofa, end tables, and several side chairs, all finished in a high-tech, high-gloss white enamel. And with the addition of some ready-made cushions from Sears, foam rubber mattresses from the camper, and a few Eskimo prints we rented from the public library, the apartment was quickly transformed into something considerably more civilized-looking than our raw, exposed stud-wall house back in California.

"It's all so simple," Micki said as she adjusted the thermostat one evening after dinner while we settled in to watch the evening news on our new twelve-inch black-and-white television, a $125 extravagance we'd allowed ourselves once we realized that life in Thunder Bay was going to be even duller than we'd feared. Push a button here, flick a switch there, and you've got electricity, hot water, flush toilets, central heat, everything. And all you have to do is pay the rent. Through the double-glazed sliding glass door we could see the lights of a shopping mall and a radio tower beyond the dying lawn and the thin woods.

It was strange to realize that this cold and desolate place, this foreign country, was much more like other places in which we'd lived than our home in California. It was a world of familiar sounds and images, of everyday conveniences and casual consumption, a reassuringly ordered world, if you didn't think too much about it. And, above all, so *easy*, compared with that life we'd made for ourselves back on the mountain.

There was the weather, for example, which directly shaped our daily life in California but here was little more than a mildly distracting consideration in frigid Thunder Bay. When storms swept in across Lake Superior or off the plains, we simply stayed in and turned up the thermostat. When temperatures didn't rise above twenty below zero for three months, we simply plugged in the block heaters that kept our car engines warm, shopped in overheated malls, and went from building to building in underground, shop-lined tunnels on campus. This was simple living: no house to finish, no chores to do in raging storms, no road slides to clear, no machinery to break down, no wind, rain, or mud to cope with—and all the electric power and hot water anyone could want.

"It's easy for us," Micki said one winter afternoon as we sat in the living room of the apartment, watching the snow come down. "But imagine trying to homestead up here. And people do it." But not us. Settled in and comfortable, we experienced a bitterly cold Thunder Bay winter that we agreed was nothing, really, compared with those we had endured in what was objectively, at least, the infinitely more salubrious climate of northern California.

The boys were quickly introduced to two of the things that dominated the lives of most children but had scarcely touched theirs: television and school. At first, our new, bottom-of-the-line television set seemed to be serving its purpose—it killed time, consuming all those extra hours that, back on the land, would have been spent clearing brush, working in the garden, hauling firewood, and building the house. The boys became fans of "Gilligan's Island" reruns, and we all watched the news. But television was even worse than we had remembered it, even though none of us had ever watched it very much before moving to the land. As the novelty of television wore off, we soon reverted to our mountaintop regimen of reading our way through the long winter evenings. We all agreed, though, that however much we preferred our life on the mountaintop, when it came to reading, electric lights beat kerosene lamps hands down.

Then there was school. If it made sense for the boys not to go to school in Boonville because there was so much going on around them and every day presented all of us with new learning experiences, apartment life in Thunder Bay didn't seem likely to offer anything comparable. Besides, we reasoned, since we were in a foreign country, it might be worthwhile for the boys to be exposed to its educational system. We wouldn't be in Thunder Bay for very long, so whatever they experienced there wasn't likely to do them any harm. The boys agreed: going to school in Canada might be something of a lark.

They enrolled in a school halfway across town and came home each day with fresh reports on the strange and amusing world they had entered. It wasn't that they disliked it, as we had feared, but rather they found it to be a terrible waste of time. How could anybody think that sitting in an overheated classroom, memorizing the products of Manitoba and doing the same math over and over again, made more sense than doing something *real*, like building a road or splitting firewood or reading a really interesting book? Besides, Mrs. Cunningham must have something wrong with her because she screeched at the class all the time; nobody paid any attention to Mr. Lawson because he gave everybody good grades no matter what; and it didn't make any sense to do all that busywork they were sent home with because none of the teachers looked at it anyhow.

Of the three, Reed enjoyed school the most. He was allowed to "skip" kindergarten when the teacher determined that he was reading "at a fifth- or sixth-grade level" and was by far the best reader in his class. He was even designated a "First-Grade Sweetheart" not too long into the year.

"A *what?*" Grant exclaimed as Reed proudly showed us the elaborately lettered proclamation. "A 'First-Grade Sweetheart'?"

Drew found it hilarious, and Reed was devastated.

"Everybody got *some kind* of award," he explained, tearing up. If they thought school was such a joke, why had they made such a big deal over his getting into first grade? They were always giving him a hard time, just as they did back in California, usually for not doing his chores. He *hated* the job of cracking acorns to feed the peacocks. Once they'd made him sit out in the rain until he'd filled a bucketful. School was a lot more fun. You could sit and read all day and nobody bothered you.

As any one of us might have predicted, Drew was the one who got into trouble—but only once, and because of a principle. For a week he put up with being told by the school bus fourth-grade "monitors" where and with whom to sit each morning and evening on the two-mile ride to and from school. Then one morning, after ignoring a monitor's order to change seats, he rallied everyone else on the bus to sit with whomever they pleased. Such insubordination could not be tolerated, of course, and upon arriving at school, he was brusquely escorted to the principal's office, where, to the staff's consternation, he sat tight-lipped, refusing to identify himself or answer any questions.

"All he had to do was tell me what happened," said the principal when Grant had been called after someone realized that he was Drew's brother.

"He just sat there, staring straight ahead and looking furious," Grant said that night at dinner.

"I didn't do anything wrong," Drew stated after Grant told us about him sitting there, glaring at the principal, defiantly self-righteous. "I didn't have to explain anything—and I didn't." He looked at Grant, who had betrayed him. "*He* did all the talking. As usual."

But school and television couldn't compensate for the sense we had of having interrupted our "real" life in California for this sojourn in academia. More than we ever expected, we missed the physically and psychologically demanding and rewarding life that our years of homesteading had provided. Only now, from the perspective of a comfortable apartment in the freezing northland, did we recognize how much real pleasure we derived from doing things together as a family, of working together to do what was necessary to survive on the mountain. Here, in contrast, our lives, our daily routines, were defined and circumscribed by others. The boys would get up and go to school, David was off teaching three days a week, and Micki substituted at the local high school on the days that David was free to stay at home with Garth. We went our separate ways and came together in the evening to talk about the different worlds in which we were living. There were none of the challenges like those we had to confront together as a family, no accomplishments that we could all take pride in together. It was the way things were, out in the world, away from the earth, and we didn't like it.

"Maybe it's only that we're up here, away from everything," said Micki when we were talking about it one evening. "Maybe if you could find a job in the States, where the students and faculty are better, where we could get back into politics, we'd like it better."

David agreed. Cecil certainly had been right about the students being a lackluster lot, most of them interested only in acquiring credentials that would land them jobs with the provincial government as social workers or teachers. And his colleagues, he found, were more interested in discussing the merits of late-model cars, what was good on television, or the hot spots in Duluth than sociology, social issues, or education.

Many of them had been enticed from dead-end jobs in the United States by Canada's higher salaries and lighter teaching loads years before and now found themselves unable to find work elsewhere. Some, such as Cecil, hated Canada, Canadians, academia, and themselves. "We're all failures here," he'd tell David time after time on the afternoons he would stop by his office on his way home after classes. "Fourth-rate teachers in a third-rate university in a second-rate country," he'd say ruefully. "Not you, though. You can always go back to California and live off the land and tell them all to stuff it." Cecil's one pleasure in life was pheasant and quail hunting. David had turned down several invitations to go out with him. "Me, I'm stuck here with a bunch of morons and with my goddamn wife," he'd say. Poor Cecil was worse off than we ever imagined: Five years after we left, in the middle of winter, he stuck the barrel of a shotgun into his mouth and killed himself.

We had gone to Thunder Bay thinking it would be a way of getting back into American academia, that a year in Canada would offset the efforts of the Washington University administration to keep David out. But to our dismay we discovered that the impact of the blacklist had grown even more pervasive. Halfway through our stay in Canada, as he had done the year before, David wrote to colleges, answered advertisements, and contacted former colleagues. This time the only result was a single interview at an Ivy League college, where he was the students' first choice for a new "distinguished professorship" and which, predictably enough, came to naught. Now, as spring approached, Cecil was pressing for a commitment to stay on for the next year—but only as an untenured associate professor.

"What do you think?" Micki asked as we sat around the dinner table one snowy evening. David had just met with the president of the university and had been told that all tenure decisions were "on hold" for the foreseeable future, and he couldn't promise anything. "You don't even *want* tenure here. They know that you're blacklisted—why else would you be here? You really don't want to stay on here, do you? Under those conditions? It's demeaning."

"Well, we know what the alternative is," said David. "It's either here or back to Shining Moon. If I don't stay on here, I might never find another teaching job."

"And they know that," said Micki. "That's why they aren't giving you what they know you're entitled to. They think you're so desperate that you'll have to take whatever they offer. Don't think Cecil hasn't talked to some of those people you've written to."

"Why can't we go back to Shining Moon?" demanded Grant.

"Yeah, Shining Moon!" Drew exclaimed.

"I can't imagine our going back to Boonville for the summer, then coming back here in September," said Micki. "Especially now that we know what it's like. The town's awful, and the university is worse. Can you imagine living here for the rest of our lives, just so you can keep teaching? You won't be able to do any of the research you'd want to do, and you can bet they'll deport us if we get politically involved the way we were in the States. I thought we went off to California so we wouldn't have to put up with some broken-down job in some god-awful place. And look where we've ended up."

"But neither of us ever thought I'd be blacklisted, for chrissake," said David. "It looks like this is the end of the line."

"Yeah, and I can just imagine how happy some of your former colleagues would be if they knew that this is where we ended up."

"Is it really any worse than Boonville?"

"You know it is, David. Playing at being a scholar, cut off from politics, teaching kids who don't care, a faculty made up of the walking wounded? Of course it is."

"But at least we'd have a steady income here. What do we do in Boonville? Cut firewood?"

"Maybe," said Micki. "Look, don't think I don't know that it'll be hard. And you can quit playing devil's advocate. I know how you feel." She glanced over at the boys, who had been listening intently.

"You boys know that if we go back, we'll all have to work together really hard, for a long, long time. You understand that, don't you?"

Solemnly they nodded together as one. "But we'll have a house and the land," said Grant.

"And we've saved some money," Drew said.

"Some," said Micki. "Not very much, though."

"You know what we're giving up, don't you?" said David. "A guaranteed annual income for the rest of our lives. You know they'll have to give me tenure eventually."

"You said the same thing in Connecticut and St. Louis," Micki reminded him. "Besides, that's not the point."

"So it's back to no electricity, no telephone, no hot water?"

"And no money," said Grant.

"That's for sure." Micki turned again to David. "You know you've been marking off the days on the calendar. Don't pretend *you* don't want to go back. Admit it."

"Yeah, Dad," said Drew. "Admit it."

"Yeah, Dad," Reed echoed.

"So we all want to be poor again," said David. "We all agree that that's what we want? It's crazy."

"It'll be better than staying here," said Micki.

"Then I'll tell Cecil tomorrow that his offer isn't good enough and that we're going back to California."

"And be sure to tell him that no offer would be good enough now," said Micki.

The boys let out a loud cheer and woke up Garth, who had been asleep in his plywood cradle across the room.

It thawed on March 1, and rivulets of water trickled out from under the hard snowpack as we loaded up the Volvo and the pickup. An hour after David met his last class we were on our way south to meet Raj, who was flying in to the Duluth airport to meet us and drive the Volvo back. "It reminds me of that day we left Morocco to come back to the United States," Micki said as we stood at the window in the airport lounge waiting for his plane. "It feels again almost as if we are escaping from some kind of prison."

"Maybe it's just that we're charging off—again—into an uncertain future," said David.

"At least it's not as uncertain as it was then. We know where we're going. We have the land and the house."

"And no income."

Micki watched as Raj's plane banked and touched down. "We'll manage," she said as we headed for the gate. "We have so far."

PART SIX

Ranchers

CHAPTER THIRTEEN

Cattle, Game,
and Timber Days

"Hello. My name is Reed Colfax and I am a member of the Anderson Valley Four-H Club. The title of my talk is 'What's Up, Doc?' and my topic is 'How to Build a Rabbit Cage.' "

We sat in the back of the Apple Hall at the fairgrounds, Garth beside us in the stroller, as Reed, tiny and serious, his eye still patched, turned to the easel. "To make a rabbit cage you will need four things." He lifted off the poster board with his Bugs Bunny drawing on it and pointed to the list, in five-inch Magic Marker letters. "Welded wire, clips, wire cutters, and a tape measure. The first thing you need to do is . . . ."

It was 4-H demonstration night at the monthly Anderson Valley Farm Bureau meetings, the first opportunity the boys had had to give the speeches they had been practicing for weeks. We recognized most of those in the audience—Mrs. Bailey, who had the roadside farm produce stand and had given us spoiled produce that first year to feed the chickens, red-faced Faye Dealey and his wife, most of the Gowan uncles and aunts, whose nieces and nephews were in 4-H, and the Johnsons, who were the biggest sheep ranchers in the valley.

Reed finished his presentation without a hitch, and as he gathered up

161

his props, Micki nudged David and pointed over to old Ward Haines, who, in his knee-high boots and overalls, was smiling and applauding appreciatively.

Poor Julie Walters stumbled through her demonstration on how to ice a cake ("She should have practiced more," said Reed, who had come to the back and joined us), and then Drew, his curly blond hair down to his shoulders, walked to the front of the room, holding a length of three-quarter-inch rope.

"My name is Drew Colfax," he said. "Why buy an expensive halter for your livestock when you can make one out of rope? The title of my talk is 'As the Rope Turns,' and I'm going to show you how to make one."

A minute later he was making his way through the rows of folding chairs, asking for volunteers, and picked out George Gowan. Grizzled old George, who had been working with ropes and livestock all of his long life, who one of the 4-H leaders told Drew would be a good sport, did his best to follow Drew's instructions but ended up tangled in the rope, amid the hoots of his Farm Bureau buddies. "You all know you can't teach an old dog new tricks," George announced, handing the rope back to Drew and eliciting a round of applause.

"You really wowed them," Micki said as we rode home that evening, the six of us jammed into the front of the pickup. "All of you."

"Drew was the big hit," Grant said, pouting.

"Well, you have to admit that old George Gowan was pretty funny," said David. "And everybody liked 'What's Up, Doc?' You can't expect them to get too excited about a thirteen-year-old's demonstration." Grant's talk had been about the care of goat kids.

"Were we good enough to win gold medals on Demonstration Day?" asked Grant.

"*I* think so," said Micki. "But you don't know who the judges are or what their standards are going to be. You know, it's not whether you win golds or not, as long as you do your best up there."

"Well, we *were* the best tonight," said Grant.

"I suppose your boys will be getting into Four-H about now," Peggy said casually one morning as Micki sorted through our mail.

"I don't think we've given it any thought," replied Micki. "Why?"

"Oh, I only thought it might be good for them. Fact is, I think my son learned more there than he did in school. Some of the old-timers here in the valley have been project leaders for years, and let me tell you, they can teach them an awful lot, especially about animals, if they're interested, as I think your boys would be."

"It might be worth checking out," admitted Micki. She'd *heard* of 4-H, of course—a paramilitary organization like the Boy Scouts, farm kids in green-and-white uniforms.

"And it'd give them a chance to meet some of the local kids as well, seeing as they don't go to school," said Peggy. "Though I can't say they'd find *that* too exciting."

To our surprise, the boys didn't object when Micki told them about Peggy's suggestion, and they returned home full of enthusiasm from the first meeting of the year at the fairgrounds, where they pledged their "heads, hearts, hands, and health" to 4-H.

"It *is* a little bit like school, with all the records you've got to keep," Grant said as they displayed the evening's spoils on the dining room table—green enlisted men's caps, pretied neckties embossed with the 4-H clover, binders for the "record books" they were expected to maintain, and a half dozen forms. "The best thing, though, is that you can sign up for all kinds of projects. I signed up for goats, cattle, and animal science."

"I'm doing rabbits," Reed chimed in.

"And animal science," said Drew. "I'm doing woodworking and cattle, too."

"Why cattle?" Micki asked.

"Bill Charles is the cattle leader, and he said you can make a lot of money if you raise a steer," said Grant. "There's a big fair in Ukiah every August where Four-H kids sell their livestock. Drew and I thought it might be a good idea."

"But we don't know the first thing about cattle," Micki said.

"Bill said he'll show us everything we need to know," stated Drew. "He said all we need is a shed and a corral. Grant and Reed and I can build those."

From Grant's diary, April 1977: *We all got gold medals at the 4-H Demonstration Day in Willits, but there was a big problem when the leader saw Reed's baby teeth and told us that he wasn't old enough to be in 4-H. We had to promise that he wouldn't go on to state.*

From Drew's diary, August 1977: *We went to Cal Expo to give our demonstrations and I screwed up. Grant got a big gold medal for his hat, and I got a smaller one. It was hot. We went on all the rides and it was fun.*

We'd been at it all morning now as they bounded through the brush, disappeared in and out of the canyon, smashed fences, and tore up pens. The 2 nine-hundred-pound steers, an Angus and a Hereford, had broken out of their corral and, wild-eyed, snorting and panting, were tearing up the homestead.

We had hustled Garth down to the safety of his playpen when we discovered what was happening, and now, once again, we moved in to surround them. "Go more to your left," shouted David as the Hereford threatened to break out of the ragged circle the five of us had formed, waving two-by-fours and poles at the beasts like bull ring picadors. Grant, farther down the ridge, had for the third time succeeded in working Amon to within a few feet of the open corral gate. But this time, instead of backing on past and bolting into the woods as he had done before, he stopped abruptly, pawed the ground, snorted angrily, and charged at Grant, head down.

"Run, Grant!" screamed Micki, horrified. He didn't hear her. He'd stopped and was facing the charging animal, waiting, the two-by-four he'd been carrying held high above his head. Micki let out a scream as he waited until the last possible instant and brought it down squarely on top of the steer's head. The Angus stopped as surely as if it had run into a wall, bellowed loudly, lurched backward, turned, and loped off unsteadily into the fir forest.

"God," panted Micki, running up to Grant, who stood there half-dazed, the two-by-four dangling from his hand. "He could have killed you. What if you had missed?"

"Well, I sure knew I couldn't outrun him," said Grant. "He would have trampled me for sure. You know, that's what he was trying to do. Trample me, after all the good care I've given him." He laughed nervously. "I sure surprised him with that bop on the head. The big sissy. Did you hear him bawl? It couldn't have hurt him *that* much."

"I could have gotten away," said Reed.

"Sure you could," retorted Grant. "If he trampled *you*, there'd be nothing left but a grease spot in the dust."

"Let's let them go." Micki sighed. "They'll have to come in on their own. They're not worth one of us getting hurt." She put down her pole and turned to Grant. "Are you okay? You can't imagine how terrified I was. My heart stopped there for a minute. It really did."

Over lunch we talked about what would happen if they wandered into the canyon and managed to join up with the Bradfords' herd. We had several thousand dollars—all the money left from our months in Canada—invested in them. We agreed that we might never see them again.

"And after all the work," Micki said as she pushed back her plate. "It's more than the money. All the building, the sheds, everything."

We would never have thought of raising cattle as our first "cash crop" if Bill and the boys hadn't been so persuasive.

"But we don't even eat beef," Micki objected when, after a cattle project meeting, the boys returned home to tell us that we'd have to buy a couple of young steers within the next few weeks if they were going to be eligible for the auction. We'd been on a bulk-food, low-cost cheese, eggs, bulgur, and brown rice diet since returning from Canada. Besides, beef production was notoriously wasteful—it took huge amounts of grain to produce a pound of beef.

"But we'll raise *organic* beef," Grant explained. "We wouldn't use steroids or anything."

"Yeah," added Drew. "We'd raise really good beef."

It seemed as good an idea as any that we'd come up with since returning from Canada. We'd cut firewood and delivered it locally all summer and fall—David had bought a new chain saw, which made it a little easier—and we'd talked endlessly about how we could best use the few thousand dollars that we'd managed to save back in Thunder Bay.

Now, guided by Bill, the idea was that Grant and Drew would take care of their steers, fattening them up over a period of eight or nine months, and sell them for an inflated price at the auction. Then they'd invest their profits in breeding stock, and if everything worked out, we'd be on our way to becoming cattlemen.

We had had some building to do—a cattle shed, corral, loading ramp, and sideboards for the pickup. Before we went to Canada, we'd put up a pole-frame tool shed and had, in the process, come to appreciate how much easier—if a bit more costly—it was to use milled lumber. This time we invested more than we could afford in two-by-fours and plywood for the cattle shed and kept the fir saplings—wet, debarked twenty-footers, each of which took all five of us working together to move—for the corral.

We eventually located a four-hundred-pound Angus for Grant, chest deep in mud on a ranch ninety miles down Route 101, and, for Drew, a locally grown young Hereford that already was as tall as he. Grant named his steer Amon, after the "head god of the New Kingdom Egyptians," whom he'd been studying for months, and Drew, who was doing some reading in Greek mythology, named his Zeus. Bill came by to show the boys how to tie them to the redwood posts to which they'd be tethered, condemned to do nothing more than "eat, sleep, and shit," as Bill put it, until just before the fair, when the boys would have to begin "settling them down" for the auction.

It was what they called a "bale and bag" operation, one that "if you had about a hundred more cattle, it'd be a feed lot," Bill said. It wasn't exactly what we had in mind, recalling the sight and smell of the cattle pens we'd passed somewhere down along Interstate 5. Our long-term plan was to establish a few acres of redwood and fir-shaded pastures on which, eventually, a carefully regulated number of cows could be sustained. But until then, for the first year, we'd truck a ton of corn over the hill from Ukiah every Thursday and spend hours on the fairgrounds' pay telephone in search of ranchers who could help us locate good alfalfa.

We'd been aware that steers were inefficient, but it had never occurred to us that under the confined, "hot feed" conditions we were raising them, they were disconcertingly *fragile* as well. We had had them only a week before discovering that they were inclined to react violently if we gave them too much corn—that it could cause them to bloat up and drop dead on us. On the other hand, if we gave them too little grain, they wouldn't weigh enough to qualify for inclusion in the auction. The boys' job—it became a twenty-four-hour one—was to monitor them closely, to maintain a balance between overfeeding and underfeeding. One would break into a cold sweat and they'd adjust its feed, watching and worrying until it seemed all right, and then, a few days later, the other would go off its feed and they'd frantically break open bale after bale of alfalfa in search of a flake of hay that the animal could be enticed to eat. The boys had spent hours, every day, for more than six months, watching over and caring for the beasts and had managed to produce a pair of imposing, sleek-muscled giants. And now they were running wild through the woods.

"Two thousand dollars," moaned Grant. "Wasted."

"More than that," Micki commiserated. "Think of the wear and tear on the truck."

"And the money for the wood for the shed," Reed added. Like the rest of us, he had become adept at calculating cost-benefit ratios.

"Well, let's get working in the garden," said David. He slid his chair back and stood up. We could hear the steers trampling about in the woods as we spent the rest of the afternoon hoeing and picking vegetables.

"It must be weird for them," said Grant. "Imagine spending months staring at a wall, and then suddenly finding yourself out there in the brush and trees. No wonder they're freaked out. I bet they'd rather be back in the shed right now."

"Yeah," Drew agreed. "Only they're too hyped up to find it."

"They'll be back," predicted Reed.

And they were. The next day Grant and Drew sneaked up to the cattle shed to find them standing docilely side by side, next to their empty water buckets. While Grant watered and fed the exhausted animals, Drew repaired the latch that had allowed them to escape in the first place.

"Whew," Drew said at breakfast. "That was a close one. Only a month to go until we finally make some money on those guys."

We'd passed the "second district fairgrounds" hundreds of times on our trips to Ukiah to pick up supplies and had seldom given it more than a passing glance. A dreary conglomeration of badly maintained, dilapidated buildings and a stadium in which stock car races and obscure country-and-western singers provided weekend entertainment, it came alive every August when hundreds of 4-H'ers from across the county arrived with their livestock and the pigs, sheep, and cattle that they'd groom and show over the five days preceding the Saturday livestock auction. Grant and Drew had devoted a couple of intense weeks to "gentling" their steers the way Bill taught them—leading them around in halters and prodding them into show stances—"setting them up"—with their chrome-plated "show sticks." Then there were hours of brushing—"carding"—them, trimming hooves, and braiding tails in preparation for the big afternoon when their months of hauling feed and shoveling tons of manure and nights spent nursing them through chills and diarrhea would pay off.

We had signed on as chaperones to the two dozen Anderson Valley 4-H'ers and spent hours in the barns watching other 4-H leaders demonstrate how to outfit and show their animals. The boys were given special attention from the outset, since their steers, the biggest and showiest of livestock, automatically conferred high status upon them.

It was a strange world, light-years removed from the counterculture enclaves up in the hills, a world of rednecked, tobacco-chawing fathers in pearl-buttoned best western shirts and pressed jeans; of pasty-faced, big-bottomed mothers in oversize sweatshirts emblazoned with too-cute slogans and spandex pants fussing over their teenaged children before they entered the show rings; of 4-H leaders huddling together to assess their clubs' standings in the competition. Amid the braying and snorting, the smell of urine and manure and straw and feed, a half mile downwind from the smoking particle-board plant, it was hard to say where we felt more out of place—here or down by the river with stoned hippies. We obviously lacked what all the *serious* parents possessed: an "RV"—recreation vehicle—or a cab-over camper, and we took a bit of good-natured—but pointed—kidding about the two of us sleeping in the back of our pickup after the boys hosed it down. Once again, as had been the case so many times over the years since we'd left St. Louis, we found ourselves watching, listening, learning a vocabulary, making our way in a world we scarcely knew existed not too long before.

By the time auction day rolled around, we considered ourselves old hands. We knew we had been accepted when Bill asked David to help with the "weigh-in" and "taggin'" and Micki was invited into one of the RVs to help tabulate "break-even" points. Drew started off well enough: his steer had the best feed-to-weight ratio, which meant that it had put on the most weight on the least amount of corn and hay, and he was awarded an engraved tray for the accomplishment.

Drew, barely tall enough to see over the animal, led Zeus into the auction ring toward the middle of the sale. Five hundred sweating people—potential buyers, parents, and fairgoers who simply happened to wander in on the event—jammed into the bleachers, drinking Coors and sipping margaritas, talking and calling back and forth across the rows, waving sales lists in a largely futile effort to get some air circulating in the big metal structure.

"This is Drew Colfax from the Anderson Valley Four-H Club," intoned the auctioneer, looking very much the part in his ten-gallon hat, bolo tie, and Simon Legree mustache, up on a stage festooned with banners proclaiming the virtues of pork, beef, and lamb. The routine was that after the sales list number was announced, the 4-H'er would lead his or her perfectly groomed lamb, steer, or pig into the sawdust ring, where, as the auctioneer made a comment or two about the animal or its owner, a changing cast of local luminaries serving as ringmen—a county supervisor, a judge, the sheriff—cajoled members of the audience, most of whom they seemed to know, into bidding on the animal.

"Don't let those blond curls fool you, folks. He's a real cattleman, and his steer had the best rate-of-gain record of any here this year. His break-even price is sixty cents a pound. Do I hear a dollar?"

Nobody bid.

"Seventy-five cents?" Nothing.

"Sixty cents?"

A pause, and then, "Sixty."

"Do I hear sixty-five?" An even longer pause, as Drew stood there, halter rope in one hand, show stick in the other, scratching the steer's belly. "Sixty-five cents, ladies and gentlemen?" Nothing. "Sixty-two cents, do I hear sixty-two cents?"

"Sixty-two."

"Sixty-two once, sixty-two twice. Sold! Sixty-two cents, to Mendocino Farm Supply. Lead him on out of the ring, Drew."

A leathery-faced old rancher leaned across his wife to speak to Micki. "Your little girl shoulda gotten a better price than that," he said consolingly. "He's a *boy*, Clyde," the wife said with a disapproving look at Micki.

We met Drew as he came out of the building. "Well, that was sure worth it," Drew fumed, blinking his eyes angrily, his face flushed. "What'd I make, sixteen dollars?"

"More than that," Micki consoled.

"Not much more."

"Remember that you got the silver dish for the best rate of gain," said Micki. "That's an honor worth something."

"Big deal," he said. We followed as he led Zeus back to his stall and watered him, then took our seats in the stands and waited for Grant's turn, knowing now what to expect.

Grant left the ring with a final bid from the farm supply that, like Drew's, was only a few cents over his break-even point.

"All that work—for nothing," Grant said as we stood next to the pens. Down the aisle another 4-H'er was celebrating the three dollars a pound she'd gotten for her steer. "You *know* we got the worst prices of anybody."

"Well, at least the Farm Supply bought your animals," Micki told him. "They didn't have to, you know."

"Well, we sure spent a heck of a lot of money there for feed," said Drew.

"Not that much, really," she replied.

And that, of course, explained it. The boys had done a good job of raising their animals, and as the rules specified, they'd put on their 4-H outfits and gone to a half dozen businesses to line up bidders. But a thousand dollars was a lot of money to spend on steers raised by two kids whose family really didn't do much business in the community. We hadn't bought a new car or truck from any of the auto dealers sitting up there in the stands, didn't have an insurance agent, hadn't borrowed money from any of the banks, and didn't make much use of the veterinarian. The county Farm Supply had come through with enough to keep them from losing money, but nobody else in the community had any reason to bid up the price. It all made sense, but it didn't make any of us feel any better.

"Thirty-five dollars over my break-even price," Grant moaned after having received his check the next morning. "It doesn't even pay for the gas to get them here or the wear and tear on the pickup."

"Or your labor," added Micki. "The hundreds of hours, going up there three times a day, back and forth, all spring and summer."

"Well, at least they didn't run off or die on us," Drew said as he absentmindedly turned his silver plate award over and over in his hands. "Did you hear about that girl from Potter Valley who screamed and cried when they put her lamb on the truck?" All the animals were loaded onto a stock truck and sent to the slaughterhouse at six A.M. the morning after the auction.

"How'd you handle it?" Micki wanted to know, watching him closely.

"I felt kind of sad," he said, blinking rapidly. "But I told myself that's what we raised him for . . . for meat, right?"

"I'm going to do a lamb next year," Grant decided. "You only have to raise them for three months, and you can get three dollars a pound. One girl got eight dollars a pound for hers, and it wasn't even a champion."

"I guess we're lucky to have come out as well as we did," Micki said later that night after the kids had gone off to the midway with the five dollars that we'd allotted the three of them for carnival rides. We were sitting at a picnic table next to the pickup. "But all that work. And the risk! We should have known better. Cattle's a rich man's business. We really shouldn't have let them do steer anyway, you know. They're so damned wasteful. Just look at all the feed and water and labor it took to produce one pound of beef. It's disgusting, really."

"Yeah, and I'm sure you'd be saying that if they'd gotten two bucks a pound for them," David retorted. "I didn't notice any of us worrying too much about that when we thought we were going to make some money on them. If you want efficient feed conversion, you raise ducks. Remember how much fun that was? A half a day to pluck a four-pounder?"

"That's true." Micki sighed. "Well, anyway, so much for our future as cattle barons." She got up to check on Garth, who was asleep on the seat in the front of the truck. "Now what?"

From Micki's diary, September 1977: *Boys have been sleeping on the deck all summer and say they plan to stay out all winter. It's become a kind of contest. Drew scared us last week when he didn't show up for breakfast and didn't answer our calls. Finally found him sound asleep in a pile of brush halfway down the hill in front of the house. Told him he was lucky a rattlesnake didn't get him and that we'll tether him if he does any more sleepwalking.*

From Grant's diary, September 1977: *My projects: Two letters per week, my new book, Neolithic man, Roman emperors, gardening, India's vanishing tigers, the Depression.*

From Drew's diary, October 1977: *We went apple picking yesterday at an old orchard Mrs. Bates told Mom about. We picked 100 pounds and a man named Mother Bill came with his hidralick press and made 45 gallons of juice. We gave some to him and froze some.*

From Reed's diary, November 1977: *Bred my rabbits, Doe 1 to the new buck and Doe 3 to the old one. We leveled a place near the swing for a rabbitry.*

In the year and a half since we had returned from Canada and had become increasingly engrossed in trying to make a living off the land, we'd seen a surprisingly large number of our neighbors abandon their dreams of rural self-reliance as the glamour of country life paled, as their money ran out, and as they grew tired, as one of them put it, of "living poor." Even some of those who appeared to have been getting their homesteads together quietly gave up and moved away, and we'd hear about them from friends. Dulcimer was getting a teaching credential, Reddog had opened a law practice in Menlo Park, Deerheart was working for the Bank of America in San Francisco. Others stayed around but abandoned the idea of living off the land. There was Moonglow, the best gardener in the area, whom David had hired to work on the Sloan job; he joined the carpenters union and went off to work in Ukiah. Pogo went to work as a choke setter for one of the small logging outfits, and Steve took a job as the manager of one of the vineyards that had been planted just north of town. Several had begun working their way into the ranks of the biggest employer in the county, the public schools, some as teachers, others as aides. For those who could stand the bad hours and low pay, there were always openings at one of the "licensed children's institutions"—group homes for kids who were wards of the court—which had recently emerged as a cottage industry in the valley. And then there was Peter, who had been one of the earliest back-to-the-landers in the valley. He had spent two or three years trying to survive by producing hand-milled exotic local woods such as black oak and pepperwood and selling it to area craftsmen, but he gave it up and opened a cafe in town. When that went broke he got a real estate broker's license, got rich, and boasted that he was the only hippie in the county who had *really* succeeded in "living off the land."

But the very sight of so many of those around us who were giving up and making their compromises only strengthened our resolve; *we* were going to make it on the land. Clearly, though, it was not going to be in the cattle business, and for a while, after the steer episode, we fell back on the firewood business. And even if we didn't make much money at it, we at least had the satisfaction that what we were doing was ecologically sound. It made sense to clear out the big, overgrown, and dying oaks now, while the wood still had some value, and to encourage the resurgence of the firs and redwoods in what had been their natural habitat before the logging onslaughts. But we could not expect to live off the firewood indefinitely. It was harder as the trees that needed to be thinned became more and more inaccessible. Surely, we kept telling ourselves, there had to be something that would allow us to make use of the land, our brawn, *and* our intelligence.

One of the many ideas we came up with was that of building a dam in the canyon between the house and the access road so we could collect winter runoff and use it to irrigate several acres of vegetables that we could sell at the farmer's markets in the city. We'd heard that government money was available to help pay for such projects, and indeed there was: one fund would provide several thousand dollars if we came up with twenty thousand dollars of our own to build a dam that conformed to the government's specifications. Anything less just didn't qualify, said the forester who spent a morning examining the proposed site with us.

"Besides," he said when it became clear that we weren't about to proceed any further, "you really don't think you can make a living on forty acres, do you?" Didn't we know that recent Department of Agriculture research showed it was impossible, now more than ever? That's why so many people had left the farms in the first place. And here we didn't even have a farm to start with. But if we were serious and wanted to make a little money, he continued, he'd be happy to approve a "conifer release project" for two or three acres. We'd collect two hundred dollars for every acre we cleared of brush and hardwoods. "If you're cutting firewood, you might as well take everything else out, too—and get paid for it."

We dutifully completed the necessary forms and carefully measured out two acres—four hundred and eighteen feet by four hundred and eighteen feet each—opposite the orchard. Conscientiously, assiduously—we didn't want to do anything that would jeopardize our getting paid—we cleared, thinned, and piled brush according to the regulations. The larger logs we cut into firewood lengths, then split and stacked them, and after six weeks we called in the forester to pass approval on our work.

"You did all this by hand?" he wanted to know as he stood on the road next to the orchard, holding his clipboard and looking up the hill. "How long did it take?"

"About a month, full-time," said David. "Why?"

"That's a lot of time for a few hundred dollars. Most people would have brought in a cat."

"A bulldozer? We'd have lost money doing that," said Micki. "And torn up the land in the process."

"Well, I sure never heard of anybody doing it by hand, the way you obviously did. 'Course it makes for a nicer job, though. You certainly earned your four hundred bucks." He checked something on one of the forms on his clipboard and looked up. "I can give you approval to do two more acres if you're up to it."

"Sure," said David. We had to keep all options open.

But we never followed through. We'd learned that when you cleared land according to government specifications, you weren't permitted to save a grove of healthy oaks, to spare a particularly interesting madrone, or to leave a patch of underbrush where quail and rabbits might find shelter. There was nothing in the regulations that allowed for diversity or anything that encouraged the kind of careful thinning and clearing that respected the character, the lay, of the land. From the perspective of the land management bureaucrats, their job, after the loggers had come in and torn up the forest in the quest for profits, was to encourage not restoration, but homogenization, factory forests of same-age, uniformly spaced, same-variety stands of "sustainable yield," readily marketed trees. It was a perspective that gave little or no attention to other values—the protection of watersheds, provision of wildlife habitat, or perpetuation of ecological diversity, all of which were too intangible to merit government recognition.

A year later, when we resumed clearing land to create a wooded pasture for our newly purchased sheep, we didn't give the regulations-ridden government program another thought but set about doing it on our own terms, which included a proper respect for the integrity of the forest into which we'd intruded, had made our home, and were committed to restoring.

From Drew's diary, November 1977: *Garth has learned to climb down off the deck and can go anywhere he wants. He is 100 percent double trouble! Reed and I designed a rabbitry using three pieces of plywood. It'll hold eight cages.*

As the months wore on, we found ourselves becoming increasingly reliant upon game for food. We harvested rather than hunted—the brush and steep lay of the land provided too many escape routes, and we didn't have the time, as Michael did on his occasional visits, to sit in a tree blind for hours waiting for a buck to come by. Our quarry were the jackrabbits and deer that appeared in the clearing behind the house, on their way to or from the garden, which, no matter how secure we thought we had it, they were drawn and regularly got into, occasionally wiping out our corn, peas, and lettuce crops. We'd asked around, as casually as we could, and found some old-timers who said that it was legal, taking a deer or rabbit anytime it was destroying your crops, but one or two said that even so, you had to get a special permit. We didn't want to draw attention to ourselves by asking the Fish and Game Department to clarify the matter, for we suspected that a special permit was, in fact, required. But how were we to know when a big buck would appear in Grant's garden on a foggy morning, or when we'd come upon a yearling, blithely munching away in the zinnia patch we'd painstakingly nurtured all summer? It would happen most often early in the morning when we were all in bed, and one of the boys, whose bedroom was closest to the garden, would awaken to the unfamiliar sound of something big moving around outside. "Dad," he'd call softly. "Dad, *deer*." David would snap awake, stumble out of bed in an undershirt, load the gun, slowly open the door, and, if the animal hadn't yet heard him and bolted—most of the time it did—he'd fire.

"Get it?" one of the boys—they'd be all awake now—would call out as the shot echoed through the woods.

Usually the answer was a disgruntled "No," for David missed more often than not. The family joke was that he always had an excuse—a dirty barrel, misaligned sights, or the sudden appearance of the dog from under the house—for David, despite all evidence to the contrary (as he was regularly reminded), considered himself a crack shot. "Well, at least we don't have to spend the day dressing it out," he'd say. After all, he'd imply, we had more important things to do, and maybe it was just as well that he'd missed. But it didn't work: we all knew that we could always use the venison.

When he didn't miss, we all worked together to transform the carcass into something resembling the familiar cuts of meat found in any supermarket. It became something of a ritual as we got better at it. The boys would carry the animal up to the big fir that became known as our "hanging tree" and set up the rope and pulleys. David would make an incision just above the hocks of each of the rear legs of the carcass and work a two-foot-long piece of galvanized pipe through them, and then, after tying a rope to the pipe and threading it through the pulley, they'd hike the lifeless form into the air and secure the rope to the trunk of the tree.

Skinning a carcass is easier if you don't want to save the hide, for then you don't have to worry about punctures and tears. At first we did our best to produce perfect hides, but eventually, after having gone through the tedious—and not always successful—process of scraping, salting, tanning, and softening a dozen or so hides that turned out not to have much use, we didn't try to save them, and the work went easier. The first few times David did the skinning himself, and the boys were mainly responsible for keeping the knives sharp, having buckets of rinse water available, and hauling off the offal; later, as they grew older and David more confident, two or three of them would work on a carcass together. Standing on opposite sides of the animal and rotating it slightly, back and forth, they'd work their way down the animal's back, cutting gently through the translucent, effervescent fascia that lay between the muscle and skin, proceeding down along the brisket and around the neck until the hide fell away from the glistening scarlet-and-purple carcass.

"It looks like something out of a Francis Bacon painting," Micki said the first time we did an animal. "Death imitating art." Butchers who specialize in "custom ranch slaughtering" could do an animal from start to finish in five minutes—we watched one skin an old goat at a friend's house one afternoon. But even when we got good at it, it took the three or four of us that long just to do the skinning.

The boys would always leave the gutting to David. They'd done it and didn't like it. It could get pretty messy. The idea was to avoid puncturing the internal organs and get them out of the body cavity in one unbroken piece, and David always found it a challenge. He'd make a small slit at the animal's groin, where the flesh, drawn thin and as taut as a drum head, tapered into the flank. With the intestines visible through the thin film of the peritoneum, he'd puncture it and step back as a warm, sickeningly sweet smell rushed upward and the body deflated slightly. The next step was to cut the urethral cord away from the belly and pull it upward, tying it into a knot so that the contents of the bladder wouldn't contaminate the meat. Then David would take his knife in one hand and insert his other hand, palm out, into the body between the intestines and the abdominal muscles. Pushing the guts inward with the back of his hand to keep from puncturing them, he'd draw the point of his knife and hand together down the belly of the animal, stopping at the breastbone. As the intestines and stomach—a steaming, almost irides-cent mass of tubes and sacks in shades of pink, tan, and gray—strained downward and out, he'd slice through the taut muscles under the loin, which caused the guts to lurch downward and partially out of the body. Reaching down into the blood-engorged chest cavity with one hand, he'd cut out the lungs, heart, and trachea, and then, as he pulled them up together with both hands, the animal's entrails would pitch out in one piece onto the plywood board at his feet.

Sometimes—too often—the job didn't proceed so neatly. An overfull stomach or intestine would rupture and spew its foul-smelling, half-digested contents into the body cavity. Or a gall bladder would break and pollute the liver with bitter green bile. Or an intestine would split and threaten to spoil everything near it. Under such circumstances only one thing mattered: getting everything out and the carcass hosed down as quickly as possible.

We usually quartered the deer carcasses, putting them on ice in two old picnic ice chests that we kept for that purpose until they cooled down and "aged" for a week or so. Then, armed with a meat saw, cleaver, knives, and a generator-powered meat grinder, we'd turn them into roasts, chops, and ground meat, wrap and label them, and take them down to town and store them in a friend's freezer in exchange for some of the meat.

From Micki's diary: November 1977: *Last night after the boys were in bed David shot a deer grazing on some oats about sixty yards from our deck. From 9:30 until 1:30 in forty-degree weather we struggled to hang it up to bleed, gut, and skin, all of which had to be accomplished in half-moon light with the aid of one kerosene lantern. Boys were astonished to find a hundred-pound deer carcass strung up on the oak tree near the house this morning. Our winter meat is in now; can see how pioneers survived.*

Pigs, though, required more work. We'd done several deer before one of the black-and-white wild pigs that we'd seen only from a distance appeared behind the house one rainy morning, rooting up the wet earth.

"Bacon!" Grant exclaimed as he handed the shotgun to David, who was fumbling with a new box of shells. He opened the back door a few inches stuck the barrel out, fired, and missed. "Damn it. The sights must still be out of alignment."

"Jeez, Dad," Drew said disgustedly. "That was such an easy shot, too."

An hour later Reed came running down from the goat shed. "The pig," he said breathlessly. "He's up behind the tool shed."

This time David sneaked in closer, the boys right behind, steadied the gun on a big old redwood log, and fired. This time he didn't miss. It was a young boar weighing perhaps a hundred and fifty pounds.

"Now what?" Micki asked, standing in the rain, as the boys examined the animal, commenting excitedly on the size of its tusks, the length of its snout, and how much damage the shot had done to the meat.

"We have to dip and scrape it," said David. He'd read that in the

Morton Salt Book, which we used when carving up other carcasses. "You guys get a fire going over there on the road where we can back the truck in."

While the boys gathered wood, David chiseled the end out of a fifty-five-gallon drum and set it up on some broken concrete blocks. Grant dragged a hose up from the garden and half filled it with water. Reed and Drew managed to find some dry manzanita branches and built a hot fire under it. We retreated out of the steady downpour to the shelter of the cattle shed, one of us emerging every ten minutes or so to add wood to the fire.

It took nearly three hours for the water to come to a boil. Micki pulled the pickup as close as she could to where the pig lay and, after we pulled it up onto the tailgate, backed up to the steaming drum of boiling water.

"Now," said David, standing in the truck bed with the boys, the pig at his feet. "We lower him into the water for a few minutes, then pull him out. You two"—he gestured toward Drew and Reed—"find something to brace the drum so we don't tip it over."

He and Grant each took a rear leg and pulled the pig as close to the drum as they could before being driven back by the heat. Then they took the pig's front legs, swung it around, and pushed the animal into the drum. The animal pitched backward, and for an instant it looked as though the drum were going to tip over. Then the pig bobbed up out of the water, steam billowing up around it, its head and shoulders exposed, a macabre grin on its homely face.

"It looks just like a fat man taking a bath," said Drew. "It's creepy."

"I think he might be starting to cook," said Micki. "How do we get him out?"

"I'm not sure," said David. "Maybe we can lift him if we all get up here and pull together." Garth stood on the seat of the truck, watching through the rear window as we lined up on the tailgate and, reaching forward over the steaming drum, positioned our hands on the pig's legs. "All together now, pull!" David ordered.

Nothing happened. "I can't get a grip on it," Micki told him.

"Neither can I," said Grant. "It's too wet and slippery. One of us is going to fall in."

Tying a rope around the pig's legs didn't work, either: we couldn't get the angle right, couldn't get it up high enough. The pig slumped against the side of the drum, its head lolling, the grin even more grotesque than before.

"He's been in there too long," said Micki. "Why not tip the drum over and then hose him down?"

"Good idea," David said as they climbed down from the truck bed.

Drew and Reed found a couple of long two-by-fours and pushed against the top of the drum, toppling it over. It slammed to the ground, and the pig surged out into the mud in a cloud of steam. After pulling the carcass up onto the truck tailgate, we set about scraping the hair off the hide with inverted jelly jars, the way David remembered his grandparents doing it thirty years before. It didn't work. After a half hour of leaning into the jars and rotating them in the circular pattern that was supposed to loosen the thick hog bristles, we called it quits.

"Maybe we overcooked him," ventured Drew.

"Maybe wild pigs have tougher bristles," said Grant.

"We'll have to skin him, just like a deer," said David. "It'll make the hams and bacon look a little odd, but we'd better get going or we'll be out here working in the dark."

"Then what?" asked Micki. "You just don't hang pork. We'd all end up with trichinosis or something. We probably have to cool it down, and pretty quickly now, since he's been dead for quite a while. I'm going to check out the *Morton Salt Book*."

A few minutes later Micki headed for town to buy the ice and salt the book said we'd need. By the time she returned we'd managed to skin and gut the pig and were ready to cut it up. Book in hand, water dripping from the brim of her battered Mali hat, Micki directed the operation, reading and pointing: cut the legs off there for hams, across here for ribs, and down along here for bacon. David tossed the big chunks of meat into the drum, which the boys had refilled with cold water and ice and where, according to the book, they would cool down after several hours.

"That was not exactly the way I had planned to spend my day," Micki said as we sat down to a late, improvised dinner. "I hope we don't all come down with pneumonia after all this," she added as Reed, who almost never got sick, sneezed.

"But think of all the ham and bacon," Grant fantasized. "I can't remember the last time we had bacon."

"I just hope it turns out."

"It should, shouldn't it?" wondered Micki. "It'd be terrible to spoil all that meat."

"Well, we did the best we could," David said. "The conditions weren't exactly what you'd call ideal for butchering." We didn't inject the hams with salt water with something called a meat syringe the way the book recommended, but it said that wasn't absolutely necessary. We had carefully followed the instructions for "dry curing" the hams and bacon, by burying them in two packing boxes filled with rock salt. Over the next three weeks the boys turned the meat and drained off the accumulated moisture twice a day, until it was ready to eat.

"I hate to say it, but it doesn't smell quite right." Micki took the big ham out of the oven while the rest of us gathered around expectantly.

"Maybe it's just because we haven't had any for a long time," said Grant.

Micki cut off a piece and tasted it.

"How is it?" David asked.

"You taste it," said Micki. "I don't want any of the kids getting sick."

David took a small bite. "It's a bit sour," he said tentatively, and cut off a larger slice. He chewed it slowly, then spit it out with a grimace. "It's edible, I guess. Barely."

"It's ruined," Drew sulked. "I knew it."

"It's not that bad," said David.

"Then why'd you spit it out?" Reed asked with impeccable logic.

"I don't want any of you eating it," said Micki, covering the ham with a cloth. "If we don't get sick, you can try it tomorrow—if you want to. But I think it's rancid."

We didn't get sick, but the ham didn't improve overnight. Our "dry cure" was a colossal failure: none of the hams were any good, and neither was the bacon, which we tried several mornings later. We never did figure out what went wrong, but we weren't inclined to try it again. We had better, more productive things to do than spend all day in the rain and end up with bad colds and a batch of lovingly tended meat that turned out rancid. The next unfortunate pig that found its way into our backyard provided us with bacon and hams that we cured in a mom-and-pop meat plant in Ukiah. Giving them the job ran counter to our do-everything-ourselves philosophy, but we all agreed it was something we could live with if it guaranteed us edible hams and bacon. It wasn't as if we had turned the *whole thing* over to the custom-ranch-butchering man, and we *did* get good at doing all the rest of it.

Later, though, we didn't have to rely upon wild pigs for our pork. As Grant's goat herd expanded, we had more than enough milk to raise several domestic pigs every year. We'd buy fifteen-pound "feeder pigs" from a 4-H'er who had done well at one of the local fairs and feed them goat milk and "cob"—corn, oats, and barley—until they grew to about

250 pounds. At that point we'd lure them out of their pen, which we had prudently set up a good distance from the house, with a bucketful of corn, and entice them down to the hanging tree, where David would quickly dispatch them with a rifle shot. Then we'd string them up, skin and gut them, and take them down to the house to cool off overnight.

"I thought I'd seen it all," Jim said as he came by one afternoon shortly after we'd slaughtered two of them and encountered their two bloody heads, which sat grinning at him on the kitchen counter. "Just what the hell are you going to do with *those* things?"

"Make headcheese," said Micki. It was an all-afternoon project. We'd scrub the heads, skin them, remove the tongues and jowls, and simmer them for hours in a kettle of water seasoned with a blend of coriander, mace, and cinnamon that we'd perfected over the years. When that cooled, we'd shape the reduced mixture into loaves of pâté-quality headcheese.

"You know, you guys are seriously *weird*," said Jim.

"Oh, if this bothers you," Micki said, "come on in here." She led him through the living room and opened the bathroom door.

"What the hell!" exclaimed Jim. "Pigs in the bathtub?" The two carcasses, resting on a bloody sheet, all but filled the tub.

"It's the coolest place in the house," Micki said as Jim, shaking his head, followed her back into the kitchen. "Don't worry," she added. "We scrub it out before we put them in *and* after we take them out."

"Hey, I never said you guys didn't have *class*," said Jim. "I won't say what kind of class, but pig heads in the kitchen and dead pigs in the bathtub—that's a class act of *some* kind."

"But you don't do *everything*," sniffed the little old woman, an old-timer, at the counter when she overheard Micki telling Postmaster Bates how well the current batch of headcheese had turned out. What she said was true enough. We didn't save the thick layer of "fatback" and render it into lard or mix it with wood ashes to make the kind of rough brown soap that David remembered his grandparents making on their farm back during World War II.

Micki smiled at her politely.

"I *know* you don't do blood sausage," the old woman persisted. "My mother used *everything*. I bet you never even *tasted* blood sausage." She glowered at Micki for a moment, then turned and hobbled out of the building.

"I guess she put me in *my* place." Micki laughed.

"Some of these old-timers, they just don't like seeing you new people coming in here and doing these old-timey things," said Peggy Bates. "I guess they think they own them or something."

"I bet she never made headcheese," said Micki.

"No," said Peggy. "But her *mother* did. That makes her even madder that you're doing it."

From Drew's diary, December 1977: Reed and I started the Shining Moon Stamp Company today. We ordered $56 worth of stamps from Sweden and $24 worth of supplies from New York. When we get them we will sell topical packets to the stamp shop in Ukiah and keep some good ones for ourselves. Reed is doing athletes and I'm collecting railroads. Grant is doing mint U.S., which gets really expensive, so he doesn't have many.

Will, our old friend the lumber truck driver, came by one rainy afternoon with some cheese and crackers and a bottle of wine, and we sat talking about how we still hadn't come up with an answer to the question of how we could live on the land and earn some needed cash to do things like finish the house.

"Well, hell," said Will, "I never thought you kids would get this far. I figured that once you went off to Canada you'd never be back."

"Maybe we should have stayed there for another year or two," said David. "The firewood business sure isn't the way to go."

"Or being cattle barons," Will said, laughing. We'd told him about the boys' steers.

"One thing you *could* do, though—and don't get me wrong, I know how you feel about the land—is take off some of these redwoods."

"Never," Micki said emphatically.

"Now I know how you feel about it," placated Will. "But my brother and I—we got my dad's equipment now that he's passed away—could do it real careful. You could clean up a little after us, and you wouldn't even know we'd been here."

"How much wood do you think we have?" David asked with a quick look at Micki. It wouldn't hurt to check it out.

"Let's just go out and cruise it," said Will, standing up.

Drew disappeared into the boys' room and came out with his jacket on. "I'm going with them," he told Micki and the other boys. *He* wasn't going to let them get away with anything.

They were gone for most of the afternoon. Will started near the house and worked his way out. He'd approach a grove of redwoods or a stand of firs, squint up into the rain and fog for a minute or two, then call out a series of numbers, which David would record on a page of the "Lumberman's Notebook" that Will had given him. Drew walked on behind them, keeping his distance, glaring angrily at David as Will commented on the size and location of the trees and the direction they'd have to be felled and taken out. After several hours Will said he had all he needed, retrieved the notebook from David, and began doing some calculations as they stood protected under some big redwoods. Drew motioned for David to come nearer.

"You're not going to let him log it, are you?" he whispered angrily.

David shrugged. He'd been adding the numbers in his head as they'd been going along. "I think Will's figured that we have about eighty thousand dollars' worth of trees. Eighty thousand dollars! We sure could do a lot with that. A new truck, barns, fencing, lots of things."

Drew looked away, furious, blinking away the tears.

"We wouldn't have to take them all."

Drew spun around at him. "You'd really let him log? You really would, wouldn't you," he said disbelievingly.

"We'll talk about it later, okay?"

Will ambled over to them, his calculations completed. "Well, it looks like you have about eight thousand dollars' worth of trees here. That's not too bad."

Eight thousand dollars? It wasn't even enough to buy a good used truck. Drew, who a moment ago had been on the verge of tears, broke into a big grin. The trees weren't worth anything at all. And neither was his father's math.

"We could start next week and be out by the end of the month," continued Will. "Whaddya say?"

"Let me think about it," said David. "Hell, I sure thought we had more than eight thousand dollars' worth."

"Well, the trees don't grow as big or as fast up here on a south slope. It gets too hot. And of course they took out all the big ones years ago. But what the heck, I know you kids could use the money."

"So that's all they're worth?" said Micki, disappointed and yet pleased, as we sat around the dinner table that night. There was no question of taking any of them out. "And here we always thought that they were really worth something."

"They are," Drew said. "As long as you don't cut them down."

"Mr. Sensitive!" exclaimed Grant. He was always being accused of being the sentimental one and Drew the tough guy.

Drew ignored him. The trees were safe, and that's all that counted.

"They might be worth more," said David. "Maybe we should get Pardini or somebody else in here to give us another estimate."

"But even if they're worth twice that much, it wouldn't be worth taking them out," said Grant. "It would take us three or four years to clear up the mess, no matter how careful they are. I don't care what Will says. You know what kind of a mess logging always makes."

"And besides, we wouldn't make much money," Reed piped up.

"Don't worry," said Micki. "We wouldn't even be talking about this if Will hadn't come by."

"Or if Dad hadn't gotten greedy," said Drew. "You should have seen his face when he thought they were worth eighty thousand."

"Well, they should have seen yours when you thought that we might be going to log it," returned David.

"Well, in any case we won't be doing any logging," said Micki. "And here we thought the trees would be there to save us if things really got bad."

From Reed's diary, December 1977: *We sold $12 worth of stamps to the stamp shop. He says he'll see how they do.*

From Drew's diary, December 1977: *Catch-up list. Here are some of the things that have happened to us. 1. We butchered our pigs plus eight wild ones and have a quarter ton of pork. 2. We planted the winter garden—broccoli, carrots, and cauliflower are already up. 3. Both sets of grandparents came and left. 4-H news: I was elected historian and Grant was vice-president. 4. We built the frame for a ferrocement WATER TANK! but haven't poured the cement yet.*

CHAPTER FOURTEEN

A Living with Livestock

From Grant's diary, December 1977: *Drew, Reed, and I finished the new chicken shed roof. Reed showed Garth how to sort nails. Then we brought firewood up from next to my garden. We ate venison stew for dinner. Delicious! But the best part of the day is that Mom and Dad said I can buy a purebred goat!*

"The judge said she had good legs," Grant informed us as we loaded Prudence, our mellow old dairy goat, back into the pickup. We'd gotten her when Essy—the kid we'd bought that first month on the land—had failed to conceive, and over the two years since we'd returned from Canada she'd steadily produced a couple of quarts of milk a day and didn't seem to mind being tied out to a tree.

"But didn't she rank her third?" asked Micki. "Out of three?" She and Grant had happened upon the goat show that morning at the fairgrounds when they'd gone into town for the mail, and they had gone home to get Prudence for Grant to show.

"Yeah, but I learned a lot about goats," said Grant. "The judge said that you can make a lot of money breeding really good ones."

"Umm," Micki said unenthusiastically. We had not had much better luck with them than we had had with the cattle. Checouan had died on us, Essy had dug up that yellow jacket nest, and for a month there was Susie, a mean ten-year-old long-horned doe that a friend gave us, who would break loose and terrorize the boys—until we took her to the auction.

Over the next few weeks, with the same energy and sense of purpose that he had put into his studies of Indian, Egyptian, and Mayan civilizations, Grant immersed himself in the esoterica of dairy goat breeding. He borrowed a half dozen books and a stack of back issues of the *Dairy Goat Journal* from the county library and spent days poring over them, comparing photographs, memorizing show records and lineages, sharing his newly acquired knowledge at mealtimes with his less-than-entranced brothers and parents. We really ought to get into goats, he enthused. Not with what we had, though. Prudence, despite her "good legs," had too many other faults, which he enumerated endlessly in terms that meant nothing to us then: She suffered from slabbiness, steepness in the rump, weak pasterns, a huge pocket, and a lack of smoothness and dairy character. What we needed, he'd concluded, were a few really good goats. And he was certain they'd pay off. We could sell the milk or raise pigs on it. He'd do all the work. And besides, then we'd have a use for the cattle shed that we'd put all that work and money into and was just sitting there empty.

Drew and Reed weren't exactly taken with the idea. They had sold lambs that fall at the junior livestock auction and had cleared several hundred dollars each over the cost of buying and feeding them for three months. They were in the market for some breeding ewes that they could use to produce lambs for themselves and to sell to other 4-H'ers.

"Goats!" exclaimed Drew one evening after Grant had been going on and on about goats. "You know what Bill Charles says: 'There are two things in this world I can't stand: goats and blowflies.' "

"Oh, sure, Drew," said Grant, rising to the occasion. "And Bill Charles is really an expert, isn't he? We sure made a lot of money when he was the cattle project leader, didn't we?"

"Goats and blowflies," repeated Drew, having the last word. It sure was easy to get a rise out of Grant.

From Drew's diary, February 1978: *It was a super rotten day. I cleaned the shed (mainly Dad's tools). We only ate two meals, which were also rotten. I hate bulgur.*

A few weeks later we piled into the pickup and drove down to the Santa Rosa County fairgrounds to spend the day at an official "American Dairy Goat Association Sanctioned Show." Even Drew had to admit that the sleek, well-groomed animals that were paraded around the ring over the course of the morning didn't look anything like the goats we knew and bore no resemblance to the tin-can-eating cartoon stereotypes that people joked about. Grant led us from pen to pen reciting lineages and pointing out the strengths and faults of animals from the various herds represented. He happened to mention his interest in getting some good stock to a breeder who suggested that we check out a famous goat dairy nearby that was dispersing its herd. If we got there right away, he might be able to get a good deal.

"We're not going to buy anything," Micki warned as we pulled into a driveway next to several long, collapsing chicken coops sitting side by side in an overgrown field. Junk cars, rusted farm equipment, and ragged pieces of building materials littered the area. This was the place, Grant assured us. A grossly fat old woman greeted us at the door of one of the sheds and beckoned for us to enter.

The darkened interior reeked of sour milk, and flies swarmed around the stacks of dirty buckets and pans piled in the corner next to an ancient stove and cot. "Sit down, sit, down," cackled the old woman after Grant told her why we'd come. The old woman shook her head impatiently. "First, I'm going to show you my beauty," she said as she disappeared into the shadows.

"This is a famous herd?" Micki wondered, looking around at what appeared to be the old woman's living quarters as well as a goat shed.

"That's why they're selling," Grant said uncomfortably. "They're just overextended. They really do have some good stock." He rattled off some names that meant nothing to us.

The woman returned, leading a doe that Grant recognized from its picture in the dairy goat journals. "Of course she's not for sale," the old woman declared, almost belligerently. After giving us more than enough time to admire the doe, she led her back into the shadows, then reappeared and took us down a garbage-littered path and into another shed, where, she told us, she had a dozen "very special" yearlings for sale. For the next hour she and Grant moved about the pen, the old woman pointing and prodding the animals, lifting their legs, positioning them so that Grant, who had dozens of questions, could evaluate them.

"Four of them are really good," he told us as they joined the rest of us, who had been entertaining ourselves by swatting flies. "Could we afford them? They could be our foundation stock. And we can sell their milk next spring."

"You've got your sheep money," said David. "We could put up the rest if you think you know what you're doing. You know we don't know the first thing about it. The whole operation'll be up to you."

"We can make money on them," said Grant. "I know we can."

David wrote a check for $500, and we loaded up the four yearlings and headed for home as Grant told us about his breeding plans and did his best to reassure us, now that we were beginning to have some second thoughts, that we'd made a good investment.

From Grant's diary, April 1978: *I had the best day of my life! We went to Playfair Dairy and I got four purebred French Alpine does for $125 each. Drew, Reed, and I formed the SHMDGA (Shining Moon Dairy Goat Association), and each paid a dollar to join.*

A few weeks later, after he'd converted the cattle shed into a goat barn and had an opportunity to do further research, Grant informed us that we had probably made a mistake: the new yearlings, he'd come to realize, were not as good as he'd thought. We could sell their milk, of course, and upgrade their offspring, but if we were ever going to be very serious about dairy goats, we'd have to get better stock. Much better.

"Just what I was afraid of," David fumed later, out of Grant's hearing. "I thought that old woman saw us coming. That's really unfair, taking advantage of a young kid like that."

"Grant thought he knew what he was doing," said Micki. "Don't say anything more to him. He already feels awful about it."

"Yeah, and we're five hundred dollars poorer," said David. "You realize we're almost broke again, don't you?"

"I'm perfectly well aware of that."

We were standing next to one of the large glass cases in the Arts and Crafts Building, where Micki's Cuban bread and hummingbird cake were on display, when Grant charged into the building, breathless. "They're selling Classic Example," he exclaimed. He had been over at the livestock barns with his brothers. It was a warm day, late in September, county fair time.

"Whoa a moment," said David. "Look here. Mom has a chance to be the sweepstakes winner in baking. Look at all the blue ribbons she's won." He pointed to the display case.

"Yeah, that's great," Grant said with a perfunctory glance at the rows of cakes, breads, and cookies. "But Classic Example's for sale, Dad, Mom. Do you know who he is? He's one of the best bucks in the country. A grand champion. They're never for sale. I just talked with the owner over in the livestock barn."

"Grant, you know we couldn't afford him," Micki said without taking her eyes from the three gray-haired women who were huddled together around a table behind the display cases, intently tabulating prize points.

"Come on, Grant," said David. "We can't spend any more money on goats. Look what happened with those yearlings."

"But that was *before*," pleaded Grant, undaunted. "I know a lot more about goats now. They're asking only five hundred dollars. Five hundred dollars! He's worth *thousands*."

"If he's worth so much, why are they selling him?" asked David.

"The owners are retiring and moving to Hawaii," Grant said. "It's a sudden thing. They haven't told anybody else about it."

"You're sure it's a good deal?"

"I'm sure. We'll never have another chance, Dad. Mom, we *need* a good buck."

"I know that," Micki said, exasperated. "You've told us that at least a dozen times." Grant had become convinced that if we were ever going to make any money with goats, it would be through the production and sale of world-class animals and not milk. We were too far away from the northern California cheese factory that kept most nearby goat dairies in business, and everybody knew—or had learned the hard way—that there was little profit in feeding goats in order to produce milk to feed pigs. The key to success, if Grant had read it right, was to develop an outstanding herd, out of which you could sell kids to other breeders. That was why we needed to buy Classic Example.

One of the gray-haired women finished her calculations, stood up, and smiled at Micki. "You've won the sweepstakes, hon. Congratulations."

"That means you're the best baker in the county, doesn't it, Mom," said Grant.

"Well, at least it's worth fifty dollars. Only four hundred and fifty more and we'd be able to pay for that buck."

"Seriously, Mom," said Grant. "It's a great deal."

Micki turned to David. "Well?"

David shrugged. "I don't know of any other good deals out there. Do we have the money?"

Micki opened her purse and leafed through the checkbook. A month before, each of the boys had again sold a lamb at the Ukiah fair. "And you're sure you know what you're doing this time?"

"I know a lot more now, Mom, I really do. It's a good deal."

"And it'll pay off?"

"Yes."

"Well, it better." She wrote a check for $500 and handed it to Grant. "Get over there and buy it before somebody else does. And while you're at it, see what else they have for sale," she called as he hurried off.

"What?" said David, shaken.

"We still have six hundred dollars left."

From Micki's diary, May 1978: *Garth decided to help out yesterday by "washing" all fifty of our new batch of chicks, which we had in a big box in the kitchen. Was working in the garden when I heard them cheeping, ran in and found them covered with liquid Ivory soap. Thought they were doomed, but washed each of them off with warm water and put them in the oven set at low, making sure not to bake them. Miraculously, all are alive and apparently none the worse for the experience.*

Micki entered only a few baked goods in the fair the next year. By then we'd become full-time livestock breeders and were more interested in how our animals would do in the show ring than in whether or not Micki could repeat her triumph as "the best baker in the county." Drew had used the money he and his brothers had made on the auctioned lambs to buy four bred ewes, big black-faced registered Suffolks, naming them Minnie, Mabel, Myrtle, and Maud. They were our "foundation stock" and, at $400 a head, represented our biggest investment in anything since we'd bought the pickup. Drew was responsible for taking care of them and planned to get his money back by selling two ewe lambs to Reed and Grant each year to raise for sale at the junior livestock auction. Local big-time sheep ranchers would buy his rams, which, being Suffolk, were not as hardy as their smaller, white-faced range ewes but whose size and "growthiness" provided the hybrid vigor they needed.

Through yet another dry autumn—the media told us we were in a drought, but we had more water than ever since we'd developed our new spring—we cut and barked redwood saplings for fence posts, strung fences through half-cleared woodlands, and built gates, feeders, and more sheds. Our stock—a dozen goats, now, and the four new ewes—were bred, and as we moved into January, the boys began their morning, noon, and evening rounds of the sheds and pastures, checking for any signs that the lambing and kidding seasons had begun. We had a pretty good idea when the goats were due: Months before Grant had led each of his in-heat does down to Classic Example's pen, where, with a lasciviousness so gross that it could only be forgiven as a bizarre trait that had evolved to ensure the perpetuation of the species, he "serviced" the seemingly disoriented but receptive animals. It was different with the sheep: the rams had been let into the pastures with the ewes in the late summer, with the result that we didn't know precisely when any one of them was due.

Early in February we awoke one morning to the sounds of one of the boys running up the deck steps. "Mabel's having trouble," Drew shouted as he burst into the kitchen. "She's been in labor for two hours and nothing's happening."

We pulled on our clothes, woke the other boys, and ran up the hill. Drew had run back ahead of us and was kneeling next to the panting ewe, his sleeping bag crumpled in a corner. He'd been sleeping with the sheep for the last week after bringing them into the shed, out of the mud and driving rains that were now upon us.

"She seems to be giving up," said Drew. He turned to Grant. "What do you think we should do?"

Grant shook his head. "Go in, I guess."

When we'd delivered a dozen kids, Classic Example's progeny, the spring before, we had learned that every birth was different. Most were fairly routine: the doe would get restless, her vulva would swell, and within a dozen hours or so she'd go into labor. Grant, who slept in the pens every night when a doe was within five days of her delivery date, would rush down and get the rest of us when the contractions began, and we'd settle into the hay with our flashlights, rubber gloves, towels, iodine for the umbilical cord, and molasses water for the postparturient doe and watch for the appearance of the kid. If things went well, the tiny, gelatinous hooves would emerge first, followed by a few inches of the forelegs, a nose pressing hard down upon them, and then a face. After a few more contractions, the head would "crown," and the blood and mucus-covered kid would slide out easily into the fresh hay that we'd been assiduously working in around its mother. Grant would hook a finger into the kid's mouth to clear out any mucus that might impede its breathing, then check its sex. An enthusiastic, "It's a buck!" or "It's a doe!" if we had an order for one or the other, a disappointed, "A buck," or "A doe," if we didn't.

But sometimes the feet didn't appear, or only a single foot would emerge, or nothing would seem to be happening as the goat brayed in pain. We'd wait and watch until there was a consensus that we'd better "go in." After returning from the house, where he'd thoroughly washed his hands and forearms, Grant, synchronizing his movements with the goat's contractions, would gently work his way into the vulva, feeling for the kid's legs and head and arranging them so that it could be delivered.

"Will you do it?" asked Drew, hopefully.

"They're not *my* animals," Grant said haughtily. Drew was always telling him how obnoxious his goats were, and now he wanted help with his stupid sheep.

David leaned into the big ewe, and Micki cradled her head in her lap as Drew began to work his way into the vulva. The ewe brayed and struggled to get up.

"I can't do it," he said, looking around at us helplessly. "She's too tight. Grant'll have to do it." He backed away from the ewe and stood up, wiping his hands.

"Dad should do it," said Grant. "His hands are smaller than mine."

"He's right," Micki said.

The ewe was glassy-eyed by now, a sign that the contractions were taking their toll and she'd be giving up soon.

David moved around behind the animal and hunched over. "Just hold her, then. You know I don't know what I'm doing."

"Just work your way in with each contraction," explained Grant. "The way Drew did, only harder."

The boys pressed against her while David, slowly, with each weakening contraction, worked his way up the birth canal as the ewe twisted and bleated. After ten minutes he was almost prone, deep in the hay behind her, halfway up his forearms into the ewe.

"What am I supposed to feel?" he asked. "God, this is hard work."

"Try to get the feet forward," Grant instructed. "You should be able to feel the head and feet."

"I feel a *bunch* of feet," said David. He closed his eyes. "Four—no, five—legs, and two heads, and . . . my God, they're all tangled up." He felt around, then moved two legs forward and pushed another pair back.

Now, in his mind's eye, he could visualize them. Triplets, badly tangled. He pushed them farther back into the birth canal, grasped the nearest one, and pulled it toward him. There was room now to arrange the legs of the second one and straighten the head of the third one. Gripping the two nearest legs firmly, and hoping the head would not twist back again, he pulled the lamb toward him as the ewe let out an anguished cry. It was on the ground, breathing. A minute later the second and third lambs emerged easily.

"They're all alive!" exclaimed Micki. "I don't believe it."

Reed and Grant wiped them dry as Drew injected the ewe, who was now back on her feet, with penicillin, and Micki gave her a bucketful of molasses water. David leaned against the shed wall, wiping his bloody hands and arms, his face drained. "I hope the rest of them aren't going to be this hard," he said. "I don't have the strength for it."

Over the next week Minnie, Maude, and Myrtle each gave birth to twins, easily and without assistance. Drew kept the two best ones for breeding stock and sold the others to Grant, Reed, and a local rancher, using the profits to buy a four-hundred-pound young ram, which he named Spectacular.

Good as he was—and the county 4-H sheep leader, with his reputation on the line, had made sure he located the very best Drew could afford— Spec was not in Classic Example's league. Unlike buck goats, nationally known rams sold for tens of thousands—rather than hundreds—of dollars. One could make a mark on the national scene with a relatively small investment in a goat buck, but it took big money to buy a ram that would be noticed by serious sheepmen. Knowing this, we devised a plan that would allow us to take advantage of three different markets: Drew would produce animals for the *local* market with his sheep, Grant would tap into the *national* market with his goats, and all the boys would take advantage of the various fairs and shows by entering, showing, and selling both sheep and goats wherever possible.

Even as we identified and carved out something of a niche for ourselves as producers of top-quality, intensively managed breeding stock, we realized that it was going to take several years of showing, culling, and marketing before we could expect to see any real return on our investment of time and money. Until then, we knew, we'd have to muddle through— growing our own vegetables and selling firewood, an occasional goat or lamb, milk, and eggs to come up with some cash every month. It meant forgoing clothes, entertainment, medical care, and, perhaps most irritating of all, much needed work on the half-finished house while we attended to the feeding, housing, and medical needs of the livestock. Fortunately we were all in good health—Reed's eye no longer needed treatment, and we owed next to nothing on the land. Our taxes were low, and we didn't have monthly utility or telephone bills. All we really needed on a regular basis was some propane for the stove and refrigerator, kerosene for the lights, gasoline for the vehicles, pump, and generator— and feed for the animals. We had little time to reflect on just how close to the edge we were living or how this bag-and-bale operation was going to turn out. Indeed, there was no question that it *had* to turn out, because we couldn't imagine any other options. We were too *poor*—"land poor," to be sure—to buy fence posts or hardware or machinery that would have made our work easier, and we compensated for our lack of money by doing what people generally have had to do in such circumstances: work harder.

Considering our inexperience, it took us relatively little time to become recognized as serious breeders of good animals. Not "us," perhaps, so much as Grant, Drew, Reed, and, little by little, as he shared more and more of their responsibilities, Garth. Spectacular, Drew's ram, upgraded his flock within a couple of years to the point that they began to take prizes at the fairs and even grizzled old-time sheepmen ambled by his pens to talk about buying "one of them-there rams" from him. And Grant, having successfully shown his goats in one of the most competitive regions in the country, was shipping his four- and five-week-old kids to breeders across the country and writing articles on optimal herd size and artificial insemination for dairy goat journals.

Still, we had our share of setbacks. There was the first spring that Kupie, the doe Grant was relying upon to produce his first good kids, gave birth to a single buck that he couldn't sell since she wasn't yet a champion—and who several days later expelled a blackened, mummified doe fetus. "It happens," said Dr. Bob, our veterinarian. There was the expensive, painstakingly selected doe with the famous bloodlines that never produced any kids worth keeping, who went into labor in the backseat of the Volvo as we brought her home just hours after the breeder from whom we'd purchased her had assured us that she wasn't due for another month. And worst of all was the sleek young doe Breathless, who somehow—and, given her name, ironically—tangled a tiny piece of baling wire around her collar and strangled to death.

The reality was that every loss of an animal, and every animal that did not meet our standards and had to be culled, represented a loss of a generation, a setback in our program for turning out top-quality animals. A proven doe or ewe was worth a half dozen unproven animals, and because of that we took very good care of each of them. Unlike some ranchers, who wouldn't call a veterinarian in the belief that "a sick animal is a dead animal," we couldn't afford to let ailments go untreated. Still, there were times when we had to improvise—such as when two of Drew's pregnant second-generation ewes, Ewella and Number Five, developed prolapsed rectums, a potentially fatal condition if not corrected before giving birth. We had dutifully called in Dr. Bob, who, while stitching up the protruding flesh, warned us that it "might not work." When it didn't, and when their condition worsened, we called Dr. Bob again.

"There's really not much else I can do," he said. "It's a hereditary thing, and the best thing to do is probably get rid of them."

"We can't do that, Bob," Drew told him. "They're my best animals." He was tactful enough not to remind Dr. Bob that we'd just paid him a hundred dollars for his most recent visit.

"There is one thing you *might* try to do," said Dr. Bob. "But I'm not going to recommend it. You insert a piece of plastic pipe into the rectum, then tie off the protruberance with a loop of baling wire and draw it tight."

"Plastic pipe?"

"About ten inches of three-quarter-inch PVC. The idea is that if you do it right, the flesh will die, then you just slice off the dead part. It's something I heard about from some of those old coots over your way."

"Sort of like a castration?" asked Drew. All the boys had learned how to do that in the 4-H lamb project.

"Something like that. *I* wouldn't do it—it's too iffy—but you might want to try."

We did. A week later, as Grant held down first Ewella, and then Number Five, Drew amputated the dead and swollen gray mass with a razor as the rest of us watched from a distance. Both ewes lived to produce lambs for the next ten years—lambs that, unfortunately for them, we had to butcher, since they inherited the condition.

From Micki's diary, April 1979: *Dr. Bob came by yesterday to check the abscess on Kupie's neck and lanced it. After he left Garth asked, "What's a people vet called?" Maybe we are paying for Bob's new swimming pool. Did in three chickens. Michael is up hunting; I pickled* *forty pints of organic peaches he got in Geyserville. The swelling on David and the boys' faces has finally disappeared. Last week we accidentally burned some poison oak vines and they inhaled the smoke. Rushed them to the hospital as their faces ballooned up. Was afraid that they might have trouble breathing if it got any worse.*

But the greatest test of Micki's devotion to the livestock—as if worrying over them, providing them with better feed and medical care than most people receive, and sleeping alongside them when they were due to lamb or kid were not enough—came one afternoon when one of the ewes broke into the feed shed and, when we found her, was down on the ground, bloated with grain. Micki rushed into town and put in a call to Dr. Bob, who was halfway across the state and wouldn't be able to get back in time to do any good.

"You've simply got to get the gasses out before they kill her," he told her. There were two ways to do it. The quicker way was to stick a knife into one of the stomachs (ruminants have four) and relieve the pressure. The trouble was, if you didn't do it just right ("And it hasn't always worked for me," said Dr. Bob), it was just as likely to kill the animal as to save it. The other was to get the digestive juices that were generating the gas out of the rumen.

"We don't want to try puncturing her," Micki told him. It sounded too risky. "What else can we do?"

"There's a special device, which even I don't have, for pumping it out. About the only thing you can try doing is tubing it out."

Micki came back to the ranch and told us what Dr. Bob had said. The ewe's eyes were glazed over by now, and she was having a hard time breathing. David and the boys held her down while Micki worked the flexible, transparent plastic tube into its throat the way Dr. Bob had told her to do. "I think I've got it in," she said as she handed the end of the tube to Grant. "He said to suck on it and try to get a siphon going."

Grant put the end of the tube in his mouth and inhaled. An instant later his head snapped back as he pitched the tube aside and, with a loud "*Ahhhgg!*" spewed out a mouthful of fluid. He bent over, spit, wiped his mouth, and spit again. "It's *awful*," he said finally. He picked up the tube and thrust it at Drew. "Here," he said. "You do it."

"Not me," exclaimed Drew, recoiling.

"They're your sheep," Micki reminded him.

"Yeah, but it was your idea to do this," said Drew. "*You* do it."

Micki turned to David with a pleading look.

He shook his head. "Not me," he said. "I'll hold her."

"Then *I'll* do it," she said. "Reed, run down to the house and see if there's any juice in the refrigerator. Hurry up."

Reed was back in a minute. "There wasn't any juice," he said breathlessly. He handed her a bottle. "How about beer?"

"It'll have to do."

It took the better part of an hour. David and the boys watched, bemused and nauseated, as Micki, with the beer bottle in one hand and the tube in the other, repeatedly sucked the juices out of the animal's rumen and, spitting the tube out just before the liquid reached her lips, emptied it on the ground. "It's awful," she repeated each time as she rinsed out her mouth with the beer. "Just awful." We all sympathized with her but weren't inclined to take her place.

"Let her up," she said eventually. "I can't get any more."

The ewe struggled to her feet and ran up toward the pasture.

"She'd *better* live, after that," groaned Micki, who looked as if she were about to be sick.

"At least you never had to do that with the *goats*," said Grant.

"Yeah, well, at least we didn't waste sixty dollars on a vet, like you're always doing with your goats," countered Drew.

"You know what, Drew?" Micki said as she wiped her hands on an old towel. "I'd have gladly paid it. Even twice that amount. And you would have, too, if you'd had to do it."

"Yeah," said Grant. "You wouldn't even *try* to do it."

The ewe survived. A few weeks later a friend who heard the story sent Drew a custom-lettered sweatshirt. "Yo' Mama Sucks Rumen," it said.

From Grant's diary, March 1980: *I received a letter from Can-D Farm confirming and reserving as many kids as Pentimento will have for $200 each. My first big order! Finished planting the field peas in my garden. We docked the lambs' tails and gave them pulpy kidney and tetanus shots. Reed and I slept with Kupie a couple of nights before she did it. Yesterday at six A.M. she went into labor. It took her forever, but finally a kid came out. I held my breath as I checked to see what it was. It was a doe! She finally had one. I named her Classic Cabaret, and she is beautiful. Kupie is coming into more milk, and her udder looks super.*

CHAPTER FIFTEEN

Getting By

Afterward we shuddered to think what might have happened if Grant had been at the wheel that day. We had taught both him and Drew how to drive the pickup, Old Green, and they had gotten pretty good at it as they moved equipment, building materials, livestock, feed, and firewood around the homestead. Grant was old enough to get his license but had been putting it off, since the truck was in such bad shape. We were reluctant to let him drive anywhere but on the ranch and knew that if he showed up in it to take his test, the Highway Patrol was almost certain to find any number of things wrong with the battered old hulk. It had served us well, all things considered, over so many years, and we'd formed a collective love/hate relationship with it. Unlike the Volvo, which had given us over two hundred thousand hard miles and then went— transmission, engine, body, and electrical system—all at once, Old Green, almost from the moment David picked it up in St. Louis, died a piece at a time. By the time we'd had two rebuilt engines installed at cut-rate prices by self-taught "shade tree" mechanics, and after we'd replaced what seemed to be virtually every identifiable part, we should have given up on it. But, instead, each time telling ourselves that it would be the last cent we'd put into it, we continued to pour money into the beat-up, gas-guzzling, and oil-burning wreck. We'd done so much scrounging for parts—starters, radiators, water pumps, carburetors—that Ukiah junkyard proprietors would hold on to them for us—"a good rear end," a transmission, an alternator—keeping them "back there for when you need it."

Unreliable as it was, it was, for better or worse, *our* unreliable old pickup. Even though it had left us stranded dozens of times, and had transformed David's previous lack of interest in machines into a finely honed hatred of anything mechanical, we were reluctant to spend what little money we had on another vehicle that might turn out to be equally troublesome. After all, our friend who found Old Green for us had been fooled into thinking it was "a great find," and we couldn't afford to make—or have made for us—that mistake again. Besides, we'd replaced most of the parts over the years. Still, with the loose steering and the trouble with the transmission and the electrical system, it was wearing out. . . .

It was just another routine run into town to get the mail and deliver some milk. Micki, Drew, Reed, and Garth were in the front of the pickup, which was half-loaded with firewood. There were four big turns on the county road that twists down into town: a notorious hairpin just below the dump, where four members of a vacationing family were killed a few years before when their brakes burned out after a trip across the mountains from the coast; two more, one worse than the other, just below that; and one that cuts between an orchard and a steep embankment at the bottom of the hill. Micki shifted down, as she always did, at the first turn and kept in low gear as she went into the second. She tapped the brake pedal lightly as she rounded the turn, and nothing happened. Quickly she hit it again, sharply, harder, pushing it unresisting to the floor. She slammed it down to the floor, again and then again, pumping frantically as the truck picked up speed. "The brakes!" she screamed in terror. "We've lost the brakes!"

"Go into the ditch!" shouted Drew. "Slam into the hillside."

The truck lurched into the drainage ditch and back out again as Micki struggled to keep control. They were going too fast now, the firewood in the back bouncing and slamming against the cab window, the boys clasping tightly to each other, slumped down in their seats.

"The hillside, Mom!" yelled Drew. "Hit it hard!"

They were going too fast. Micki pulled hard to the right, but the front wheel kicked back out of the ditch and tore the spinning steering wheel out of her hands for an instant. Again into the ditch and back out as the truck ricocheted off the embankment and careened downward, picking up speed, tearing up bushes and overhanging branches, the boys slamming against the dashboard and falling over each other, milk and broken glass everywhere.

"Get down," ordered Micki, clutching at the steering wheel with all her might, forcing the truck against the hillside again, pumping on the brake pedal wildly, uselessly, as they came around the bend and the orchard curve loomed before them. "Get down low!" she shouted. They'd never make the turn, they'd turn over, on the kids' side, even if she managed to avoid the trees.

"The rock!" screamed Drew. "Hit it!"

It was round and gray, the size of a refrigerator, half-buried in the ground at the edge of the Eubanks's driveway, the last thing between them and the trees, the curve. "Smack it," he cried. "Now!"

There was a horrible scraping, tearing sound, and they all slammed forward against the dashboard as the truck hit, lurched upward, fell forward, and gently coasted across the broad lawn, coming to a stop in a clump of blackberry bushes.

"Are you hurt?" Micki shouted at the pile on the floor next to her. "Reed? Drew? Is Garth all right?" Her hands still grasped the steering wheel, and she was shaking. The boys untangled themselves slowly, their eyes wide.

Reed was the first one to react. "Get out, *quick*! We might catch on fire!"

Micki had to jump out first, and they rolled out after her—the passenger side door was jammed. Now, a safe distance from the truck, Micki examined the boys for injuries. To her amazement and relief, apparently there weren't any. Slowly the boys edged back to the truck to survey the damage. The front right fender was crumpled tightly against the wheel, and the side was ripped and torn. The bumper had been jammed back into the radiator, which was dripping and steaming. Drew peered underneath the truck.

"Wow," he said "Radiator, transmission, everything." He walked up the hill to the rock. It was deeply gouged where the truck had scraped across it and had been pulled a few inches out of the ground from the impact.

"You oughta see this rock," he shouted.

Micki was sitting on the ground now. Reed and Garth huddled close, and some cars had stopped out on the road. There were sirens now; somebody must have called the fire department.

They'd been lucky, everybody agreed. Lucky that they hadn't lost the brakes on the first turn, because then they'd have never made it around the second one and would have gone off the edge. And hitting the embankment was the smart thing to do. Hadn't Jeff, only a month before, told her about the logging truck driver who'd recently lost his brakes on the Ukiah road and stupidly, in an effort to save the load, tried to ride it down, only to be killed? "You always go into the hill," Jeff had said. "No matter what, you hit the hill." Before he opened his garage, Jeff had driven logging trucks. We were in his garage now, unwinding, while he checked out the damage. An old-timer from town who'd stopped had gone up to the ranch to get David and Grant. "Your wife and kids are okay," he'd greeted David, "but your truck ain't in such good shape."

"It's not as bad as it could have been," said Jeff, wiping his hands on a shop cloth. Of course we'd need to replace the broken brake line, and we'd need a new exhaust system and radiator. He'd have to check out the U-joints; you could never tell about the transmission until you got it on the road—

"Tell David about the brakes," Micki interrupted.

"Well, like I was telling the little woman before you got here, this wouldn't have happened in a newer model. They all have dual braking systems on them now." He went over to his truck and opened the hood. "C'mere and I'll show you."

"So we could have been killed because it's an old truck," prompted Micki. "And the line could break again, right?"

"Well, it could," Jeff said warily. He was not about to be drawn into what looked like a marital dispute in the making. "I couldn't guarantee that it wouldn't. You just don't have a backup in these older trucks."

"I'll never drive it again," Micki said emphatically. "And the kids aren't getting in it again, either."

"Billy Palmer was talking about selling his GMC," said Jeff. Bill had worked for Jeff for a while before he inherited the family ranch up on the Ukiah road. "It's in pretty good shape for a seventy, except for where his kid smashed it into a tree one night. It don't look too bad, though."

"How much do you figure he'd be asking?" said David.

"Oh, maybe fifteen hundred dollars or so."

"And you're sure it has this dual braking system?" asked Micki.

"They all do, sure, that year."

"Tell him we're interested," said Micki. "And that we can't afford to pay much for it."

A week later we had our new truck, a still jaunty top-of-the-line model complete with a genuine imitation-embossed-leather "western" interior, two-tone paint job, and lots of chrome. If we parked it so that the crushed-in panel above the rear wheel well didn't show, it blended in nicely with the other rigs at the fairs and shows that had increasingly become a part of our lives.

From Micki's diary, April 1980: *Added two new milk customers and now have eight. Peggy's calling me the "Milk Lady of Boonville." Takes forever for the door-to-door deliveries and would be easier with a drop-off point somewhere—but where? Saw Homer on the access road for the first time in a long while. Poor Homer. Sold his paper, lost his job as judge, and is now running the dump.*

Fair time, show time—from early spring to late summer—was when your reputation was on the line, when you laid the groundwork in the show ring for the prices you'd get for your animals over the next year or two. To get good prices for your animals, you had to show them, and that meant traveling up and down the state, to fairs and shows on the edge of cities and in dusty little farm towns, collecting ribbons and earning the "legs" toward livestock championships that generated publicity and sales.

From April through September, week after week, the six of us piled into the front of the truck and jammed together, Reed on Grant's lap, Garth on Micki's, to head off for yet another show, another fair, in yet another bleak and dusty town, the goats and sheep crowded together behind us almost as tightly as we were in front. If we were lucky, we'd make it to our destination without the animals becoming so "stressed" by the trip that they'd show poorly in the ring. But sometimes the weather—the Sacramento valley heat, coastal fogs, mountain winds—would take its toll, and they'd show poorly. It was then, as we found ourselves facing another weekend of meals on the run and restless nights, the two of us sleeping in the back of the pickup and the boys, for security reasons, in the tack pen next to the animals, that we'd wonder if it was worth it.

But even as the work with the animals expanded, so did the boys' interests in other areas. Grant, Drew, and Reed all continued to show goats and sheep—and even turkeys for the three years there was a 4-H pre-Thanksgiving rate-of-gain turkey auction. Garth, as soon as he was tall enough to reach the pens, took over Reed's rabbitry, which allowed Reed to devote an hour a day to running up and down the access road in preparation for the northern California five- and ten-kilometer races. Before long, on those weekends when livestock shows didn't take precedence, we were taking him and then, inspired by his brother, Drew to races around the state. There, with the four of us lined up along the course to cheer them on, they competed in this new arena with the same intensity they had in the show ring, and before long they were making space for running trophies among the dozens of livestock awards they'd been accumulating over the years.

From Micki's diary, February 1982: *Reed and Drew are busy organizing a 10K race in town; plan to call it the "Boontling Classic." They measured the course last night and are working on posters today.*

Grant's interest in dairy goats took him off in several different directions. When he was trying to decide if it made sense to expand his herd, he conducted a survey of dairy goat herd owners across the state, and published the results in a national dairy goat periodical. When he was developing his breeding program, he reviewed the literature on artificial insemination and wrote another piece for the magazine. He interviewed breeders at shows, published their stories in *Goat Notes*, laid out our advertisements, and wrote our annual herd brochure and sales list.

From our 1982 sales list: *Shining Moon Ranch has been raising quality dairy goats for four years. We began to show Alpines two years ago and started Dairy Herd Improvement Association testing in 1978. The ranch is located among the Redwood, Fir, and Madrone forest of Mendocino County in northern California. Milking does are fed 3 lbs. of a natural dairy goat mix per day and have alfalfa pellets and hay available at all times. Kids are bottle-fed until they are 4½ months old and eat grain, pellets, and hay. The goats are frequently allowed to graze in the forest. The herd is small and strictly limited to quality does. In 1979 our does won 11 firsts, 1 reserve grand championship, 6 grand championships, and 2 best in shows. Our projected herd average for this year is 2,248 lbs., and a third of our milking does are yearlings. We attribute a great deal of our herd's success to our herd sire, Grand*

Champion Redwood Hills Classic Example, to whom most of our does are bred. We feel you can consistently expect from Example deep, long kids who will freshen with tightly attached udders that milk well.

We do not accept deposits on unborn kids, but you may reserve "buyer's first choice" on any given doe. Prices listed here do not include a $25 delivery charge to the San Francisco Airport. The buyer is also expected to pay for health certificates.

If you would like pictures or further information on our herd, feel free to inquire anytime. Thank you for your interest in our stock.

Very truly,
Grant Colfax

Grand Champion Redwood Hills Kupie Doll AMA 3666: Born February 1976. Cou Blanc. Disbudded. . . . Kupie Doll is one of our best does. She has an outstanding udder attachment, both fore and rear. She is very dairy and open and stands very wide in the rear. She also has strong pasterns. . . . Kupie Doll freshened as a yearling but did not finish her lactation on test. Kupie will be bred to Laurelwood Acres Nobility and will kid in April. Her kids are priced at $600. . . . La Sierra Lizzie A302295: Born February 1977. Cou Blanc. Disbudded. . . . Lizzie is a very dairy, open doe with a snugly attached udder. When she finishes milking this lactation she should be a four-star milker. Lizzie's topline is long and level. We plan to show her as a three-year-old. Her production is projected at 1,980 lbs. Lizzie is bred to Example and due in April. Her kids will be priced at $400. . . .

Drew, who never became anywhere near as engrossed in sheep raising as Grant did with his dairy goats, didn't take long to develop an interest of his own: astronomy. It had begun the Christmas when he was thirteen. It had become a tradition that our gifts to the boys had to be educational or immediately practical. There were always books, of course—favorite authors, books relating to their special interests, reference volumes, and, one year, a new encyclopedia set—and starkly utilitarian items such as stainless-steel milk buckets for Grant, wool-carding brushes and woodworking tools for Drew and Reed, a set of rabbit watering bowls for Garth. That year, though, as a follow-up to one of our lunch- and dinnertime discussions, in which both of us had to confess to knowing little about astronomy, we thought we would get them all a good telescope, only to discover that they were so expensive as to be out of reach.

"You don't want a toy telescope," said the Bay Area optical shop proprietor who a few years before had given us a good price on that year's "family present," a microscope. He reached under the counter and pulled out a tray of Ziploc bags. "One of your kids has got to be good at making things, right? What you want is to have him *make* a telescope. It'll beat anything you can buy."

A half hour later we left the shop loaded down with an assortment of materials we'd been told were necessary to build a telescope. That Christmas we laughed together as a puzzled Drew—"Is this a joke or something?"—opened in order a dozen packages of abrasives and strange-looking parts that Micki had carefully wrapped and numbered so that he wouldn't know until he opened the last one, a book on how to build a telescope, what in the world they were for. Over the next year he spent hundreds of hours carefully standing in his room grinding and shaping a telescope mirror on the fifty-five-gallon drum that served as his worktable and sink and then, the mirror finished, took a few more weeks putting together the rest of it. The next summer he and his brothers built a sliding roof observatory up near the orchard, where he spent long hours scanning the sky. One early morning he awoke us with the news that he thought he had succeeded in doing what every "deep sky" observer hoped to do someday: discover a comet.

"It's out there, Mom, Dad," he said, standing at the foot of our bed, his face red from the night cold. "I've checked and double-checked my sky charts, and there's not supposed to be anything out there. I really can't believe it, though. People spend years looking for something like this, and I've only been at it a few weeks."

"What do you do next?" asked David.

"Report it to one of the big observatories. I want to go into town the first thing in the morning and call. They'll probably tell me I was looking in the wrong spot or something."

"You get to name it if you're the first to see it, don't you?" said Micki.

"Yeah, if I'm the first. I really can't believe I spotted one so soon, though."

The observatory confirmed his sighting. Three other people had also reported seeing it, but there was no need to establish precedence among them since it had been first identified by a NASA satellite earlier in the day. "Well, you can't beat out a satellite," Drew said when he told us the news. "But they said I was the first person in northern California to see it. And after only three weeks of viewing, too."

All of Shining Moon might have gone up in flames that July morning, we later realized, if Reed hadn't been there and in such good shape as a result of his daily two- and three-mile training runs.

David and Drew had gone to Ukiah for feed and Grant was up cleaning goat pens when Reed came charging out of the woods shouting, "Mom, Grant, the pump's exploded! It's on fire!"

Micki ran out of the house, followed by Garth. "What happened?"

"It blew up when I started it. Quick, get some tools."

"Grant, go call the fire department," shouted Micki.

Grant was halfway down the ridge, armed with rakes and shovels. "Reed, you go for help. Let's go, Mom, now!"

"Run, Reed," Grant shouted as he disappeared into the woods.

Both sides of the gulley were on fire, thirty feet up the ridge, the fire feeding on the tinder-dry leaves, the melting plastic pipe sending up a thick, acrid smoke. Grant had already begun digging a trench farther up the ridge when Micki and Garth arrived.

"My God!" she exclaimed. "Grant, we can't let it get out of the draw." The small oaks were beginning to ignite, one by one, as the ground fire moved upward. If it made it up to the black oaks, there would be no way to stop it.

"You two work over there," Grant called through the smoke. "I'll try to trench it."

Gagging and coughing, eyes stinging, they stumbled back and forth across the draw, alternately side by side, raking and beating out the flames together and then alone, and falling back, little by little, as the fire crackled and advanced up the ridge through the brush.

"Garth, Grant!" Micki screamed. "It's getting worse. Get back before you get hurt."

Suddenly Reed was there beside her in the smoke, shovel in hand. "They're on the way," he told them as he began digging.

"Up here, Reed," shouted Grant. "Mom, Garth, get up here."

Amazingly they were all over the ridge, sliding into position, spraying and digging and cutting out brush: two dozen forestry department fire fighters, looking more like science fiction creatures than human beings in their yellow outfits, visored and helmeted, oxygen packs on their backs, all working silently and methodically.

"Do you think they'll stop it?" Micki asked as she and the boys pulled out of their way.

"They'll call in the planes if they have to," said Reed, pointing to one of the fire fighters standing off from the others. He was speaking into a walkie-talkie and appeared to be overseeing the operation. "It'll be okay."

"How long did it take you to get to the Gibsons?" asked Grant.

Reed glanced at his watch. "Darn it," he said. "I forgot to set it. But I know that I got over there before you could have with the car. Only fell twice, too, going through the woods."

It took the forestry people two hours to get the fire out completely. The chief told Micki we'd been lucky that it hadn't happened later, when the afternoon winds came up. They were gone by the time David and Drew returned from Ukiah.

"A phone," David said after getting all the details. "We've *got* to get a phone line in."

We'd become used to living without the convenience of silent, unlimited, plug-in electricity, for we always had the use of the generator when we really needed it to operate tools, the vacuum cleaner, or, on occasion, a food grinder or blender. And as much as we missed having hot water on tap, we had gotten used to heating kettles and pots of water on the stove every morning for bathing and washing. But we'd never gotten used to living without a telephone. Almost from our very first weeks on the land we were made aware of how much easier it would have been if we'd had a telephone—when we had to drive into town to make calls to lumberyards and hardware stores, when one of us went off to Ukiah and couldn't find a needed part and couldn't call home, and when visitors dropped by without warning or invitation with the excuse that there was no way to reach us. But until Micki was attacked by the yellow jackets that summer, we'd presumed that running a telephone line down to the county road would be as difficult as, if not more so than, putting in an electric power line.

We quickly discovered that we were wrong. The investors who owned the land between our forty-seven acres and the county road still wouldn't allow power or a telephone line to run up alongside our access road, but upon hearing about Micki's experience with the yellow jackets, they readily agreed to let us run a "farmer's line" across a corner of their holdings and down into the canyon to the lines on the county road. Unlike high-voltage electric power lines, which, because of their hazard potential, had to be accessible on year-round roads to power company equipment and the workers who maintained them, farmer's lines could be run just about anywhere since they posed no danger to individuals or the environment and had to be maintained by the parties who used them.

But it wasn't that we'd have to clear nearly a mile of brush through some steep and overgrown terrain, or the logistics of running a line from tree to tree, that made us put off the job year after year; it was the cost. We had immediately rejected the offer of a moonlighting telephone company employee who had offered to put in the line for us for about $8,000. Materials alone, he told us, would cost well over $1,000. There was no way we could afford to put in a line, no matter how much easier it might have made things—until Michael came through for us again, just as he had nearly ten years before when he came up to help build the house.

He'd sent us a card saying he'd be up to go pig hunting, and when he arrived the boys, as always, went out to help him unload his equipment and tie up his dogs.

"I, uh, got something here for you," he said as he opened the tailgate of his truck. "How much wire did you, uh, think you needed to, uh, run that farmer's line?"

"About three-quarters of a mile," said Drew.

"Yeah, well, that's what the guy who sold me this said was on here," said Michael, pushing aside some boxes and revealing a big wooden spool of black wire. "And there's all the hangers and stuff in these boxes that he said you'll need to, ah, put it up."

It happened that Michael had been doing a remodeling job on some-one's weekend place in the Santa Cruz mountains when he'd come across the materials. The owner had planned to run a farmer's line and then found that he didn't have to when the phone company agreed to put up a conventional line to his house and some newly constructed homes nearby. After Michael had told him about us, the owner gave him everything for fifty dollars.

"I, uh, hope that wasn't too much," Michael said apologetically. We happily assured him that it wasn't and began work on the line immedi-ately.

Even with the right tools and with all our years of clearing brush behind us, it was a challenge. It was far more difficult than laying the water line over to Cervetto's, since we had to clear a swath wide enough for the wire to be hung on trees every forty feet or so without touching any branches. That meant taking down scores of trees and limbing those that remained to a height of fifteen feet or so as we descended the face of the ridge into the deepest part of the canyon, aiming for the pole on the other side of the canyon that the telephone company people said we should hook up with.

It took nearly two weeks for all of us, working together, to cut the trail, drill holes in the trees for the hanger bolts, and attach the wire "twisties" to which the line was attached. Then it took less than an hour for Reed and Drew to pull the wire down into and back up out of the canyon, while the rest of us fed it down to them from the reel mounted on a piece of pipe and sawhorses next to the house. Two days later the line was hung and the lines into the house were in place. One morning a week later, while Drew was in town putting in his one day a week on his new job at the nursery across from the high school, the telephone rang.

"My God," Micki exclaimed as she picked it up. "It works."

"Just testing, and it sounds like everything is in order," said the lineman down on the county road.

"Now, whom do we call first?" wondered Micki, hanging up. Everybody agreed that it had to be Drew, at the nursery.

"We just wanted to know what time we should pick you up," Micki said when Drew came on.

"Okay!" exclaimed Drew. "We're connected!"

There was no question but that having a telephone made things easier. Now Drew was able to use it to schedule his one-day-a-week job at the nursery around our need for him on the ranch. Potential goat buyers were able to talk with Grant directly instead of sending letters asking him to call. Now we could call back and forth to town when we were chasing down odd-size and hard-to-describe pieces of hardware. And Micki could call the vet without having to make a trip to town when a goat had problems. We were immediately reminded of its inherent capacity for being demanding and intrusive, as its ringing shattered the quiet we'd become so used to in our isolation over the years. Still, it made things both easier and safer and that made it worth the price.

From Micki's diary, March 1982: *A good day yesterday. Managed to fit two air kennels into the back seat of the car and took Kupie's two doe kids down to San Francisco airport. Shipped one to Michigan, other to Maine. Kept pig on ice in the trunk and delivered it to the Hayes*

Street Grill; they plan to feature it as "Boonville bacon." A two-thou-
sand-dollar day!

Little by little, and perhaps more than a bit reluctantly, as the boys
grew older, we found ourselves being drawn back into activities that we'd
all but abandoned as we carved out our livelihood as livestock breeders
in the middle of nowhere. A young lawyer who moved into town had
started a "reel classics" film series, and we immediately became its biggest
fans. The six of us would join twenty or so others in his office every Sunday
evening, grateful for the chance to see often scratchy and barely audible
versions of everything ranging from *The Battle of Algiers* and *Ramparts of
Clay* to *Tom Jones* and *Topper*, which, as a matter of course, provided the
texts for our lunch- and dinnertime discussions over the next few days, all
of us becoming, in the process, film buffs and social critics.

From Grant's diary, March 1982: *Saw a GREAT movie last night,
"Children of Paradise," made in occupied France during World War
II. Fantastic crowd scenes that Dickens might have written.*

We began spending more and more time, now that we had some time
and could be reached by phone, attending political meetings—supporting
a liberal candidate for supervisor, opposing aerial spraying of hardwoods
by the timber corporations, organizing against nuclear power plants,
protesting cutbacks in the library budget. It was all pretty tame, we
reminded ourselves, compared with our life-and-death grass-roots efforts
back in St. Louis and Connecticut, but at least it allowed the boys to
get a taste of what social activism, being a socially responsible person,
was all about. It was part of their education.

Anyone who came by our place on one of those rainy winter days could
fairly have concluded that our ten-year-old home education program was
not too different from what they might have found in a conventional
classroom. That morning they might have found Reed and Drew in their
room sitting at the plywood sheet that served as their desk, surrounded
by bookcases, Reed doing algebra and Drew trigonometry. They might

have found Grant on the living room sofa reading a physics textbook, and Garth would be next to him going through one of the programmed readers. Later in the day, after we'd sorted through the day's mail and read the newspaper over lunch, they might spend the afternoon reading—novels, *Astronomy, Running,* the *Dairy Goat Journal, Natural History.*

But if the same visitor had come by on another day, when we were working on a fence, splitting wood, docking lambs' tails, or butchering a pig, he would have seen a very different kind of home school, one in which the boys, sometimes together and sometimes separately, were learning lessons that were not in books—discipline, cooperation, self-reliance, problem-solving—all taught by real-life experiences.

Unlike some parents who had moved to the land in the sixties and early seventies with the idea of teaching their children at home, we had stayed with it over the years. We had succeeded in avoiding problems with local authorities at first because of our isolation and later because the boys' performance in 4-H events made it obvious that they were learning far more at home than most kids their ages did by going to school.

When they were young, our efforts to restore the land, to plant gardens, and to improve our livestock stimulated the boys' interests in biology, chemistry, and nature in general, and we were always on the lookout for books and materials that would encourage them to widen and develop these interests. We'd virtually plunder the county library on our weekly trips to Ukiah for feed and building materials and spend whatever little cash we were able to generate on educational materials that ranged from chemistry laboratory equipment to movie reference books. From the outset it was apparent that the boys' natural curiosity provided the motivation to learn and that our job was to be there to provide support, materials, and, when it was requested, direction. We seldom *taught* the boys in the conventional sense of the term. We learned together, and we *talked*—about politics, literature, religion, and economics, about breeds of cattle and brands of feeds, about arts and crafts. Initially, when they were younger, they relied upon us for information and direction, but as they grew older they'd turn more and more to each other as they carved out their different areas of special competence, Grant becoming our livestock expert, Drew the botanist and astronomer, Reed the athlete and musician, and Garth the naturalist-artist.

As time went on, we found that what would come to be called "homeschooling"—for years we simply said that the boys "didn't go to school"—was becoming easier in many ways and more demanding in others. It was becoming more demanding largely because we had been able to cover the basics without much trouble, but our few years of Latin and French did not prepare us to teach languages, for example, nor were we always able to draw upon our smattering of college math when the boys needed help with a trigonometry or physics problem. But it was becoming much easier in general primarily because Grant was there to help his brothers as they progressed through the materials we had provided him and because he, who had borne the brunt of our sometimes mistaken choices of texts and other reading materials, was there to tell us what had and hadn't worked. We all recalled the year that he had used the "new math" text we had selected only because it was assigned in a University of California correspondence course and had come perilously close to becoming convinced that he was "bad at math." (We switched to another series that guided him—and, subsequently, his brothers— almost painlessly through precalculus.) There was a bookcase full of high school history, literature, and science textbooks that Grant had considered and rejected before finding those that often were little more than the best of a bad lot, which he could recommend, with reservations, to his brothers.

Throughout it all, we knew that the boys were receiving the kind of education we would have wanted for ourselves at their ages. But how would that education translate into "real world" competence? It was the question we had been asked dozens of times by friends, relatives, and strangers whose reactions to what we were doing ranged from mild skepticism to outright hostility, and it was one we had asked ourselves many times as well. And as the boys grew older, we found ourselves wondering more and more about how well we had prepared them for a world in which creativity, intellectual independence, and love of learning were not held in the highest esteem. It certainly wasn't a question of whether they'd *survive*. If nothing else was clear, we knew that they were already far better prepared in that regard than either of us had been before we had come to the land.

PART SEVEN

Moving On

CHAPTER SIXTEEN

Backwoods Scholar

From Grant's diary, March 1982: Decided to get my act together and started to study to go to college. I've been doing schoolwork nearly full-time since Christmas. In the last four months I've done 420 pages of math, 800 pages of English, 200 pages of chemistry, and have almost finished second year Spanish. Major events since last fall: County fair: Kupie won Grand Champion, and this ended the show season. What a way to go! Stock sales are up and still climbing. I have sold almost all my kids in utero. People from Washington, Nevada, Indiana, Michigan, and California have reserved kids. I wrote a short story that the entire family gave rave reviews. I've decided to become a writer despite the odds of getting a short story published running about 25,000 to 1. Have added "Rebecca" and "David Copperfield" to my top ten best movies of all time list.

We had parked the pickup in front of the Baltimore County Museum, just around the corner from the Johns Hopkins University Admissions Office. Drew, Reed, and Garth were in the camper shell behind us, reading, while Grant did his interview.

"How'd it go?" Micki asked as Grant reappeared and climbed in beside us.

"Terrible," he snarled. "Just terrible."

"What happened?"

"The interviewer said I'd have to be considered along with the *foreign* applicants since my schooling was so different. I knew this was a waste of time. I'll never get into any of these colleges."

"You might not," said Micki. "We talked about that."

"Not that I'd be considered a *foreign* student."

"What was the interviewer like?" David asked as we pulled out into the boulevard that bordered the campus.

"Well, when I told her my parents were visiting the museum, she said she'd never been there," fumed Grant. "Never been there even though it's right across the street!"

"That says a lot about her," said David.

"Yeah, but *she's* the one who makes the admissions decisions."

"You wouldn't want to go to school here anyway," said Micki, unfolding a city map. "I didn't know Johns Hopkins was in such a bad area."

"I'd go here if I could get in," Grant said petulantly. "You know I would."

"You have ten more interviews," David reminded him. "Don't make it miserable for us just because of a bad start."

"We should have stayed at home," sulked Grant, slouching down in his seat.

"Yeah, maybe we should have if this is the way you're going to react," said David.

We were heading north to Pennsylvania. Grant had interviews scheduled at Swarthmore and Haverford the next day.

We had always assumed that the boys would one day leave the homestead, that there would come a time when they would want to strike out on their own, to explore and experience the world on their own terms. But when we came onto the land, those days seemed infinitely far in the future. It wasn't until Grant was sixteen that we began to think seriously about his—and the other boys'—off-the-land future. We didn't have any reason to worry about how well they might do in college. They'd read extensively—certainly to a greater extent than we ever had—and their interests were even more wide-ranging and arcane. Because they were self-directed and enjoyed learning—whether it was building a house or solving a math problem—we were confident that they would have no trouble managing whatever they might encounter in a college setting.

The real question was how we'd ever be able to pay for it. Room and board at a state school would run at least several thousand dollars a year—about what we managed to bring in on a good year. We simply weren't generating enough money to pay even for the cheapest of college educations.

"I'd go where the money is," Eric advised the summer before when he and Pat had come by on their annual pilgrimage down from Washington. We were talking about our children and their college plans. Both Larson kids were star athletes and were almost certain to be given athletic scholarships in track or basketball. Or they could attend Evergreen College, where Eric had been a professor of anthropology for a dozen years. Grant, we asserted, didn't have those kinds of options.

"I'm not kidding," said Eric. "Grant's smart enough. He ought to apply to a school like Harvard or Yale, where they have all kinds of scholarship money."

"We were thinking about one of the state schools," said Micki. "But even they're too expensive, by the time you figure room and board. You know we don't have five or six thousand dollars to pay for that."

"I'd really check out those rich schools," Eric persisted. "Hell, they'd love to have Grant. I'd love to have any of your kids in my classes after seeing what they've done around here. Except Evergreen doesn't have any money for scholarships—and it's really expensive for out-of-state students."

The problem, of course, was getting admitted to one of Eric's "rich schools." For one thing, Grant's credentials were not exactly conventional, and we had no way of knowing how admissions officers might regard a home-taught applicant. For another, Grant had never taken any kind of standardized test. We had never felt the need to test the boys ourselves, for we did not subscribe to the classroom-driven notions of "age specific" or "grade level" performance. To the extent that we had a theory of learning, it was simply that we tried to respect and build upon their individual differences—in social, emotional, and intellectual development and in interests and abilities. Our job as parent-educators was to suggest options, to identify opportunities, and to provide support and not to demand conformity and attempt to control the way most schools did. And in sharp contrast with the organizationally driven conventional wisdom of the professional educators, we believed that it was not important that they master any or all subjects at any particular age, in any particular time span, or in any particular sequence. And now Grant, untested and with that background, had to confront one of the most intimidatingly conventional and formidable of hurdles: the Educational Testing Service's Scholastic Aptitude Test—the SATs—and Achievement Tests.

"Well, here goes the rest of my life," he said only half-jokingly one January morning as he headed off to Fort Bragg High School to take his first test, the SATs. "If I screw up today, it's all over."

"I'm sure you'll do just fine," Micki assured him.

We were waiting for the results of Grant's tests when we received a note from Toby, Raj's wife. Raj was in an intensive care unit in a Los Angeles hospital. The diagnosis: leukemia. Micki and Grant drove down immediately and, as his condition deteriorated rapidly, watched and waited, ran errands, and spent long hours in the waiting room, consoling friends and meeting his relatives as they flew in from Toronto and Trinidad. By the end of the second week, as Micki was being readied as a donor for a last desperate bone-marrow transplant operation, he died. He was thirty-five. A draftee in Vietnam, a member of a helicopter ground crew, he had been routinely exposed to Agent Orange.

"They killed him," Micki sobbed when she called to tell David and the boys of his death. "That goddamn war. That goddamn war." It seemed that it would be a part of our lives forever.

Grant received his SAT scores a few days after he and Micki had returned from Los Angeles, but now it didn't seem all that important. He'd done better than any of us could have ever hoped, with scores in the ninety-ninth percentile, but the shock of Raj's death put things into perspective. It wasn't the boys' first encounter with death: David's father had died five years earlier while the boys were showing animals at the fair, and Drew had gone into the show ring with tears streaming down his face a few minutes after we received the news. But Grandpap was old and had been sick for many years; Raj was different.

One afternoon a few days later, an uncharacteristically subdued Grant sat in the living room compiling a list of colleges he thought he might be interested in attending. After an hour he drifted into the kitchen, where Micki was just taking some loaves out of the oven.

"What do you think about my becoming a doctor?" he asked casually as he broke off a steaming crust.

"That would be fine," Micki said. We'd always assumed that Grant would go into anthropology or become a veterinarian.

"Here he comes," Micki said apprehensively as Grant emerged from one of Swarthmore's hallmark gray stone buildings. We'd been sitting in the bright sunshine in front of the library for most of the morning. Drew had gone off to check out the observatory, while Reed and Garth tossed a football back and forth on one of the playing fields.

"You were in there long enough," Micki said as Grant approached, a wide grin on his face. "What happened?"

"I got the director of admissions," Grant announced. "He said to tell Johns Hopkins to go to hell."

"What?"

"He used to be in Four-H, and we really hit it off. He said that if Johns Hopkins can't deal with my background, just tell them to go to hell."

"It sounds like it was a good interview, then," said David, greatly relieved. The trip up from Baltimore had not been a pleasant one.

"Yeah," said Grant. "But of course he didn't say I'd be admitted."

We made our way up the coast as Grant interviewed at Haverford, Princeton, Yale, Brown, and Harvard, then turned west to Dartmouth, Amherst, and Williams. The interviews that had begun so poorly at Johns Hopkins had turned into something very different: Each of the scheduled fifteen-minute interviews lasted at least an hour or two, while the five of us wandered the campuses, taking in the local color and checking out points of interest. The interviews had become performances, each of which Grant would rate in terms of previous ones: this one was better than the one at Brown, that one was worse than the one at Yale, he was too emphatic here, forgot to mention this or that there.

"You must just go on and on," Micki said with a sigh after an especially long interview at Yale.

Grant laughed, exhilarated and suddenly self-conscious. "Yeah. Pretty much. I go right down the list—from not going to school to living without electricity to raising goats. They really get into it. I guess I come across as being pretty unusual."

"I can't imagine why," said Micki.

We made it back home in time for the Redwood Empire Dairy Goat Show and to plant the corn. We agreed that it had been a good trip, but we were not about to try to read too much into the reception Grant had received, remembering too well the trip east seven years before when David was looking for a job.

It was a busy summer and autumn: goat shows, the fairs, preparation of the goat sales list, the summer garden harvested and the winter garden planted, breedings to arrange. Grant took a math achievement test, did very well, and spent October writing and rewriting the personal essay that the college admissions officers told him was so important. He'd decided that he wanted to go to a large urban university—an environment as different as possible from the one in which he'd grown up— a decision that eliminated more than half the colleges at which he'd interviewed. Harvard cautioned him against applying in November for a December decision—the "early action" procedure—since his score on the English achievement test wouldn't be available in time for consideration, but Yale said they could make a decision without it. It wasn't a conventional application. In lieu of a transcript, we wrote a letter explaining his "unique educational background," described his "course work," and listed textbooks he'd used over the last four years. In place of the usual high school counselor's report, he submitted a half dozen letters of recommendation—from fellow dairy goat breeders, 4-H project leaders, the editor of the dairy goat publication for which he'd been writing since he was eleven, and co-workers at the new health center at which he'd been doing volunteer work one day a week since deciding that he wanted to become a doctor. There were his current sales list, reprints of articles he'd done for the *Dairy Goat Journal*, *Goat Notes*, and the *Dairy Goat Guide*, and a long essay about his life on the ranch and his reasons for wanting to go east to a large university.

It was rainy and gloomy, the fog still so thick in the middle of the afternoon that we couldn't see the redwood tree that hung out over the canyon in front of the house, an ordinary December day in every regard but one. It was December 15, the day that "early action" decisions were announced.

Grant picked up the telephone for the tenth time to make sure that our farmer's line hadn't shorted out in the wet weather.

"They should've called back by now," he said. "It's almost five o'clock there." He'd telephoned Yale a few hours earlier on the pretext that our road was blocked by a slide and he wouldn't be able to get to town to pick up the mail for several days. "Maybe they didn't believe me."

"*I* wouldn't have," said Drew, looking up from his book. It seemed that all they'd done since the trip east was worry about Grant getting into college.

Grant ignored him. "If they don't call back by five, it means I'm not in. Twenty more minutes." He checked the telephone again, and it rang, startling him, as he set it back into the receiver.

"Yes," he said, his jaw set. "Yes, I'm sorry to have bothered you. . . . Well, that's great," he continued, his expression unchanged. "Well, thank you for calling me." He put down the telephone and turned solemnly to the five of us, who had gathered on the other side of the room. "I'm *in*!" he shouted, throwing his arms into the air. "I'm *in*. I made it!" The dog jumped out from under the table and began yapping excitedly.

Micki rushed across the room and hugged him, tears in her eyes. "That's wonderful, Grant. I thought you'd make it, but we just couldn't be sure." She wiped her eyes and laughed. "I just don't know how we'd have managed if you hadn't been admitted. You would have been unbearable."

"I know," said Grant. "But you know what this means? Now I can apply to Harvard."

"And it really won't matter," said Micki.

"What do you mean it won't matter?" Grant said. "Of course it will."

"Here we go again," muttered Drew.

From Drew's diary, December 1982: *Reed, Garth, and I spent the morning putting shingles on the woodshed. In the afternoon we just stood around and smiled because we found out that Grant was accepted by Yale.*

From Drew's diary, August 1983: *It was a good fair. I placed second in sheep showmanship behind Wade again, had first place yearling and champion lamb. I was county winner with my astronomy record book. Went to the carnival with Suzie Charles and everyone teased me. Two people came up from the* San Francisco Examiner *and interviewed Grant. On the last night of the fair we watched crashcars while Mom and Dad went out to dinner. We didn't get home until one A.M.*

"Just put the animals away," Micki called to the boys as they pulled in behind us in the car. It had been one of our best fairs ever, but we were all exhausted. "We can clean up this mess in the morning. Let's get a good night's sleep."

There was a note thumbtacked next to the kitchen door. "Please call me before talking to anybody else," it said. There was a woman's name, a telephone number, and, in large black letters, CBS.

"I told Grant this might happen," David said as Micki lighted a lamp. "I wonder how she found us. The article mentioned only Boonville."

"I don't know, but we're certainly not calling anybody tonight," said Micki.

The telephone rang at four A.M. It was David's mother. "Grant's on the Paul Harvey news," she said. "About how he had never been to school and was going to Harvard."

"Mom, it's four A.M. out here," David said sleepily, shaking his head at Micki, who had sat up beside him, a worried look on her face. "You've known he's going to Harvard for six months."

"I know that, but I thought you'd want to turn him on. Would you believe it? The Paul Harvey show!"

"I'll never get back to sleep," Micki muttered irritably as David hung up. "Paul Harvey, for God's sake."

We had dozed off when, an hour later, the telephone rang again. "It's probably *my* mother this time," Micki groaned.

"This is NBC in Los Angeles," said a voice. "Is there room to land a helicopter at your place?"

"What?" asked David.

"Hasn't New York contacted you?"

"No."

"Oh. Well, we'll get right back to you," the voice promised, and hung up.

A moment later New York called. Grant's story—the one that had appeared on the front page of the Sunday *San Francisco Examiner* the day before—was "on the wire," and they wanted to send a crew up from San Francisco to do something for the evening news. They'd need to get in and out in a hurry. Did we have a spot where a helicopter could land?

No, said David, but the Boonville airport—a paved landing strip, really—was four miles away. No, they wouldn't be able to rent a car in Boonville, but one of us could pick them up. In an hour? No, that wouldn't be a problem.

"I wonder who else'll be calling," said David, pulling on his shoes. "It's a good back-to-school piece."

Grant and four of his goats had been pictured next to a long piece, complete with a map that showed where Boonville was, entitled "Backwood Scholar Heading to Harvard." The reporter had contacted us the week before, and we had arranged for him to interview us at the fair.

The telephone rang again, and as David answered it, Micki pulled on a robe and charged into the boys' room. "Everybody up!" she shouted. "A television crew is going to be here in an hour and this place is a *mess*. Let's go. Now!"

"That was another station," said David. "They're flying in at eight-thirty." The telephone rang again. Grant answered it, listened for a moment, then covered the mouthpiece. "It's 'The Today Show,' " he said. "They want to send up a limousine to take us down for an interview in San Francisco."

"Tell them you'll call them back," said Micki.

The plane broke through the cloud cover, circled the landing strip, and taxied to a stop next to the GMC. "I'm David Barrington," said the first man out, followed by the sound technician and cameraman.

"I'm afraid the back of the truck isn't very clean," apologized David. "We just came in from the fair late last night."

"Oh, they won't mind," Barrington said as the other two climbed into the back. The boys had hosed down the sheep stands for them to sit on. The smell of wet sheep dung permeated the truck. "We've ridden in worse," said the cameraman, knocking a piece of manure-encrusted straw off his designer jeans. Barrington climbed into the front of the truck with David.

After introducing himself to Micki and the boys, Barrington set the scene and established the sequence that the other crews would more or less follow over the course of the morning. There was the long interview with Grant, who looked more preppy than farmboy in his button-down shirt and khakis, a few shots of him with his goats, the younger boys feeding chickens and sheep, David in the garden, Micki baking bread and filtering milk, and the whole family posed on the deck with the mountains in the background. But we rejected his request, as we later rejected requests by virtually every other interviewer, for a shot of the boys "just sitting around the table, with Mom or Dad teaching them," explaining that we didn't do it that way, that that was *not* what home-schooling was all about.

On the way back to the airstrip—the crew from a San Francisco station was due in a few minutes and another from Los Angeles in a half hour—Barrington leafed through his notes, frowning. "You know," he said halfway down the ridge, "this really isn't the story we thought we'd get. You folks sure aren't 'Ma and Pa Kettle on the Farm.' "

It was a line we'd hear over and over all morning, along with the one that annoyed Grant the most: Andy Warhol's "Everybody will be famous for fifteen minutes"—these, presumably, being Grant's "fifteen minutes." "Every one of them says it, as if nobody had ever heard it before," marveled Grant after his fifth interview, each of which he worked in around the incessantly ringing telephone. "These guys aren't very original, are they?"

But they were efficient. A half dozen television crews were in and out by noon, each one mining the same story, each one with an at least locally famous correspondent whom none of us recognized and who asked the same questions as his counterpart before and after. Was he excited about being accepted at Harvard? (Yes, of course, when he was accepted back in April, four months ago.) Did he think he'd be able to handle a classroom setting? (He'd been in school before and didn't find it intimidating.) Was he a genius? (Hardly. Ask his brothers.) Were his parents able to teach him everything? (Not at all. We teach ourselves.) What will he miss most? (His goats, of course.)

We had the limousine meet us in front of the post office, since the road up to the ranch was dusty, and besides, Postmaster Bates said it was the only decent thing to do.

"You just have to let everybody see you," she told David, who stopped in for the mail on one of his back-and-forth trips and of course had to bring her up-to-date on all the activity up at the ranch. "Boonville needs all the celebrities it can get."

"I'm completely exhausted." Micki sighed as she settled back onto the seat as the limo pulled away from the curb. "I don't know how you managed to keep going," she said to Grant. "How many calls did we get this morning?"

"Fifty-six," said Drew, who was examining the reading light and the push-button window console. "This must be costing them a fortune. We should have just told them we'd drive down and stay in a Motel Six and they could pay us the difference."

"Not me," said Micki. "I plan to enjoy this." We were booked at the elegant Stanford Court. She closed her eyes. "We're going to lose sleep again tonight, you realize." We—Grant, David, and Micki—were scheduled to be at the studio at four A.M. Two more crews and some newspaper reporters were supposed to meet us back in Boonville the next afternoon, and if Grant was going to be on "The Tonight Show" next week, he'd have to reschedule his flight.

"I always wondered who rode around in these things," said Grant. "Now we know."

"Yeah," said Reed. "Media freaks."

"No, poor white dirt farmers," David said. "You know, it'll be just our luck that today the Santa Rosa revolutionary brigade decides to blow up all limousines going down Route 101."

"There aren't any revolutionary brigades anymore." Micki yawned sleepily. "You don't have to worry."

From Drew's diary, August 1983: *We stayed at the Stanford Court Hotel and spent $300 for dinner and $100 for breakfast. It was all paid for, of course. The three hotel rooms cost $500! They even had a phone in the bathroom. We watched ourselves on national television, and our place looked really good.*

Johnny Carson introduced him. "The young man who is our next guest will be entering Harvard University as a freshman next week. That may not be so unusual in itself. But this freshman has had no formal education. He was educated at home by his parents. Let's welcome Grant Colfax."

Grant acknowledged the applause with a grin and a small wave as he came onstage and settled into the seat between sitcom actress Betty White and Carson as easily as if he were a seasoned veteran of the talk show circuit.

"You must be happy to be going to Harvard," said Carson.

Grant said that he was.

"You have three brothers. And they were all educated at home? How about a little bit of the reasoning behind where you live and how this came about."

Grant told the story again, as he had dozens of times during the week since the media barrage.

"That's truly an amazing story," Carson said as Grant wound up the part about his being admitted to Harvard. "Now, is it really true that you didn't have *television?*" Carson arched his eyebrows incredulously.

"Right," said Grant. "For most of the time we were growing up. My brothers, though, got interested in pro football last year, so if they want to watch a game, they have to take the battery out of the truck, haul it into the house, and hook it up to an old TV."

"Because you don't have electricity?"

"Yes. Then after the game they have to unhook it and take it back to the truck and hook it up again. Sometimes when they don't do it quite right and Mom gets stuck in town with a dead battery, things get a bit tense around the place."

The audience laughed. "I can't imagine why." Carson chuckled, shaking his head. "So your brothers are watching us now using the truck battery?"

"If they managed to hook it up right."

They had, and were gathered around the flickering screen with David. It was the first time the boys had ever watched the show.

"And now you're off to study premed. I'm sure you'll make a terrific doctor," said Carson. There was applause and a cut to a commercial.

"He didn't screw up even once," Drew said admiringly. He got up to turn off the set as Carson welcomed his next guest, Shirley MacLaine.

Micki and Grant flew to Boston the next morning, where they were greeted at the airport by a crew from a local television station. Grant vetoed their plan to record for posterity his entry into Harvard Yard and his first meeting with his roommates. It was one thing to be in the limelight back in California, where it was okay to be the "goat boy," but this was Harvard, and it was time to get serious.

Micki returned to California a few days later. "Don't expect too much," she had reminded Grant as they stood on the sidewalk on Harvard Square, reluctantly saying good-bye. "We educated you back on Shining Moon. From here on out it's all training and credentials."

"I know that, Mom." Grant waved a cab over to the curb and kissed her quickly as she got in. "I'll do okay."

Would he? She wondered as the cab headed down Memorial Drive. She'd thought about it many times before. Harvard, that bastion of the smart, rich, and powerful, could be a pretty intimidating place for a kid from Boonville. But Grant was smart and tough, and he'd learned how to take care of himself. There was no reason to worry about him. She settled back onto her seat. The only thing she needed to be concerned about, she had to admit to herself, was how *she* would do back at Shining Moon now that the goats were all hers.

CHAPTER SEVENTEEN

Cottage Industry

From Garth's diary, January 1984: *We cleaned goat pens today. Dad used the Rototiller and Drew hauled. Reed and I loaded. It smelled awful. Mom said Grant will do the other pens when he comes home in June.*

It was one of those sparkling clear, crisp winter mornings that always drew us up short and made us remember why we had chosen to live where we did. The rays of the sun were just beginning to filter through the redwoods to the west, a wisp of fog drifted across the canyon, and in the distance the staccato hammering of a woodpecker echoed through the hills.

Micki hurried up the hill, a mug of coffee in one hand and bucket lids in the other, a milking bucket hooked over each arm. She was running late. The boys were already in the feed shed, jostling for position in the cramped space as they took turns at the storage cans, noisily filling their buckets with lamb pellets, chicken grower, alfalfa pellets, pig maker, and cob. Setting the buckets and lids on the table next to the milking stanchions, Micki took a sip of coffee—in a moment, with a squirt of goat milk direct from the udder, she'd have her morning cappuccino—

and went over to the milker pen, where the goats were crowded around the gate.

"Let's go, girls," she called as she opened it. They knew the routine. Three at a time, the oldest ones first, they'd hurry across to the stanchions for their morning ration of grain. Printer, one of the senior goats, was not in her usual position as one of the first ones to be let out. "Printer?" Micki called. She was back in a corner of the shed, and on the ground behind her was a glistening mass that Micki recognized immediately.

"Drew! Reed!" she shouted as she pushed into the pen past the other goats. "Garth!" She knelt down and inspected the two half-formed kids. "Printer's aborted," she said as the boys ran over and clustered around the gate. "Our best goat."

"What were they?" asked Reed.

Micki picked up one of the mucus-covered kids. "A doe," she said, putting it down and picking up the other. "A buck."

"Did you have orders for them?"

"Both of them," said Micki, holding the lifeless form to her chest. "Eight hundred dollars for the buck. Six hundred for the doe." She stood up and patted Printer on the head. "Poor girl."

"Fourteen hundred dollars," said Drew, shaking his head, as Micki led the doe over to the stanchion.

"Make sure you bury them deeply enough so that nothing can get at them," she told Garth as she poured some molasses into a bucket of water for Printer. Reed and Drew came out of the shed loaded with buckets of grain and flakes of hay. "Wait until Grant hears about this," she said. "He's going to be very upset. He expected really good kids out of this breeding."

"It's the money, Mom," Drew repeated over his shoulder. "Who gives a damn about the breeding."

"It's more than the money," said Micki.

"Oh, sure."

It was only the beginning. A week later one of the younger does aborted, followed by another abortion two days later. Micki had been in contact with Grant on a daily basis. "Just hope it isn't something that's going to affect all of them," he told her after hearing the news about Printer. Now it was clear that something was going through the herd, something that had to be stopped if we weren't to lose the entire kid crop. Dr. Bob came over and took blood samples; the fetuses were packed in ice and put on the Greyhound bus to the lab, where they could be autopsied; Micki was on the phone to every breeder who might have some idea of what was wrong and what could be done.

The blood tests and the autopsies showed nothing. It was probably chlamydia, said Dr. Bob, even though it wasn't showing up in the lab. And whatever it was, it wasn't likely that there would be anything much we'd be able to do about it. And in the days that followed, confirming our worst fears, the does aborted, one after the other.

"Another one this morning," Micki announced dully on the fourth day as she brought the milk into the kitchen to be filtered. And, a day later, "Two of the yearlings last night." There was no stopping it, our only consolation being that we didn't have orders for some of the kids that had been born dead.

"It's something you've just got to expect," Jennifer Bice said fatalistically. She had been one of Grant's mentors and was now Micki's. "It happens to everybody eventually. Your vet's right. There's nothing you can do about it." And other goat breeders, who had been in the business longer than we, agreed.

They called it an "abortion storm." By the time it had passed, two-thirds of our does, and every one of our best animals, had aborted. We'd lost a year in our breeding program and the source of our meager income. Another season like this and we'd be in serious trouble.

From Micki's diary, March 1984: *Had a terrible scare today. Michael was up for the weekend and took all the boys off in his jeep to go pig hunting. They weren't back by chore time, and by eight o'clock we really began to worry that maybe they'd had an accident. Drove the truck all over looking and shouting for them, without luck. They showed up a couple of hours later: Michael had gotten the jeep hung up on a log and they had to dig it out. We gave them all hell for not sending one of them back to tell us.*

We'd always known, although we seldom gave it much thought, that at some point, as the boys grew up and began moving away, our life on the land, the way we had managed to survive, would change. We'd spent more than ten long years working toward self-sufficiency and, in spite of our inexperience and problems, had achieved it. We were growing most of our own food and selling enough livestock to pay for their upkeep. We were eating well—a variety of fresh vegetables from the garden on a year-round basis, organically fed lamb, chicken, turkey, goat, pork, rabbit, and, occasionally, venison and quail. We owed next to nothing on the land and house, even though the latter was still far from finished. Our taxes were low, thanks to recent "timber preservation zone" legislation that gave forest land owners tax breaks so they would not have to sell off their redwoods and firs before they reached "maturity." All things considered, over the years we'd managed to pull together a working homestead that any early seventies back-to-the-lander would have had to respect.

But now we had to face the fact that we had managed to get as far as we had only because the five, and then six, of us had worked so long and hard together at it. Now Grant was gone, Drew would be leaving in another two years, and in all likelihood Reed would be following him shortly afterward, and those days would be behind us. If we'd been able to get by from the sale of livestock, on a hundred dollars here and fifty there from the sale of firewood, 4-H lambs, homestead goats, rabbits, an occasional pig, milk, and eggs, it was going to be harder to do in the future when the boys left and we had to cut back on our livestock. We had succeeded in making something of a living in an area where few families succeeded primarily because of the attention we gave to the animals; indeed, close and careful management of a relatively small number of top-quality animals had been our salvation. Now we were facing a future in which we'd be losing the resource—the boys—that made that kind of management possible.

There was more to it than losing the boys' labor. We had adjusted to living on the economic edge, getting by with next to no money, counting every penny, and putting every spare cent into the ranch and books. We had learned to live without automobile, life, or health insurance, knowing that we couldn't afford to have an accident, die, or even get sick. And we didn't need anything more than our "new" thirteen-year-old GMC and the eighteen-year-old "classic" Plymouth convertible that Bill Charles, the 4-H cattle leader, had sold us for $600 when our trusty Volvo died after years of faithful service. As long as we could afford replacement parts, David could keep them running. We didn't miss eating out, since the food at home was better than anything we could find in a restaurant, and we didn't have to worry about keeping in style as long as Micki had a sweater or two from her college days and David had a few patched-elbow sport coats that were serviceable enough for weddings and funerals. But with Grant's admission to Harvard, we found ourselves having to contend with a world in which airline tickets, clothes, and long-distance telephone calls were anything but luxuries. Grant had managed to capture everything he could in the way of scholarships and loans and was working at a part-time job, but even these did not cover all of his expenses. And every time we mailed off a check to him to cover the cost of books or to buy a pair of shoes, we were made very much aware that as the other boys went off to college, we were going to have to do much more than merely subsist, as we had been doing for so many years. Our needs were becoming greater as the boys were growing up and moving off the mountain, and in the aftermath of the abortion storm, we realized that we couldn't rely upon the livestock, the firewood business, and growing our own food to pay the bills. We'd gone about as far as we could in terms of subsistence and self-reliance.

When Charlene and Vernon Rollins came by to buy a couple of goats from us, we didn't pay much attention when they told us about their plans for the old Boonville Hotel, a ramshackle two-story balconied structure that sat in the middle of town across from Hiatt's logging equipment yard. Over its hundred-year history it had served as a stagecoach stop, a bordello, and, most recently, the home of a series of not very successful bars. Charlene and Vernon were like a lot of people we'd seen who'd passed through town, the kind who had a little money and an oversize vision. An almost shy, owlish-looking, earnest couple in their thirties, they told us they were fixing up the hotel and planned to turn it into a restaurant. When we mentioned that that had been tried before—in the same place, by the very realtor who had sold the building to them—they said they were going to do something a bit different. Had we heard of Chez Panisse in Berkeley? Of course. We'd read about it in the *San Francisco Chronicle* and had stopped there for pizza and a salad in the cafe one afternoon after we'd delivered a high-priced buck to the airport and felt that we could afford a small splurge. It was as good as they said; California cuisine, they called it.

"Charlene served an apprenticeship there," said Vernon. "She's really a great cook." Charlene in turn assured us that Vernon was also a good cook. They planned to raise most of the food they served, but they'd be interested in buying any produce we might have for sale, once they were open.

"That's why we want the goats," Charlene said brightly. "We want to get used to raising animals so we can serve our own meat, eggs, and milk."

"We already have a bunch of ducks and some banty chickens," said Vernon.

We loaded Firefly and Gloworm—two of Grant's does who, in their old age, were suffering the ultimate indignity of being downgraded to "homestead goats" since neither of them had ever produced progeny that had amounted to anything—into the back of Charlene's father's red pickup. After offering Charlene and Vernon a few last-minute suggestions on the care of goats, we wished them well in their new ventures and watched them drive away. As the sound of their truck faded into the distance, we agreed that theirs looked like just one more of those familiar country-living fantasies destined to collide with reality. We'd seen a lot of them by now—Peter's burl and board company, Dino's resort, Marvin's canning factory, Beth's health food store, the downtown feed store. Even Mother Bill's One-Man Apple Pressing Company had gone broke when the local organic apple juice market became glutted with the output of every back-to-the-lander's backyard apple tree. It was true that new wineries were just getting started in the valley, but they had a lot of money behind them and, in most cases, didn't have to show a profit in order to stay in business. ("You can end up with a small fortune in the winery business," ran an industry saying, "provided you start out with a large fortune.") The truth was, all of Anderson Valley seemed barely able to support little more than a couple of grocery and hardware stores, two or three service stations, and, on and off, a coffee shop or two. About the only ones who seemed to be thriving were the half dozen or so realtors who traded on people's fantasies, especially would-be entrepreneurs fresh from the city with some spare cash and a hope of living out their dreams in the country. But we did have to agree that Boonville certainly could use a decent restaurant.

We didn't hear from them for months, and then we received a frantic call from Charlene. "Firefly hasn't been eating," she told Micki. "And both of them are having a hard time walking."

"Did you worm them?"

"I don't think so. No."

"When's the last time you trimmed their hooves?"

"I—I don't think we've ever done it," she said. "We've really been so busy," she added apologetically. "Is there any chance you can come down and take care of them? We'd pay you, of course."

The goats were a mess. Micki and the boys medicated them while David, muttering to himself, trimmed their overgrown, rank-smelling hooves. "This is a disgrace," he said as he nipped off a large, manure-encrusted piece—loudly enough for Charlene, who was hovering in the background, to hear. We refused payment for the hour's effort. "It's enough for us to know that the goats are feeling better," Micki said pointedly.

A few weeks later Vernon telephoned to invite us down for the opening of the hotel. He meant the restaurant, actually: they hadn't started work on the rooms yet. There weren't even windows on the second floor, where rough-framed, black openings stared out on a rickety balcony and the highway below. The rest of the building didn't look much better: It had been given a coat of white primer, and there were deep, abandoned-looking trenches around the foundation, surrounded by sawhorses. Except for a big black slab of a sign, utterly out of character and protruding over the treacherous-looking front steps, that identified it, in fuchsia letters and an arty swirl, as "The New Boonville Hotel," there was no reason to assume that the place was anything more than a run-down old building in the very early stages of restoration.

It was an exterior that didn't prepare you for what was inside. On the right as you entered was a long, exquisitely sculpted, vaguely art nouveau bar of polished eastern maple and local madrone wood. Hanging on the opposite wall, above several handcrafted bird's-eye maple tables, were a half dozen black-framed hand-pulled prints, oversize broadsides illustrating poems by Gregory Corso, Philip Whalen, Lawrence Ferlinghetti, Charles Olson, and, rather disconcertingly, the young Chairman Mao. In the rose-carpeted main dining room, the walls were adorned by large, stark, abstract expressionist paintings by good artists. The room was illuminated by a single exposed blue neon tube that ran the length of three walls, looking like a minimalist installation in an upscale New York art gallery. A dozen white tableclothed tables, set with handmade glassware and decorated with sprays of flowers in cut-crystal vases, surrounded a lustrous, black-lacquered Japanese baby grand piano.

"This sure isn't Boonville," Micki whispered after Vernon had seated us and we'd looked around the almost deserted, hushed room. Only two other tables were occupied, by people we didn't recognize.

"It certainly isn't what I'd expected," said David. "Let's just hope the food's edible." It was the first time that we'd eaten out in months.

The food was more than edible. It was elegantly simple: herb salad with rabbit terrine, chicory chowder, grilled leeks with bacon, caper, and cream sauce, sautéed peppers with okra and marjoram, pit-roasted boned leg of lamb stuffed and rubbed with a peppermint, garlic, and red pepper paste and marinated with something called "verjuice," mashed potatoes with peppermint and garlic chives, chocolate coffee cake, and raspberry tart. The menu noted that most of the ingredients used came from the hotel garden and local producers.

"I can't believe this," Micki enthused. "It's better than Chez Panisse."

"It's too bad we won't be able to afford to come here again," said David. "Maybe on your birthday or our anniversary."

"It's really not *that* expensive. My lamb chops were only ten dollars. I can't imagine the locals eating here, though. They want a steakhouse where you get a soggy vegetable, mashed potatoes and gravy, iceberg lettuce, and all the trimmings."

"You know, you're really a snob," said David.

"Maybe they're appealing to snobs," said Micki, sipping her coffee. "I love it." We agreed that it was a far cry from the mushy tofu, squash, and brown rice casseroles of the countless solstice and birthday parties we'd gone to and stopped attending when we realized that the main reason we were being invited was in the hope that Micki would show up with one of her chicken-and-almond dishes or a big tray of lasagna that would compensate for the otherwise meager fare that graced such events.

Vernon called again a week later. It was Saturday night and there was nobody in the restaurant. Could we come down and have dinner with them? Business was slow, he explained after pouring David a tumbler of one of his single-malt Scotches. They'd expected that. But if they wanted to get any more money out of their investors—it was a limited partnership—it would have to pick up. The locals had come by, a few of them, and tried the place, but only a few had come back. They'd have to learn to appreciate the kind of food that Charlene was preparing, he said.

By midnight and a bottle of wine later, David had agreed to search the records, prepare a report, and file the the documents that would qualify the old building for the National Register of Historic Places. This would entitle Vernon and Charlene to some tax breaks and would make the partners happy. Payment would be in meals. "Don't worry about how many," said Vernon. "We like cooking for people who appreciate our food."

It didn't seem to bother them, all through the spring, that there would be nights, weekend nights, when nobody came by, and the four of us would sit in a corner of the big empty dining room, trying out Charlene's latest concoctions, drinking wine, and talking about food, art, politics, education, and animal husbandry. Night after night, in the empty dining room, Vernon elaborated his vision of what the hotel would become: a country inn, an *auberge*, in which local workers would come in from the vineyards and logging sites and mix with the artists and poets who lived in the hills and with travelers from the city. There would be music, good food, and conversation. When Micki suggested that working people wouldn't be able to afford the prices, Vernon declared that they'd simply have to reorder their priorities: nothing was more important than good food, good wine, and good company—in that order. He was confident they'd have plenty of business as soon as the right people discovered Charlene's cooking.

It happened one Sunday. Even as we were sitting in the deserted dining room the evening before, San Franciscans were reading about what the Sunday food critic called "the best restaurant in California" and were making plans to drive up to Boonville to check it out. Micki went into town to pick up the paper the next morning and found it jammed. Cars were parked alongside the highway a half mile in both directions, and there was a crowd of people clustered around the front door of the hotel.

Micki burst into the kitchen. "What's happened?" she shouted over the noise of the equipment and the staff, racing back and forth.

"We've been discovered," Vernon shouted with a grin. "We're famous."

Over the next several months the New Boonville Hotel and its huge garden, which was presumed to be the source of all the fresh vegetables that made it onto the restaurant menu, captured the imagination of dozens of food writers, who along with hundreds of others made the pilgrimage to Boonville to eat at what one of them called "a foodie's mecca."

At first we took advantage of the hotel's success by providing them with eggs, the occasional wether goat, turkeys, chickens, and rabbits. But the low volume and the time it took to butcher or hand-pluck the smaller animals didn't cover much more than our costs.

"We can take all you can produce," said Vernon, who was well aware of how precarious our economic situation had become, especially with Grant off at school. We sold them goat-milk butter at eight dollars a pound—"It looks terrific on the menu," said Vernon—and provided some of the goat cheese that had become a *de rigueur* item on the menu of every self-respecting "California cuisine" restaurant. We were paid in meals, once or twice a week. Sometimes we'd be called down to provide local color, to entertain food writers as well as celebrity chefs—James Beard, Alice Waters, Jeremiah Tower—while Vernon and Charlene, who never let a dish go out of their kitchen without attending to it personally in one way or another, prepared one of their celebrity dinners. Sometimes we'd take down something special—one of our pork loins or some venison medallions—and Charlene would cook them up after the restaurant closed. One night it was the rattlesnake that David had spotted as it worked its way along the edge of the garden—the first one we'd encountered in a dozen years of watching for them. Charlene thought it would be interesting for the patrons in the bar to have a chance to see the writhing creature, which Micki had curled into a large Pyrex dish after David shot and beheaded it.

"Ugh!" said one perfectly groomed young matron who was waiting for a table, as Vernon set the dish on the end of the bar. "What's that?"

"A rattlesnake," Micki said as matter-of-factly as if we supplied them on a regular basis. "We're going to eat it."

"You're kidding," exclaimed her boyfriend, scrunching up his face. "Will it be on the menu?"

"Not tonight," said Micki. "Tonight it's the hermaphrodite goat we brought down yesterday."

"A hermaphrodite goat?"

"That's one with both sexes," Micki informed her, enjoying the horrified looks on their faces. "Be sure to order it."

It was too much for the matron. "Honey, buy that woman a drink," she declared as she backed away from the bar.

It was Micki's idea to turn the cabin into a guest house. Vernon said that if it were done right, it would perfectly complement the hotel. Almost all of his out-of-town customers, when they made their reservations, asked him for suggestions about places to stay. There were only a few places in the area that he could recommend. If we had an upscale place, he'd send plenty of business our way.

The cabin in question was little more than a weatherbeaten, twenty-eight-by-sixteen-foot shell that sat up the hill past the orchard. We'd begun work on it years before, shortly after we'd discovered that Micki was allergic to bees, with the idea of renting it out and having somebody there to get her to the hospital in the event of an emergency when David wasn't around. But by the time we got the roof on and some siding up, we realized that it was going to be too expensive to finish, so it sat there year after year, too good to be turned into a shed and too rustic to be livable, its windows covered with torn plastic sheeting, a back wall protected only by curling pieces of sun-bleached felt paper.

"Do you think we can do it?" David asked as we stood in front of the sorry-looking building one gray March afternoon. "It's going to take a lot of work to make it look good."

"Well, we certainly won't be able to leave it half-done, the way we did the house," Micki said ruefully. We'd only gotten the hot water connected the fall before, after Grant went off to Harvard.

Drew was busily making calculations on a yellow pad. "It'll take about five thousand dollars," he announced. "We'll have to add a whole new back section for a bedroom and bath."

"That'll include everything?" asked Micki. "Carpeting, stove, refrigerator?"

"And a deck," Reed said. "You have to have a deck." He and Drew had been working as handymen and waiters on weekends down at the Bear Wallow Lodge and had come to know something about what Bob, the owner, called "the business."

"What about a hot tub?" Drew suggested. "Bear Wallow has a hot tub."

"No hot tub," said David. "How would we heat it, anyway?"

"Well, let's get at it," said Micki. "The sooner we get it done, the sooner we can be in business."

From Drew's diary, April 1984: *We've been working like maniacs on the guest house. We have all the Sheetrock up and are now working on the windows. For the past six weeks I've been studying for the biology achievement test. My yearling died from a prolapsed rectum.*

Grant had called to say that public radio would be running the interview the afternoon we were putting down the floor. Drew and Reed were gluing parquet tiles in place in the living room, and Micki was on the deck, putting a second coat of paint on the window frames. "I can smell that solvent from here," she exclaimed through the open window. "That stuff must be terrible for you."

"Grant should be on pretty soon," said David, turning up the radio.

He and Garth were aligning trim around the bathroom door. It was "All Things Considered," out of Boston by way of San Francisco. There was the now familiar lead-in about the goat boy who never went to school, who was now at Harvard, and then a cut to Grant, who began talking about how he and his family cleared the land, built the house, raised goats.

"I need a piece cut," Reed shouted to David.

"Wait until this is over," said Micki.

"Why?" asked Garth. "We already know all this."

"This solvent is giving me a headache," Drew complained. "Let's get it done, okay? We don't need to hear Grant."

"And you studied by kerosene lights?" the interviewer asked.

"Yes," said Grant. "We put in a twelve-volt solar system just a few months ago, though."

"Oh, *sure* we did," Drew said to nobody in particular. "Grant really had a lot to do with *that*."

The interview ended. "You can start the generator now," said Micki.

Jim brought over the kitchen cabinets right on schedule. He'd trimmed them with redwood strips that matched the slab tops David and the boys had hand-milled from a downed tree that winter. After a few lean years, Jim had been getting all the cabinet work he could handle, and we had to talk him into doing some furniture for us in exchange for some redwood slabs and the promise of a little labor in the future.

"They're beautiful, Jim," Micki said as he and Drew brought in the first section. "I only wish we had something as nice at our house."

"Hey, I've been after you guys for years to let me build you some good cabinets."

"Well, someday, maybe," said Micki.

"You get this yup hut going, and I'm going to raise my prices, though."

"Yup hut?" said Micki.

"Well, that's what it's gonna be, isn't it? You're gonna be taking care of all them Boonville Hotel yuppies, aren't you?"

"We'd *never* call them yuppies," declared Micki, feigning indignation.

"Oh, yeah, that's right," said Jim. "Sorry. I know better than that. Like all these rich folks who got me doing their kitchens. We don't call them yuppies. They're *clients*."

"*Clients?*" Micki laughed.

"Yeah," said Jim. "Pretty high class, huh? But I better get going so you can get back to work here on your . . . yup hut. And don't worry. We won't tell anybody that's what you got here."

"We're never going to make it," said Micki. "We'll have to call Vernon and Charlene and tell them to send them somewhere else." It was ten o'clock in the morning, and two magazine writers were scheduled that night to stay in the guest house—the yup hut, as we now all called it.

"We can make it," said Drew. "It's worth a hundred and fifty dollars."

"But look at all that has to be done," exclaimed Micki. The entrance door lay out on the deck, untrimmed. None of the bathroom plumbing had been hooked up, there were bifold doors to be installed, the shower door was still in its package, and all of the furniture was pushed into a corner because David was just beginning to put a second coat of paint on the bedroom wall. "It'll take another week to get this done."

"Not if we hurry," pushed Drew.

By six o'clock the doors were in place and the paint had dried, but there were a hundred jobs left undone. "Call Vernon," said Micki, who was scraping paint off one of the windowpanes. "Nobody can stay here tonight."

"Go down and just stall them," said Drew. "We can finish it in a few hours." We were supposed to have dinner with them at eight and do our usual local color routine until Vernon and Charlene could join us.

"Don't be ridiculous," said Micki. "It'll take you hours just to set up the furniture."

"Would you please just get out of here?" pleaded Reed. "It'll be easier to get it done if you two aren't around. Just go down and hold them off for a while. You're pretty good at that sort of thing."

It was past midnight when we left the hotel—we couldn't stall any longer—with our first guests, who followed us up the ridge in their rented car, past the sheep sheds, to the guest house. The deck lights were on—they hadn't been connected when we'd left—and the clutter of scrap wood and Sheetrock on the deck was gone. A cluster of potted plants—where had they come up with those?—graced the entrance. We held our breath as we opened the door and flicked on the lights.

"This is beautiful!" exclaimed one of the writers. The furniture, paintings, and flowers were all perfectly in place. We—the boys—had pulled it off. It was a worthy complement to the Boonville Hotel.

"Never thought we'd do it," confessed Drew the next morning as he emerged from his room and came into the kitchen, where we were cutting up vegetables from the garden for the gourmet breakfast that was part of the package. He was filthy.

"It's beautiful," Micki told him. "When did you finish up?"

"We were there right up until we saw your car lights."

"And then you didn't even bother to clean yourself up before going to bed?"

"Hell, we were exhausted," said Drew. "While you two were sitting down there eating and drinking and having a good time, we were busting our asses. You ought to see Reed and Garth."

"Well, it certainly looks good," complimented Micki. "Now get cleaned up so you can help Dad take up their breakfast."

Over the summer months we were full almost every night—Vernon recommended our place first to anybody who called, and we were mentioned in the travel section of the *San Francisco Examiner* as well. "Colfax's Guest House, in the redwoods high above beautiful Anderson Valley. Secluded. Working Ranch. Sleeps Six. Fireplace. Solar Electric. Kitchen Facilities. Decks. Trails," read our business card.

It wasn't the kind of life, the "living off the land," that we'd ever envisioned. Still, it allowed us to pay off the feed and vet bills and invest a few dollars in livestock. The worst part of it was fending off those who expected more than a night's lodging, who were *fascinated* by our *lifestyle*, who wanted to know *how we taught our kids at home* and sent one *off to Harvard*. In their jogging outfits, L. L. Bean hiking shoes, and Lands' End jackets, they'd wander down to the goat pens and catch Micki in the middle of milking or engage David in serious conversation even as he served them their goat cheese omelets and Micki's freshly baked blueberry muffins.

"It's part of the job," Micki would remind us after yet another couple drove off in their Mercedes or BMW, after having taken up most of the morning talking with us about local real estate, making a living on the land, getting into the Ivy League, and raising goats and sheep. We did our best to appear to be the genial country folk, the colorful guest house hosts who came with the night's lodging, but our hearts weren't in it . . . .

Micki's diary, September 1984: *Goats placed well at the fair. Seemed strange not having Grant there bossing everyone around. Garth and Reed were a big help. Drew had the champion ewe and finally took first* *in advanced sheep showmanship, beating the Dawson and Schmidbauer girls from Willits. It was really close, and we kidded him about winning under the first woman judge they've ever had. Guest house is full every night. Still like doing it, but get tired of smiling and HATE swabbing the toilets. David planted the winter garden and hopes to get in a good potato crop before it freezes.*

CHAPTER EIGHTEEN

Changes

"How did it go?" Micki asked as Drew settled into the backseat of the car. It was the same question she'd asked Grant a long three years before, when he came out of his first college interview. This time, though, we were in a rented car instead of the pickup, the three of us having flown east thanks to two good years with the livestock and a thriving guest house business. It was a gunmetal-gray day in Middletown, Connecticut, a half hour down the road from where we had lived when Drew was an infant.

"Great," Drew said as he rifled through some papers, checking out the time of his next appointment, at Yale. "The woman who interviewed me was pretty sharp. They've got a good astronomy department."

"What kinds of questions did she ask?" Micki wanted to know.

"The usual. How we ended up in Boonville, how we made a living there, what it was like not going to school."

"And you didn't have any problem with them?"

"Heck no." Drew laughed. "Why should I?"

"Oh, no reason at all," Micki said lightly. "We know you can be charming when you want to."

"Damn right," said Drew.

*　　*　　*

He knew that we were afraid he might not take to the interviewing circuit as well as Grant, who seemed almost to thrive on all the attention the media had lavished on him over the years he was at Harvard. And as friends had been quick to advise us—as if to suggest that we should be doing something to prepare Drew for failure—Grant was a hard act to follow. We were concerned that Harvard might have found it interesting, in terms of diversity, to admit one homeschooled country bumpkin but might not be inclined to admit another one, his brother. But it didn't hurt that Grant was doing extremely well—one of the supermarket tabloids overstated the truth only a bit in its headline GOAT BOY GETS ALL A'S AT HARVARD AND HE NEVER WENT TO SCHOOL!—or that Drew's test scores were even a bit better than his brother's had been. ("Of course they were better," Grant would say indignantly when the inevitable comparison was drawn. "He learned how to take them from me!")

"Did you tell her about grinding the mirror for your telescope and building the observatory?" persisted Micki.

"Of course," Drew said impatiently.

"And about your sheep?"

"Yes, Mother." Drew sighed. "I didn't miss a thing."

"Good," Micki said as we headed down the Wilbur Cross Highway in the rain.

Even after he'd gone off to college Grant had remained, if at a distance and only on vacations, involved with the dairy goat operation. He edited the sales list, made recommendations for breedings, and advised Micki on what shows and fairs to attend and with what animals. But we had felt the impact of his not being around to take care of the day-to-day operations—milking, trimming hooves, medicating, negotiating sales, cleaning pens, and repairing fences. It had taken us a while to take up the slack, and now, as Drew was preparing to head off in the same direction—there was never any question but that he would go east and, if at all possible, to Harvard—we were wrapping up long delayed projects. We finally got around to taking out some tan oaks and leveling a site behind the house for a woodshed, in a corner of which we installed a water heater. ("Why rush?" Micki asked sarcastically when we told her that we were planning to connect it. "It's only been twelve years.") And we finally got electricity.

When we moved to the land we planned to live without electricity and to use our small generator only occasionally, as we'd been told by those who had tried it that it was prohibitively expensive, in terms of fuel costs and repairs, to try to power a household with a generator. And we had gotten by, for twelve years, with our half dozen kerosene lights and a propane stove and refrigerator. We'd looked into the possibility of installing a windmill to generate power that we could store in twelve-volt batteries, much as many farmers had done on similarly isolated farms back in the twenties and thirties before the rural electrification programs came into being. But we had quickly concluded that a windmill—even if we could have afforded one, for even the smallest ones were expensive—wouldn't survive very long in the turbulent winds that raged across our ridge every winter. Our one hope was that the price of the space program–developed photovoltaic solar panels, which converted sunlight into electricity, would eventually drop to the point where we could afford them. And thanks to the energy crisis of the seventies, which resulted in their further development and wider use, they did just that. The timing couldn't have been much better, for now the boys were old enough to master the intricacies of photovoltaic technology and installation and did not have to depend on David, who had always been the first to admit that he found electricity even more irrationally mysterious than automobile mechanics.

"Be careful with that," David said, standing by as Reed and Drew called instructions back and forth through the open window as they did the final hookup of the batteries to the wire that connected with the regulator in the house. They had spent a week on their backs in the crawlspace under the house, wary of the black widow spiders that Reed insisted he'd seen the last time he'd been under there to fix the water filter, working wires up into the walls and cutting outlets for the expensive cigarette lighter–shaped outlet boxes. Four solar panels were mounted on a sturdy steel post halfway down the hill in front of the house, and the four heavy-duty batteries were enclosed in a box just outside our bedroom window.

"There's nothing to worry about," Reed said for what seemed to be the hundredth time. He and Drew had researched the whole topic and knew what they were doing. We had been told pointedly that all we had to do was provide the materials and stay out of the way. "It's only twelve volts, Dad. All it can do is give you a little jolt, that's all."

"Then do it," said Garth, who had been working as their gofer. He'd seen the sparks go flying when they'd accidentally crossed wires a couple of times before.

"Not me," said Reed. "I still don't like it."

"Just don't go cross-wiring something and burn out the regulator," said David. "That's a two-hundred-dollar box there."

"We know what we're doing, Dad," Drew said exasperatedly from outside. "Do you have it plugged in there, Reed?"

"Yeah," he replied. "I'll get Mom."

They had brought down one of our old brass lamps from the storage loft and equipped it with a ballast and a twenty-two-watt Circleline fluorescent bulb.

"Turn it on," Drew shouted from outside.

Micki flipped the switch and drew back as the light came on.

"Does it work?" came the call from outside.

"Yes!" shouted Micki. "It's magic," she exclaimed as they trooped into the house to check it out. "First hot water and now electricity. If we're not careful, we're going to end up civilized."

From Micki's diary, December 1984: *Now have a fuse box in the bedroom—our own little power system with its flickering red lights.*

It was the end of an era, an end to the nightly ritual of filling the half dozen lamps, of trimming the charcoal-tipped circular wicks so that the delicately filigreed, cone-shaped mantles would burn evenly, of constantly adjusting the flame to burn off built-up patches of carbon, and of reflexively checking to make sure that a lamp was never left burning in an unoccupied room. For nearly a dozen years we'd monitored them carefully, moving them from room to room as we needed them, and we'd managed to do so without burning down the place, as one old-timer who'd grown up with kerosene lights said was inevitable if we used them long enough. They were unromantically dangerous and dirty, and we didn't mourn their passing. One day a few months after the twelve-volt system was fully operational, Micki stuffed the old lamps into some feed bags and took them to the town dump. When David protested that we could have easily converted them to twelve-volt electric lamps, nobody paid him any attention.

From Drew's diary, January 1985: *I stopped writing, but Mom flipped when she found out, so here we go. . . . The lights are working perfectly and I haven't had to do anything to the system, though we don't have*

enough lamps yet. Still writing a weekly astronomy column for the local
paper. Some former radical students of Dad's came by in their BMW:
The Big Chill?

Just to be on the safe side, Drew applied to five schools—Yale, Princeton, Amherst, Haverford, and Harvard—and was admitted to all of them. A piece on the front page of the Sunday *San Francisco Examiner*—TOP COLLEGES VYING FOR BOONVILLE WHIZ KID—precipitated another media blitz. This time around it wasn't as frenzied and was even a little more thoughtful. Drew, pictured with the "telescope he built when not tending his prize-winning sheep," was spared the John-Boy Walton, homey goat-boy treatment that Grant had cheerfully endured. That we'd managed to send yet another of the "graduates" of what *Newsweek* had called our "Little Redwood Schoolhouse" to Harvard suggested that perhaps we were doing something right, and we were always available to talk about American education over expense account dinners with reporters and producers at the New Boonville Hotel, even though we knew that little of what we said would ever find its way into their stories.

And if our celebrity had lasted for more than the Warhol-prescribed fifteen minutes, we were finding our newly emergent roles as spokesmen for what we had discovered was a substantial "homeschooling movement" more than a bit trying. Whenever an article appeared in a magazine or newspaper somewhere across the country—TO HARVARD BY LAMPLIGHT, FROM HEARTH TO HARVARD, HOMESCHOOLED AND NOW THEY'RE AT HARVARD—we'd receive a dozen or more calls from parents wanting to know "just how you did it"; many of them seemed to be working on the assumption that since they were paying for the call, we were obliged to give them as much time as they wanted.

"We've got to stop doing this," Micki grumbled as she hung up the telephone after a forty-five-minute conversation with a parent from Texas. "We're never going to get anything done if we keep taking these calls."

"You've got to keep them brief," said David. "You've got to cut them off."

"Oh, sure," Micki said. "I notice that you're really good at that. You just go on and on."

"We probably should make a list of the most often asked questions and mail that to them," David thought aloud.

"Or write a book," said Micki. "In self-defense. Why not? That way we could get something out of all this publicity and get them off our backs. God knows we've given everybody enough of our time, and what have we gotten out of it? Dinners at the hotel."

"What are we going to say? That if you want to send your kid to Harvard, all you have to do is lose your job, get blacklisted, move to the mountains, work your ass off for a dozen years, and by the time your kids grow up they'll be ready for anything, including the Ivy League?"

"Of course not," said Micki. "We could do the same thing we do on the telephone. We don't have to get political. Most people just want to know what books we used, how we handled testing, what's legal, things like that. Now that the guest house is bringing in some money, we can afford to take the time to do it, don't you think? It wouldn't have to be anything big."

"It's an idea," David mused as the telephone rang again.

"You answer it," said Micki. "I got the last one."

Postmaster Bates couldn't have been happier. "I understand there's a TV crew down at the hotel this morning," she told Micki, who'd come in to pick up the mail. "Boonville's getting to be such a busy place, I don't know how some of these old-timers are going to be able to handle it," she exclaimed. "With your boys and the hotel there's somebody doing a story around here all the time."

"Yeah, and then there's Boontling and the Moonies," said Micki.

"You know, they just don't seem to get the attention they used to. And as far as the Moonies go, that's just as well with me." Most of the Moonies had moved out in the early eighties, after the felony conviction of Reverend Moon himself, and left behind a German couple who managed a half dozen metal buildings in which they raised "American minks."

"And there's Alice Walker, of course," said Micki.

"Well, she doesn't really *live* here," Peggy sniffed. Walker had written *The Color Purple* in a cabin outside of Boonville one winter. After the success of her novel she had built a summer home up on the Holmes ranch. "She's really one of them city folks," Peggy said with a twang.

There was no question but that the area was being rapidly gentrified and becoming, in the words of 4-H rabbit leader Bob Altaras—who had abandoned his roadside "fresh-butchered rabbits" business and opened an upscale gift shop—"a destination." Bob admitted that he enjoyed raising rabbits more than selling arts and crafts, but, like us, he and his family had been living on the edge for too long and had even been considering moving back to the city shortly before the hotel became famous.

And more than a few of the visitors to the celebrated restaurant recognized that the relatively unspoiled area was ripe for development—or exploitation. As the local realtors liked to point out to the Chardonnay-dazed, fantasy-spinning urbanites who wandered into their offices after a long lunch at the hotel, Anderson Valley was destined to be "the next Napa Valley," while being careful not to remind them that the famous wine region sixty miles to the south had become something of a winery theme park—crowded, expensive, and, all in all, not a very pleasant place in which to live.

But by now the area was no longer an enclave of Arkies, Okies, and oddballs, of loggers, sheepmen, and a few scruffy hippies living in the hills. Slowly and almost imperceptibly, it had become something of a retirement community for those who were able to sell their homes in the suburbs at outrageously high prices and move to the country, where they could buy twenty-acre plots at ridiculously low prices and put up expensive homes with their equity, while others had to settle for a double-wide mobile home and a satellite dish. Some were drawn to the area with the idea of getting a piece of the action the realtors promised, playing at real estate, buying and selling properties in a hot market. Others bought up valley land, pulled out the apple orchards and livestock fences, and replaced them with rows of gleaming metal grape stakes and young vines. Where there had been only two local wineries that had been struggling for recognition since before we'd arrived, there were now ten, all prospering and expanding. And their successes attracted the attention of others, such as the venerable French conglomerate that came in, bought several hundred acres of apple and pear orchards, unceremoniously ripped out the trees, built a massive winery, and proceeded to turn out the most unlikely of Anderson Valley products, a pricey California champagne.

And like others who had somehow weathered the seventies in the hills, our concerns about the gentrification of the timber-and-sheep country were offset by the realization that the affluent newcomers, the new industries, and the Boonville Hotel foodies provided us with new opportunities. Thanks to the yup hut, for the first time since we'd been on the land we didn't have to agonize over every little expenditure—the cost of a pound of nails, an increase in the price of feed, or the need for a new truck tire. Like our former five-dollar-an-hour carpenter friends who now found themselves with more than enough work at three times that rate, and like Jim, who was now in a position to turn down business, we were for the first time in years not affluent, but at least *solvent*. Setbacks that once assumed near-cosmic proportions—the death of a prized animal, the failure of a doe to produce a kid for which we had a buyer, an abortion, or even a poor showing at a fair—no longer loomed as threats to our survival. At last we had the resources to do at least a few of the things we couldn't when we were locked into a day-to-day struggle just to get by.

"You what?" Micki exclaimed when David returned from Ukiah one afternoon.

"I'm running for the county school board," said David.

"What? I thought you went over to file for the *college* board."

"I did. But I discovered that whoever it is who is supposed to represent our district isn't up for reelection for two more years. I asked the clerk what was open, and she said there were two openings on the county school board, so I said to put me down. I had the choice of running against somebody named Kathy Matthews, over in Point Arena, or a woman up in Willits named Morningstar."

"And you chose Morningstar, I hope," said Micki.

"Of course."

"Is that her real name?" asked Drew. "Morningstar?"

"The clerk said it's the one that will be on the ballot," said David. "Apparently they appointed her to the board last year."

"Well, if you can't beat somebody named Morningstar, you'd better give up on politics," Drew said.

"I don't know about that," said David. "She's the incumbent, and this *is* Mendocino County."

"But why the county *school board?*" questioned Micki.

"The county board runs the Indian education program and group home schools," said David. "Those kids could use an advocate."

"I'm sure they could," Micki agreed. One of the things we'd worked on together back in St. Louis had been an exposé of the state juvenile detention center. "But won't it be a bit embarrassing if you get beaten by somebody named Morningstar?"

A few months before, when there had been an opening for a dean of instruction at the community college over in Ukiah, David had applied for the job.

"I might be able to do some good," he'd explained. "Maybe it's time for me to get back in. They certainly need all the help they can get." The college, established in the early seventies, had from its inception been widely regarded as little more than the private property of a tight little group of religious fundamentalists and good ol' boys and something of a joke. Now, though, the rumor was that the new administration was interested in getting some good people on the faculty.

"They'll never hire you," Micki warned.

She was right, of course. David received a mimeographed letter signed by a "Personnel Analyst II." "Thank you for your application," it read, "Unfortunately, we have reviewed it and are sorry to have to inform you that we have concluded that you lack the necessary qualifications for the position."

"A *form* letter," David fumed. "For a dean's job? At that dump?"

"You ought to write a letter to the president," said Micki.

"It wouldn't make any difference. I'm going to run for the board."

"You'd never win. You're too radical."

But the truth was that few people in the county knew us as anything more than goat and sheep farmers, as the parents of those 4-H kids who never went to school. It wasn't that we had retired from political activism over the years. On the contrary, as the boys grew older and were themselves able to understand the issues and take part, we'd become involved in a countywide campaign to ban herbicidal spraying of the forests by timber companies, and we had piled into the pickup and gone down to the Bay Area to take part in a number of antinuclear protests. But until the demands of making a living had eased, we for the most part had relegated ourselves to the sidelines of the political movements of the seventies and eighties. Now, with a few more resources, we found ourselves edging back into the Reagan-savaged political landscape, not as the comfortable, university-based radicals we had been fifteen years before, but as parents, educators, and small farmers who had years of firsthand knowledge of how hard it was to survive in an economically depressed rural economy. If anything, we had become more radical, but now our radicalism was based upon our own and our children's more immediate experiences and needs. Our years in the hills had only reinforced our commitment to fundamental social change, and as we ventured down from the mountain to reenter the political realm, we found ourselves as alienated as ever from the dominant ethos. It was almost as if we were reverting to type.

Morningstar Rainbow Medicine Woman Bridge of Light Protected by the Golden Eagle—her full name—agreed that it had probably cost her the election. She thought that she might have kept her seat if she had run as Susan Smith, but then that would have been a repudiation of her new age identity. Still, it didn't seem fair, she told a reporter from the Santa Rosa newspaper. "It's sort of like karma that the conservative people voted for someone with a real name and chose the radical," she said the day after David won the at-large position on the county school board.

It had been our best summer yet. The kid and lamb crop had been good, we'd done well at shows, and the guest house had been kept full. Grant had found a research job in Cambridge, Reed, Drew, and Garth were with their sheep at the Ukiah fair and on their own for the first time, and Micki was in Sacramento, showing the goats at the state fair. The guests had already arrived when David, back from Ukiah, went up the hill with our trademark complimentary bottle of wine from a local winery. He would be making them breakfast in the morning. Australians, it said in the reservation book. There were four of them, three men and a woman, standing on the deck, and they seemed relieved to see him.

"Perhaps you could tell us where we might be able to get dinner tonight," the tallest one said diffidently after introductions.

"You have reservations at the hotel, don't you?" said David. Why else would a group of Australian tourists come to Boonville?

"Oh, we did," said the woman. "But the hotel's closed. The owner—Charlene, isn't it?—was having a miscarriage and had to get to a hospital. There was a notice on the door. Sounded dreadful."

David suggested that they head out to the coast; the Albion River Inn was pretty good. They were very understanding.

"You're goddamned right they left," raged Irving, Charlene's father, who lived in a trailer in town and filled in as bartender a few nights a week. "Took my truck and made a goddamn fool of me, too. There was no miscarriage. I'm standing there telling the staff how Charlene had to be rushed to the hospital in San Francisco—that's why they needed my truck—and then one of them pipes up and says no, when she was coming to work she saw them heading north toward Fort Bragg. If I ever get my hands on that son-in-law of mine . . ."

We knew they were having financial troubles and had been planning to close down in September until Charlene had the baby and Vernon could refinance the place. We had heard that several of their partners, unhappy with the return on their investment in what was now an internationally known restaurant, had been talking about the need for a new manager. But Vernon and Charlene had never talked to us about their finances or the way they ran the place: Our job was to entertain visiting celebrities on occasion, in return for which we were provided with guest house customers.

Vernon telephoned David the next morning from a location he wouldn't reveal and asked if we could meet them in Portland. Irving would need his truck back. Could we loan them the Valiant? They'd explain everything when they saw us.

"You didn't agree to it, did you?" Micki said incredulously when she returned from the goat show and heard the news. "We can't do that. The boys need the car."

"I told him we'd meet him in Eureka," David explained. "But only if he'd give us the paychecks for the help. He said he had intended to pay them but left so quickly that they'd forgotten to take the checkbooks."

"Oh," said Micki. "And so we *are* going to lend them the car?"

"Only until they can get things in order."

The next night we sat in a Mexican restaurant in a shopping mall while Vernon signed the paychecks. It had gotten to be too much, they said. Charlene was exhausted, and the baby was due in eight weeks. The partners wanted to get rid of Vernon. They could handle that, but when the investigator from the state unemployment compensation office showed up the Friday before they left and confiscated as many of their records as he could get his hands on, they knew there wasn't any hope. Vernon hadn't been making payments, and they'd probably hit him with a stack of misdemeanor charges. There was no money to hire a lawyer or pay the state, and no matter what happened, Vernon would be forced out.

"All that work, those long hours, all for nothing," said Micki, shaking her head and closing her eyes. "To have to give up everything. It's terrible." We all knew what she was thinking about, for we'd spent many an evening after the hotel had closed, exchanging stories about our political pasts.

"We'll be okay," Vernon reassured us with a quick glance around the room. "Just as long as we stay out of California."

It took us longer than we'd expected to get back to Boonville with Irving's truck and the paychecks. An overturned lumber truck had blocked the highway for several hours south of Eureka, and we drove through town just as it was beginning to get light. Irving wasn't home when, after a few hours of sleep, we took the truck down to his place. He was over at the hotel with the sheriff. Somebody had broken into the place during the night and had taken almost everything—liquor, crystal and silverware, kitchen equipment, furniture. Nobody dared say it to us—after all, we were known to be their friends—but it was quickly and generally assumed that Charlene and Vernon had come back and emptied out the place after dropping off the paychecks and Irving's truck. We realized that we probably had driven through town even as the burglary was taking place—we hadn't noticed a thing—but thought it best not to mention that. At least we knew where Vernon and Charlene had been the night before and had a credit card receipt—we had picked up the check—to prove it.

The media had a field day: FAMOUS CHEFS LEAVE TOWN, FOOD MECCA CLOSED AS OWNERS FLEE, blared the San Francisco dailies. "My God, you'd think this was the biggest event since the Jonestown massacre," one veteran reporter told us. "We're getting calls about it from New York and even London. Maybe it's the Icarus thing. Nothing pleases the public more than to see the high and mighty fall. But this is absurd."

It didn't take too long for some of the locals—ourselves included—to experience the economic consequences of the closing of the hotel. No longer was Anderson Valley a "destination," for its main attraction was gone, which left few, if any, compelling reasons for tourists to put it on their itineraries. One Sunday afternoon shortly after the robbery, one disgruntled investor backed a truck up to the front door of the hotel and in broad daylight removed the only item of value that the intruders had left behind—the gleaming Kawasaki baby grand piano. A few months later another had the big black obelisk sign taken down and donated to the county museum, where it was immediately and prominently displayed in its commercial memorabilia exhibit. Charlene and Vernon, when told about it, said they were touched by the gesture. We never saw the Valiant convertible again. Vernon loaned it to a friend, who totaled it on an icy road one night a year later.

"So what *are* you going to do now?" Drew repeated as we stood in line with him at the gate as he waited to board the flight that would take him to Boston. On the way down to the airport we had talked about how the closing of the hotel had wiped out our guest house business and what we'd be doing over the coming months while he was away.

"Don't worry about it," said Micki. "You just have a good year at school."

"Well, you have to do *something*," Drew pressed as the line moved along. It was obvious that The Boss was having a hard time letting go.

"We've got the goats and sheep, and we can rent out the place," said Micki.

"And more expenses," said Drew. "Look at what this flight is costing. You've got to do more than that."

"We can manage without you, Drew," said Micki. "I know you find that hard to believe, but we will."

"Just make sure you keep Reed and Garth working," he instructed over his shoulder as he handed the attendant his boarding pass.

Standing in the entrance to the boarding ramp, he hugged the two of us. Tears welled in his eyes, then he turned and headed into the tunnel. Halfway down he stopped, turned around, and waved. "Give Grant our love," Micki shouted. Grant was meeting him at the other end. Drew grinned and nodded, then turned and disappeared down the corridor.

"That was easier than I thought," said Micki, wiping her eyes, as we backed out of the doorway. "We must be getting better at it."

"Two down, two to go."

"We're really going to miss him," Micki said as we headed home in the truck. "And I don't mean just around the place. Reed and Garth'll pick up the slack. Reed's been a big help with the goats, but I don't think either of them is especially interested in the sheep."

"Maybe we should expand the goat operation and cut back on the sheep. Or get more into chickens and rabbits."

"You know we can't make it on the livestock. Not the way we've been living for the last few years."

"Maybe we'll just have to revert to the way we were living before," said David.

"God, what a prospect," Micki sighed as we crossed the Golden Gate Bridge.

CHAPTER NINETEEN

Camp Plywood

We came up with the idea over Christmas vacation. "Not I," declared Grant. "I'm going to be working in Boston this summer. If you want to run a summer camp and have a hundred screaming kids around here, go right ahead. But count me out." We were sitting around the table after a midday meal. Grant and Drew would be flying back to Boston in a few days.

"Not a hundred," Drew countered. "Ten or twenty at the most." It had been his idea. Unlike Grant, who had worked for our congressman in Washington after his freshman year at Harvard, he wanted to get back to California for the summer. In the few months he'd been gone, we'd seen the guest house business all but disappear and were limping along, once again trying to decide where to expand and how to contract the livestock operations in order to continue to make a go of the place. "You have all these people calling here for advice about their kids," said Drew. "Why don't we put together a summer camp they could send them to?"

We bounced the idea back and forth for an hour. It would have to be a kind of academic summer camp, a tutorial kind of thing, that would take advantage of all the publicity we'd received as homeschoolers. We could do academics in the morning and the usual summer camp kinds of things in the afternoon. It would have to be coed, of course; otherwise it wouldn't be much fun. For staff, all we'd need were the five of us and a counselor for the girls. The two of us could teach English, Drew could do biology—he was majoring in it—and astronomy, and Reed could handle math. Garth would be the all-around junior counselor.

"Fine," David said after a while. "It might be a good idea. But we'd need a place for them to stay. Where would we put it?"

"What about it, Garth?" Micki asked. "Any ideas?"

"Out on the ridge below the orchard," said Garth. "Down where the pigpen used to be. We'd have to do a lot of clearing. And it's pretty steep."

"We'll need a girls' cabin, a boys' cabin, and a kitchen," Drew said as he punched some numbers into a calculator.

"And showers," Micki added. "Hot water and toilets."

Drew did some more calculations while Reed made a list of what we could offer. There would be chores in the morning, then academics. After lunch we could swim in the river or go on hikes.

"We can offer a lot," said Micki. "But how in the world are we going to put together a camp by June? With just the four of us here?"

"We can do it, can't we?" Reed turned to Garth. It was more a statement of fact than a question.

Garth shrugged. He'd only been a gofer on the guest house.

"Just so Dad stays out of the way," said Reed. "He's too slow."

"Slow?" exclaimed David. "At least whatever *I* build doesn't fall down."

"What did I ever build that fell down? Name one thing."

"Well, you're pretty sloppy."

"I never claimed I was *neat*."

"He only meant that you're too much of a perfectionist, David." Micki cast a warning glance in Reed's direction. "It'll be a big job," she continued. "We'll have to do a brochure, line up people to teach ceramics and music, that sort of thing. If we start up in mid-June, we'll at least get a few weeks of work out of you before it starts, Drew."

"You'd better plan to have everything pretty much in place by the time I get home," Drew stated, looking up from the pad on which he had been writing. He gestured for Reed and Garth to come closer. "Here's the design for the boys' cabin. What do you think? Sixteen by sixteen?" They huddled together at the end of the table while the two of us, at the other end, began roughing out copy for a brochure.

It took a month for the four of us, working around rainstorms, to take down the big rotten oaks and clear the brush on the ridge. It turned out to be steeper than we'd anticipated, but there was enough of a flat spot on the other side of a big redwood grove from the buck pen where we could put the kitchen. By the time Drew returned home in late May, we'd managed to rough out the boys' and girls' cabins and the kitchen amid a tangle of downed trees and brush. We hadn't begun work on the showers and toilet facilities.

"All I can say is that it's a good thing you two are going to Grant's graduation," Drew said after several days of feverish activity. We'd framed up the shower house, and while David worked on that, the boys began to dig out a massive pit for a new "ecological disaster area," an upscale outhouse that came to be known as "four holes, no waiting." Earlier in the spring, thinking that everything would be farther along than it turned out, we had rescheduled the opening of camp to accommodate several of our better applicants, with the result that we'd be returning from Boston only two days before camp opened.

"Once Dad gets out of the way, we can go full speed," Drew continued as we sat on the edge of the shower house deck, eating the lunch Micki had brought up. We didn't have time to go down to the house. "We're never going to make it if he keeps insisting that everything be just right," he said with a grin.

"Well, sometimes you just have to sacrifice quality if you're going to get the job done," retorted Reed.

"Yeah, right," David said sarcastically. "It's always good to work with folks who take pride in what they do."

Grant graduated with high honors in biology. Earlier in the semester he'd been awarded a prize for having an outstanding senior thesis and had been granted a Fulbright Fellowship to spend a year in New Zealand. Commencement was a grand occasion, for Harvard, we had to admit, did a far better job of that sort of thing than any of the schools from which we'd graduated. But even as we were breaking out the champagne in our favorite restaurant high above Faneuil Hall in Boston, we couldn't help but wonder how the boys were doing, how Camp Plywood was coming along, on the other side of the continent.

From Garth's diary, July 1987: *Camp is over now. It was fun. There were 35 kids helping with the chores, and sometimes they were more trouble than anything. We all went to Mendocino to see the San Francisco Mime Troupe and spent a day at a "dig" of a Pomo Indian site* *in Clearlake. We had a great stained glass project that I helped to supervise.*

We learned, over the next three summers, that there really wasn't any way to predict which kids would do well at camp and which ones would be disasters. Some of those who looked great on their applications turned out to be disappointments, while others, who seemed to have ended up with us only because their parents felt we might be a more palatable alternative to summer school, blossomed in the few weeks they were with us. When the first cohort of campers showed up that summer, just as the boys were rushing to get the hinges on the door to the girls' cabin—the roofs would be shingled and the windows screened over the first week of camp, in what we billed as a "learning experience"—we had our first taste in a long time of dealing with other people's children. There was the camper, fresh from private school, who challenged everybody to a spitting contest within minutes after her arrival; the two girls, best friends, who had been recommended to us as "budding geniuses" but turned out to have what the professional educators would have termed "serious learning disabilities"; and the homeschooled boy who giggled constantly. But for every one of these more memorable cases—and there were a few who were worse—there were a half dozen who came to appreciate the land, love the animals, and even learn a bit of formal math or English or science in the loosely structured morning tutorials. We provided good role models. All the girls wanted to be like the pretty eighteen-year-old whose best credential, we'd found when we were looking for a counselor, was that she had grown up with a dozen brothers and sisters on a farm. And if Drew wasn't the showboat athlete that Reed was, he was still "the boss" by virtue of his being at Harvard and having rowed on the freshman crew. And as our brochure promised, we provided first-rate teachers in art, crafts, and dramatics, in addition to teaching math, science, and English ourselves. We didn't make any money that first year, and eight weeks of sixteen-hour days without a break took their toll. Still, it was good to see that the vision we'd had for our own children could be adapted, if only for a short few weeks, for the benefit of other kids, some of whom, until their few weeks on the ranch, had never had a chance to be responsible for anything important. We didn't delude ourselves into thinking that we could profoundly affect their lives in the course of eight weeks, but we saw enough growth and change to make it worthwhile.

From Micki's diary, August 1988: *The second session was a great success. Didn't think we'd ever bring Jennifer around, though. She and her friend arrived with nails polished, not a hair out of place, and in designer clothes and refused to get out of her father's Mercedes until Drew appeared and started to unload their designer luggage. They stayed off by themselves, disdainful of it all, putting the return address on their many letters to friends as "Camp Hell on the Mountain." But when she came back from the pig farm, disheveled and dirty, where she, Reed, and Drew went to get two piglets, things had changed. She became the most involved with the animals of any of the kids and ended up taking two baby goats home with her! She wants to come back next year as a counselor.*

After camp, Reed spent the next winter helping us to turn our homeschooling manuscript into camera-ready copy on our recently leased, solar-powered Macintosh, editing the newsletter of the North-coast Striders Running Club, taking the battery of tests for admission to college, and sharing the chores with Garth. He flew out to Cambridge to spend a week with Drew and decided to apply for early admission.

From Reed's Harvard application, 1988: *The sun is just beginning to filter through the redwoods as I climb into the sheep pen up on the ridge. The half dozen ewes and old Rambeau charge into the shed as I scatter alfalfa pellets in the feeder. Behind them, still spooky at three months, are their dozen offspring, which I cut off and run into the lamb creep. It has been a cold and rainy March, and I have been putting off giving them their tetanus and pulpy kidney shots until the weather improved. Since Drew and Grant have gone off to school, I have been responsible for making sure the sheep and goats receive their various immunizations on schedule. All of our livestock are show quality, and we can't afford to lose any of them.*

I fill two syringes, check for air bubbles, and set them on the windowsill. I am just about to flip the first lamb when I hear a shout. It's Mom, down at the goat barn. At first I can't understand what she is saying, and then I hear enough: "Vintage," she is calling. "She's aborting." I gather up the syringes and run down the hill. Mom is in the pen with our pregnant does. All are grand champions, and Vintage is the best of them. A long string of discharge hangs from her swollen vulva. "She's two weeks early," says Mom.

"The kids can't survive." Garth, my twelve-year-old brother, who had been taking care of the poultry, joins us, and together we push and cajole the recalcitrant Vintage into the kidding pen as Mom spreads fresh straw for bedding. "Watch her while I call Dr. Bob," she says, and runs down to the house. Bob Shugart, who has been our veterinarian since we first began to raise livestock nearly fifteen years ago, lives some twenty-five miles away, in Ukiah.

I leave Garth with Vintage and pour milk into the kidbar—a contraption made of a bucket, plastic tubing, and nipples that allows ten kids to feed at once—and head for the kid pen, where nine of them are waiting at the gate with wagging tails. Mom returns just as I finish rinsing out the bucket. "Bob says to get the kids out as soon as we can," she says breathlessly. "There's no chance of saving the kids, and we should concentrate on saving the mother."

We check Vintage again. She has not begun to dilate, so it is unlikely that she will kid before noon. Leaving Mom and Garth to finish up their chores, I trudge back up to the sheep shed and give the lambs their shots.

At breakfast Mom tells us she is very upset and afraid that this might be the start of another abortion storm. Three years ago half of our does aborted within a two-week period and we lost a couple of years in our breeding program—as well as a large chunk of income. "It's different this time, though," says Dad. "The does are a lot further along." Mom agrees.

"I only hope we can save her," she says. "Bob says that even if the kids are alive, they won't survive. Their lungs and hearts aren't strong enough. If she'd only been able to hold out for another week. He said they'd have a chance if they were even ten days premature, but two weeks is too much. You'll probably have to go in after them, Reed."

I know. For the last ten years, that's been my job. When I was seven or eight, I was the one who would have to go in and straighten a leg, feel around for a dead fetus, or gently work out a breech presentation. They said it was because my hands were the smallest, and it took a while—and by then I was pretty good at it—before I realized that none of them could really deal with it. "It might get pretty messy," says Dad.

He had spent a couple of hours delivering twisted lamb triplets ten years ago and thereupon announced his retirement from animal obstetrics.

It was to have been a busy day even before Vintage set off a crisis. I wanted to get some math and English done and work on the race flyer before going to town. Two afternoons a week I coach junior soccer and tutor a 4-H computer group, and this is one of those days. Over the years I've become accustomed to adjusting my schedule to crises here on the ranch—broken water lines, downed telephone lines, sick animals, washouts—and today I'd simply have to work things around Vintage. I gather up my precalculus and English books and head for the kidding pen.

(Vintage has dug herself deep into the straw and is resting her head against the wall that divides the pen from the grain room. The discharge has disappeared, but her vulva has become more swollen. She is constantly twisting and stretching, and it is clear that she is distressed.)

I manage to get an hour of math in and am just beginning to work on English when Dad calls from the house. Vic, the president of the county running club, is on the phone and wants to know when I can have the race materials ready. "Tell him I'll have them to him for the meeting tomorrow night." I check Vintage again. It will be at least an hour before I can do anything. Garth comes into the pen, book in hand, and I head down to the house to finish up the flyer. For the last four years Drew and I have organized one of the best-known races in the area, an eight-kilometer run in nearby Anderson Valley. This year I am solely responsible for it, and things are pretty much in place. The only jobs left are to get the flyer and my budget approved by the club, which has co-sponsored the race from the beginning. I type up the budget and give the flyer to Mom to check for errors I might have overlooked. "You'd better check Vintage," she says as she sits down at the dining room table to review it.

(Vintage is standing up in the middle of the pen with about a foot of fresh discharge hanging from her. She alternately paws at the ground and gnaws on a well-worn section of the fence.)

Garth, engrossed in his book, agrees to remain with Vintage, and I head back to the house. Lunch is on the table, and Mom hands me the flyer. "When do you think she'll be ready?" she asks.

* "Not for a few hours," I answer. I don't want to miss soccer practice.*

"Take the truck," says Mom as I gather up my equipment and head out the door.

The team is on the field when I arrive. Fifteen of them, ten- to twelve-year-olds that I have been coaching for the last year. I played for three years with one of the county's adult teams, one made up primarily of Mexican vineyard workers and expatriate Englishmen, until I dislocated my shoulder in a fall last year. Now I'm regarded—incorrectly so—as an authority by local parents who have never played the sport. We do some passing exercises, and I put Carlos in the goal and have my forwards and halfbacks take shots at him. Carlos speaks only Spanish, and I have probably learned as much Spanish from him as he has soccer from me. He is especially agile today and allows only two or three of the fifty kicks to get by him. I set up a scrimmage with the older team that is practicing at the opposite end of the field and use the telephone under the grandstand to call home. Mom says that Garth has been staying with Vintage, who is having light contractions every fifteen minutes or so. "You can probably stay down there for the computer class," she says. "I'll call if she goes into hard labor." I head back to the field, where my team is behind. The fullbacks need more work, but we look good against the older boys and should be ready for our first league game next week. I gather up the equipment, toss it into the back of the pickup, and drive over to Bruce's place.

Bruce, a retired computer scientist, greets me at the door. "Good thing you made it," he says. "They're all here today."
For the last year the two of us have been teaching BASIC programming to six kids, ages eight to thirteen. Bruce interested me in computers when I was their age, and since then I've been his assistant on a variety of projects. Today we work with the random number generator and explore ways in which it can be used in their own programs, which range from complex games to simple mathematical applications. The phone rings, and it's Mom. Vintage is having heavy contractions. "She's dilated and there's no sign of a bubble, so the kids must be stuck or tangled," she says. "One of us has to go in."
Bruce winces when I tell him I have to leave. "I'll manage," he says. "But next week you handle the sine graphing program, okay?"

There is nobody in the house when I arrive; they are all up at the kidding pen with Vintage. I quickly change clothes, scrub my arms and *hands, and hurry up to the barn. Mom looks stricken. Vintage is dilated and breathing heavily, but there is no sign of a kid. "Hurry," says Mom. "You've got to get the kids out."*

I motion to Dad, who grasps the doe around the neck and shoulders to hold her down. Gently, I work my hands into the birth canal as Vintage brays and tries to twist away. I'm in up to my forearms now and close my eyes and try to visualize what I am feeling. A head? Two legs. Front or back? Another head. "There are two of them, and they're tangled," I announce.

"She's our best goat," Mom says. "Be careful."

Dad, his back to me, says, "Just get them out."

I push them farther in, in an attempt to sort things out. After a minute or two I am able to get the nearer kid into position and slowly pull it out as Vintage contracts. It is dead.

"You have to get the other one," Mom says as I go in again. The kid slides out. It, too, is dead. Vintage is breathing evenly now. "Two dead kids," Mom says wearily. "Let's make sure we don't lose Vintage." If she retains the placenta or has another kid caught inside, it will kill her, so I go in once again. It's easier now because her cervix has been stretched by the two kids. Probing, I try to locate the placenta. Something feels like a leg, and I reach in farther. I feel a head, and the other leg. Another kid, so small that Vintage doesn't seem to feel it when I pull it out.

"Another dead one," says Mom. It shudders, and a leg moves. "Clean its mouth," Mom shouts as I pull the mucus away from its face. "Run down and turn on the oven," Mom tells Garth. "Maybe we can save it."

I wrap the tiny kid in a towel and follow Garth down to the house. I set her on the oven door, and Dad arranges the towels so she won't be burned. Mom fills a large syringe with some frozen colostrum she had thawed when Vintage went into labor, and attaches a short piece of plastic tubing. We work the tube down her throat, being careful not to put it in her lungs, and inject an ounce of milk. She barely moves. Mom telephones Dr. Bob, who says we've done all we can do, but it probably won't make any difference. He's never heard of a sheep or goat born this prematurely that survived.

"You are going to make it," Dad says as he moves the tiny creature to a warmer spot on the oven door. "Yagmi," he says. "That's her name: 'You are going to make it.'" Officially, all registered goats born in 1987 are supposed to be identified with an initial letter Y.

"Yagmi?" says Mom.

"Or 'You aren't going to make it,' " says Dad. "Same name."

It's dark now. I wash up and return to the kidding pen to give Vintage eight ml. of penicillin and a bolus, and to make sure she drops the placenta. By the time I get back to the house dinner is ready. Yagmi is asleep in a box perched on the oven door. I assure Mom that Vintage is all right. After dinner I go into my room, flick on the twelve-volt light that Drew and I installed, put on a B. B. King tape, and begin another Harry Crews novel. Two hours later I put down the book and do a final check on Vintage. She is nestled deep in the straw, peacefully chewing her cud. It's been a long—and fairly typical—day on the ranch.

(Yagmi did "make it" and in so doing made veterinary history. Six months later she was as big as her later-born, full-term herd mates and was winning her share of ribbons in the show ring. Vintage fully recovered, and we had no more stillbirths. The race went off without a hitch, the computer class continues, and my soccer team has yet to win a game.)

"Well, it sure proves that genetics has nothing to with it," said one of the first reporters who had come by to do a story about the third homeschooled, *adopted* Colfax who'd been admitted to Harvard. We had gravitated into the kitchen so we could be interviewed while we prepared dinner.

"What?" David said sharply, looking up from the garlic he'd been chopping.

"I mean, it has to be the environment you provided all the boys with here, and it's not, you know, genes." He grinned at us awkwardly. "Right?"

"It most certainly *could* be genes," Micki said after a moment. "Only *not ours.*"

"Grant?" Micki asked after the international operator had connected them. "You heard from Harvard Medical School today."

"What'd they say?" Grant asked almost casually.

"You've been accepted. I wouldn't have called if you hadn't been. I'll read their letter to you. It's short."

"Well, that's great," Grant said after she finished.

"You don't sound very excited. I thought this is what you were hoping for." Grant had flown back from New Zealand two months earlier for medical school interviews. By the time he returned there, he'd been admitted to a half dozen of the nation's top schools but hadn't gotten the word from Harvard.

"He didn't sound nearly as excited as I thought he'd be," Micki said later to David, who was in bed reading. "He took it very calmly. I thought he'd be ecstatic, the way he was agonizing about it when he was home."

"Maybe he's finally mellowing out," said David, looking up from his book.

"I doubt it. He's so competitive."

Grant called the next evening and confessed that he had already known he'd been admitted when he'd talked to Micki the night before. He'd telephoned the medical school secretary on the day the admissions letters went out.

"I just didn't want to admit that I had been that anxious," he said. "Then I began to feel guilty because I didn't tell you I already knew."

"I *knew* you didn't sound like yourself!" exclaimed Micki.

"So anyway, it's pretty great, isn't it?"

"Are you going to go there? It'll cost a fortune."

"It'll be worth it, I think. After all, Harvard's the best, isn't it?" He laughed.

"Well, that answers *that* question," Micki said after she hung up. "He's as competitive as ever."

From Garth's diary, December 1988: *Everybody liked the stained glass window I did as a Christmas present surprise for the family. It's a life-sized golden eagle on a perch. We'll cut through the wall to put it in above the dry sink when the weather gets better.*

PART EIGHT

Endings

CHAPTER TWENTY

The Good Life

There must have been a bikers' rally up north, David thought as they caught up with the ambulance, in groups of ten and twelve, then fanned out around it and roared on past. Maybe he had died and this was his escort to hell, as in that scene in . . . what was it, *Black Orpheus*? How many years ago was that? He could hear the droning voice of the driver telling his partner and the nurse about a bike he had once owned. He wished he'd shut up.

He felt wide awake, yet curiously apathetic. It must be the drugs, he mused. Expensive as hell. Three thousand dollars for that one, the doctor said. At least the insurance would cover it. He couldn't move—they'd strapped him in for the trip—and there was an IV unit in his arm, "in case we have to give you something in a hurry," he remembered the nurse telling him. They couldn't tell yet if he'd had a heart attack or not; the test results wouldn't be available for several hours. But there was no coronary unit in Ukiah, and Micki had insisted that they get him down to Santa Rosa.

He was dozing in his hospital bed when the cardiologist came by. "So you're the one who was chasing the bear," said the doctor. "I suppose it would have been worse if it had been chasing you."

David smiled weakly. Cut the jokes, he thought. Just find out how bad it is.

The cardiogram didn't show anything, but the enzyme test indicated that something had happened. They'd have to do an angiogram to get the information they needed. Now, in a cavernous, darkened room, David faded in and out of consciousness as the two cardiologists worked over him. It wasn't as painful as he'd feared. After they had explained the process, he'd asked them to dope him up good—and they had. The worst of it was the explosionlike bursts of heat in his chest as they injected the ions into his system through the incision they'd made in an artery near his groin.

"David, can you hear me?" Yes. "Look at the screens over there," directed one of the cardiologists. There were two of them, thirty-inchers, black and white, with identical feathery images of what he presumed was his heart. "You see those two dark lines there?" Yes, he could see them. He felt strangely detached from the whole thing. "Those are your arteries. The one is completely blocked up, and the other is almost blocked."

"What's that mean?" he heard himself say.

"We'll have to talk about it later," said the cardiologist.

"Okay," said David. He turned his head away from the monitors and drifted back to sleep.

"You were lucky," the doctor told him later. "It's the kind of condition where you push back from the dinner table one evening and drop dead. You should thank that bear for coming around or we wouldn't have caught it."

There was no getting out of it. A double bypass. Where they take a stainless-steel circular saw and cut open your breast bone, lift out your heart and float it in a tray of frosty freeze, and sew on a couple of arteries that they take out of your legs or chest. Micki had spent hours on the telephone talking to several old friends who were in medicine, health care activists who were critical of the tendency of too many doctors to prescribe surgery when other, nonintrusive but less profitable options might be preferable.

"Not Tom," David moaned when Micki told him that they'd agreed that a bypass was necessary. We'd known Tom, an internist who had run a clinic in San Francisco's Mission District, for twenty years, and if there were any way out, he would have come up with it.

Micki shook her head. "Even Tom," she said.

Grant arrived first from Boston, followed by Drew, who had won—or lost (he wouldn't tell us which)—the toss with Reed. Grant had a thousand questions—he'd had been in medical school all of three months—which the cardiologists and surgeon answered with collegial thoroughness and courtesy; Drew looked pale.

Micki reeled backward as they wheeled David out of the recovery room. "He looks like a piece of meat," she gasped as Drew put a protective arm around her.

"He'll be all right," Grant said in what he hoped was a reassuring, doctorly voice.

"Garth says the bear hasn't been back," said Micki. "I'm a little worried about his being up there alone."

"He's a good hunter," said David. If Garth had been at home that morning, he, instead of David, would have gone out after the bear, and maybe they wouldn't have discovered the blocked arteries until it was too late.

"He says everybody's been calling," Micki told him. "Your picture— an old one—was in the Ukiah paper. SCHOOL BOARD MEMBER STRICKEN WHILE CHASING BEAR."

Two weeks before, David had been narrowly reelected to the school board, having defeated the former superintendent, who had come out of retirement to challenge him in a bitterly fought contest. In the four years he had been on the job, David had incurred the wrath of some members of the good ol' boys network by raising precisely the kinds of questions that he promised he would when he ran for the job. Some of our friends suggested that David's work on the board and the election campaign had brought on the attack.

Micki didn't buy it. "All that silly school board stuff didn't have anything to do with it," she told Grant and Drew as the three of them stood outside David's room on Thanksgiving Day. She knew what had caused the heart attack: "It was everything that went on before. The politics, being blacklisted, worrying about how we were going to survive, all that work. *That's* what did it. And don't let anybody tell you that hard work can't kill you."

"That's a cheerful thought," said Grant.

"Well, it's true," she snapped.

It had been an unusually warm autumn, and we'd been getting tomatoes and peppers out of the garden until mid-December. Then it suddenly had turned cold, an arctic weather front dropping nighttime temperatures into the teens and freezing the water lines.

"It's never been like this," Micki said as she swung two buckets of water into the doorway. Reed, just home for Christmas, and Garth had spent most of the morning hauling water from the big tank in the canyon, two buckets at a time. Micki was warming one on the stove to take up to the goats. "They say it's going to last at least until the end of the week."

David poked at the fire. It had been more than a year since the operation, and he still didn't feel up to par. They said that maybe the reason his chest seemed to bother him, especially when it got cold, was that they had used the mammary arteries instead of ones from the legs.

Micki filled a big pot and put it on the stove. "Did you take your walk today?"

"I'll do it tomorrow," said David. It had struck him as ridiculous from the outset. Regular exercise, for chrissake. Walking. As if he hadn't been working nonstop for all those years. And then to end up *walking* for exercise. Give up your nine-to-five job, move to the country, raise your own food, breathe clean fresh air, live the good life—and have a heart attack, David told friends only half-jokingly in the months after the operation.

But there was nothing funny about it. Bad genes, too much lamb (but hadn't it been *organic?*), not the right kind of exercise. Too many eggs and cheese—remember the big trays of curried eggs, the cheese soufflés, the goat cheese lasagnes, all so correctly *vegetarian*, that we'd wolfed down at least once a week for years?

"We should have known better," Micki repeated as David, slowly—too slowly, he thought—recovering, spent the winter days on the sofa next to the stove, going through cookbook after cookbook, looking for new recipes that would get his cholesterol down. We'd been eating too well, too rich, over the years, all the time assuming that since we were working so hard at making a go of the place we didn't have to worry about the kinds of things that afflicted our more conventional friends.

It was more than that, though, said Grant. "You just don't have enough receptor cells," he'd told David in one of his weekly telephone calls. He was now taking a course in cardiology, in which he said he'd "made Dad famous." They had discussed David's attack in detail, and as a result, Grant said, "Everybody knows the 'Case of the Bear-Chasing Father.' "

Grant came home now, for just a week. He'd brought his stethoscope and a couple of other gadgets with him and in what he announced as a "Christmas special" spent his first morning back probing ears, looking into eyes, and poking at chests, giving any and all "the last free exam you'll ever get from me." He'd brought *A Guide to Physical Examination and History Taking* home with him and had made it clear that he'd be spending his time getting through that and wouldn't even have time to clean out the goat pens—a fifty-wheelbarrow job—the way he'd done every year since going off to school.

Reed and Garth went down into the canyon to check out the water line there. We needed to know how soon we could expect to have water again once the lines on the ridge thawed.

"It's really bad," Reed told us, standing in the doorway of the kitchen. "There are a couple of inches of ice in the tank, the lines down there are frozen solid. And the worst thing is that it looks like the pump may be damaged."

"Shit," said David. It was what he had feared. We hadn't bothered to drain the lines—we'd never had to do anything like that in all the years we'd lived in California. It would freeze up for a few hours every couple of years or so but never caused any real damage except to some of the borderline vegetables in the winter garden. But now the state was reeling from record low temperatures, and it had gone down to nine degrees the night before in town.

"How soon will we have water?" Micki asked as David pulled on a sweater.

"If the pump's damaged, maybe a week," David said as he headed out the door. "Nobody's going to fix anything right before Christmas."

"Don't strain yourself," Micki called after him. "And don't go getting yourself upset."

The earth crunched underfoot as David headed down the trail to the pump, followed by the boys. A light dusting of snow clung to the leaves and needles of the trees along the way, and the open spaces on the ridges opposite were white instead of the emerald green they ordinarily would have been this time of the year. It was bright and sunny, and there wasn't anywhere near the snow of that first winter, but it was colder and drier.

David bent over the pump. It had frozen hard, and the casing had popped. If we were lucky, the impellers might not be damaged. If we'd only drained the line! The boys had disappeared farther down into the canyon to check the line that ran from the spring to the tank.

Reed reappeared, shaking his head. "Forget it," he said. "It's completely ruined, all the way over to Cervetto's. There's a crack or a break every three or four feet."

If any line was going to go, it would have been that one, the one that we'd installed almost fifteen years ago when we'd lowered little Reed down the cliff on a rope to make connections. It was cheap, thin-walled pipe, the best we could afford back then, and had served its purpose. We'd be able to replace it for a few hundred dollars in a couple of days. Nothing to get excited about.

Reed took a pipe wrench and smacked an opening in the layer of ice. "Let's start filling the buckets, Garth," he said. "It looks like we're going to be doing this for a long time."

Garth lowered a five-gallon bucket into the icy water.

The telephone rang, and David answered it. "U.S.A.? California? Algeria, one moment, please."

"It's Drew!" David shouted. We thought he would call at Christmastime. Drew always took charge of the Christmas celebration—finding the tree, putting it up, checking out the holiday menu, distributing gifts on Christmas Day. There was static on the line for a moment or two, and then Drew's voice.

"Dad? We're in Tamanrasset. Can you hear me?"

He and Linda, his longtime girlfriend, who had graduated from Harvard with him in June, were right on schedule, three months out and seven hundred and fifty miles into the Sahara Desert. They were backpacking down to Mali, where Drew, who had won a Rockefeller Fellowship, planned to study the impact of the drought on parts of sub-Sahara Africa. Everything was fine. They loved Algeria and planned to stay another month, then head down to Niger.

David handed the telephone to Micki. "You have to take turns speaking," he said, repeating what Drew, on what seemed to be a deteriorating connection, had told him. They'd received only three of the eight letters we'd sent. Write to them in Tamanrasset. They'd be there for three weeks. Send political news. How were things at home? Who was decorating the tree? Have a good Christmas.

"Well, at least we know they're all right," said Micki. "He sounded in good spirits. Maybe a little homesick, though."

"I'm sure he'd rather be there than hauling water," said Grant, looking up from *A Guide to Physical Examination*.

New Year's Eve 1991. It had been a deceptively sunny, unusually cold day, the end of a decade. Grant would be flying back to Boston in the morning, and the two of us had joined him in his last walk around the land.

"How are you two going to manage here when Garth leaves?" he wanted to know as we stood leaning against the yearling pen. "How could you two haul water the way we've been doing? Or fix the line?" We had been unable to obtain parts for the pump and had been without water for ten days. The folks over at Rainbow Irrigation said a new pump—when they could obtain one—would run about $450.

Micki laughed. "Grant," she said, "we were hauling water up here when you couldn't even lift a bucket. We'll manage just fine. Don't worry about us."

"But that was before Dad's heart attack."

"I can do everything now that I did before," said David. "I just have to take it a little slower for a while."

"Besides," said Micki, "there's not that much that needs to be done. It's not like before."

We were up by the observatory now.

"I noticed that all the fence posts we put in are rotted out," said Grant. "And the buck pens need work."

"Well, of course there are things to *do*," exclaimed Micki. "There'll always be that. You have to admit, though, that the place looks better than ever."

"Yeah, it does." He paused. "But what about the sheep and the goats? Are you going to keep showing them?"

"I love the goats, Grant. Besides, we're not nearly as dependent on them for income as we were when you were here. We're in pretty good shape, and won't need that much money once you guys are out of school. The land's paid for, we've got medical insurance and we have the rental." Since the closing of the Boonville Hotel, we'd been renting the guest house to a high school teacher.

"You're going to stay on, then?"

"You don't want us to sell it, do you?"

"No, of course not."

"You boys can buy it from us in a few years," said David. "Then we can retire to a condominium in Marina del Rey."

"You'd really love that, Dad," Grant said sarcastically.

"Or there could be a revolution and they'd make me the head of a sociology department somewhere." David laughed.

"The trees need pruning," Grant observed as we passed the orchard. "Now *there's* a project that really paid off. Are we getting any apples yet? Pears? Plums?"

"We had lots of apples this fall," said Micki. "I ended up feeding most of them to the goats now that there aren't enough people here to eat them."

We stood on the knoll next to the empty upper water tank, looking out over the Anderson Valley. The Ukiah ridge was still covered with snow, and the hills below were cast in a rose glow of evening.

"In another year or so those two firs there will block the view," said Grant. "I remember wrapping chicken wire around them to protect them from the sheep. Now what are you going to do, cut them down?"

"We're going to have to thin out a lot of them," said David. "It's really something, the way they've taken off."

"Well, it's been eighteen years. It's hard to believe it's been that long," said Micki. A cold wind had come up; another arctic front had been forecast. She pulled the hood of her Harvard sweatshirt—her milking outfit—over her head. We went back down the hill. It was time for the evening chores.

A Day in the Life, 1991

From Micki's diary, June 3, 1991: *Up at 5:30, a cool, sunny morning. Milked the goats, noted that Alaska, who is past due, was not eating.*

6:00. Filtered and pasteurized the milk, fed the baby goats, got David, Reed, and Garth up.

7:00. Baked muffins, breakfast.

8:00. Garth checked Alaska, called down that she'd had a single kid, said he'd stay up there with her.

9:00. Sammy Prather called to say that a sheep shearing crew was in town but that their truck had broken down. They're late this year, and we desperately need them; said we'd come down to pick them up.

10:00. Helped David move the generator up to the sheep pasture, where he and Reed set up equipment for the shearers. Rounded up the sheep and shut them in the barn. Reed and David lanced a big abscess on Ginny's neck. Gave Alaska molasses water and milked her, dipped kid's cord. Heat-treated colostrum; Garth finally got her to suckle on bottle. Picked up shearers in front of the post office. A different group of them this year. Did a better job than last year's crew—didn't cut any of the sheep the way Augie used to. Garth did math and studied vocabulary in the barn while waiting for Alaska to drop her pla-

centa—which took her nearly an hour. Took the shearers back to town, delivered milk, went to post office, picked up groceries and gas for pump.

11:00. Garth killed the old tom turkey, which David plucked and I eviscerated. Had surprisingly little fat, considering how old he was.

12:00. Open-faced cheese sandwiches for lunch.

1:00. David and I prepared mounds and set up poles for Kentucky Wonder and Blue Lake beans while Reed and Garth hauled down compost from the lower end of the goat pen.

3:00. Finally got everybody to work on a new shelter for the goat kids, who are too big now to fit in the one we've been using since March.

5:30. Picked peas, strawberries, lettuce, leeks, and artichokes for dinner.

6:30. Evening chores. Garth bred two of his rabbits who haven't produced a litter yet; it's their last chance. Brought the new turkey poults into the house for the night—the cats have been showing a bit too much interest in them during the day.

7:30. Reed grilled the salmon and did it perfectly.

9:00. Finally have a chance to read the newspaper.

Busy day again tomorrow.